THE SOCIAL WELFARE FORUM, 1971

Margaret Berry

THE SOCIAL WELFARE FORUM, 1971

OFFICIAL PROCEEDINGS, 98TH ANNUAL FORUM

NATIONAL CONFERENCE ON SOCIAL WELFARE

DALLAS, TEXAS, MAY 16–MAY 21, 1971

 Published 1971 for the

NATIONAL CONFERENCE ON SOCIAL WELFARE *by*

COLUMBIA UNIVERSITY PRESS, *New York and London*

360
N 213s
v. 98
1971

ISBN: 0-231-03587-X

Library of Congress Catalog Card Number: 8-85377

PRINTED IN THE UNITED STATES OF AMERICA

The Contributors

ROBERT R. ALFORD, Professor of Sociology, University of Wisconsin, Madison

MARGARET E. BERRY, Executive Director, National Federation of Settlements and Neighborhood Centers, New York; President, National Conference on Social Welfare

BERTRAM S. BROWN, M.D., Director, National Institute of Mental Health, Health Services and Mental Health Administration, Department of Health, Education, and Welfare, Chevy Chase, Md.

SHIRLEY M. BUTTRICK, Associate Professor of Social Welfare, School of Social Work and Community Planning, University of Maryland, Baltimore; on leave to U.S. Department of Health, Education, and Welfare

JOHN MICHAEL DALEY, JR., doctoral student, School of Social Work, Tulane University, New Orleans

LIGIA VÁSQUEZ DE RODRÍGUEZ, Assistant Professor, School of Social Work, University of Puerto Rico, Rio Piedras

JOHN J. GILLIGAN, Governor, State of Ohio, Columbus

ARTHUR J. KATZ, Dean, School of Social Welfare, University of Kansas, Lawrence, Kans.

JORGE LARA-BRAUD, Director, Hispanic-American Institute, Austin, Texas

HOWARD N. LEE, Mayor, Chapel Hill, N.C.

SOL M. LINOWITZ, Chairman, National Urban Coalition, and attorney, Washington, D.C.

GARY A. LLOYD, Professor, School of Social Work, University of Puerto Rico, Rio Piedras

LEVI A. OLAN, Rabbi Emeritus, Temple Emanu-El, Dallas

JUAN J. PATLAN, Executive Director, Mexican American Unity Council; Chairman, Board of Directors, Economics Opportunities Development Corp., San Antonio, Texas

CHARLES B. RANGEL, United States Representative, New York

WILLIAM RYAN, Chairman, Psychology Department, Boston College, Boston

ROLAND L. WARREN, Professor of Community Theory, Florence Heller Graduate School for Advanced Studies in Social Welfare, Brandeis University, Waltham, Mass.

LEONARD WOODCOCK, President, International Union, United Automobile Workers of America, Detroit; Chairman, Committee for National Health Insurance

The National Conference on Social Welfare

THE NATIONAL CONFERENCE ON SOCIAL WELFARE is a voluntary organization of individual and organizational members whose major function is to provide a national forum for the critical examination of basic problems and issues in the social welfare field.

These annual forums furnish a two-way channel of communication between paid and volunteer workers, between social welfare and allied fields, and between the service organizations and the social work profession.

Since 1873, through its annual forums and its comprehensive publications program, the National Conference has reflected the history and dynamic development of social welfare in this country. Its national office serves as headquarters for state conferences in social welfare; as the secretariat for the U.S. Committee of the International Council on Social Welfare; and as a clearinghouse for educational materials for use on local, state, national, and international levels.

Among the newer services developed by the Conference in recent years is its insurance program and information services, including a library of unpublished Annual Forum manuscripts; its document retrieval program of which the data-processed production of the KWIC Index of its publications since 1873 is a part; and its Selected Bibliography service.

Foreword

THE THEME OF "Human Aspirations and National Priorities," selected for the 1971 Forum, was comprehensively treated in the vast array of papers presented during the Forum week. The articles selected for this volume represent, in the view of the Editorial Committee, the most significant contributions reflective of the theme.

Throughout their history social welfare and the profession of social work have struggled toward the objectives of aiding the realization of human aspirations, namely, self-actualization and self-fulfillment within a framework of communal responsibility. Today, such efforts by social workers take the form of attempts to influence national social policy.

It is only recently that this country has fully emerged as a truly national society. Yet, strong pressures exist to reverse that process and return more policy prerogatives to regional and local structures. Recognition of the significance of the concept of a national society is crucial in order to deal effectively with major social problems which thwart human aspirations. Without a national social policy orientation, little impact seems possible on the process of determining national priorities.

These papers are primarily concerned with issues of national social policy developed and implemented by federal legislative and administrative systems. Some analysts have commented that this nation has neither clarified nor resolved the crucial differences which prevent our policy-makers from enunciating clearly and vigorously the goals and social purposes of this society, which could fulfill the legitimate aspirations of its citizen-members.

Conference President Margaret Berry points up one seminal conflict as being the struggle between human rights and property rights. A number of papers focus on economic security as a fundamental aspiration of all citizens and the low priority designated to this objective by federal policy-makers.

Once again, the Forum papers reflect an increasing preoccupation with the issue of racism, which consistently frustrates the natural aspirations of this nation's nonwhite populations. Another major focus relates to the aspiration of our citizens for a more equitable participation in the social dividends. The vast amounts of public funds invested in health and mental health research and demonstrations, according to these observers, are designed to develop knowledge and skills necessary to improve the health of the American people. The delivery of services, however, remains primitive, unevenly distributed, and for the most part, subject to the forces of the market place. A strong national policy to correct this imbalance is of prime consideration.

Several papers are concerned with influencing policy formulation. How are we to offset resistance to establishment of a vigorous policy to support equalization of opportunities to meet human aspirations? Citizen participation, community control, and political action are suggested as ways of influencing national policy.

The issue before us is how to achieve a meaningful response from federal legislative and administrative systems that have for too long been preoccupied with priorities that emphasize the disastrous and destructive Indo-China military adventure. The "war," it seems, has represented during this past decade the single greatest force defeating human aspirations in this nation. No prescription for either goals or methods of influencing national social policy is possible until this nation has completely extricated itself from Indo-China and has renounced war as an instrument of national policy.

A companion volume, *Social Work Practice, 1971,* will be published separately by Columbia University Press. The Chairman extends his deep thanks to the Editorial Committee, who contributed a great deal of time and energy in reading and selecting papers for publication in the two volumes: Delwin M. Anderson, Virginia Tannar, Harold R. White, and Anne Wilkens.

The Editorial Committee wishes to record its gratitude to

Joe R. Hoffer, Sara Lee Berkman, and Mabel E. Davis of the Conference staff for their continuous help. Mr. Hoffer, who will be retiring as Executive Secretary of the National Conference on Social Welfare, has provided critical leadership to the work of the Editorial Committee throughout the years.

The committee also wishes to offer its grateful appreciation to Dorothy M. Swart, of Columbia University Press, for her significant and invaluable technical assistance in the preparation of these volumes.

ARTHUR J. KATZ
Chairman, Editorial Committee

Greetings to the Conference

from PRESIDENT RICHARD NIXON

THE 98TH ANNUAL FORUM of the National Conference on Social Welfare meets at a notable time in our nation's history. Your theme, "Human Aspirations and National Priorities," eloquently headlines the urgency of the problems.

As a people we now have the capability to achieve significant social reform in America. The challenge of the coming years is to join our will with our wealth in a concerted effort to build a just and peaceful society. I believe that the welfare reform measures now before the Congress are a vital step in this direction.

As we press forward in this endeavor, the nation looks to your deliberations to provide a constructive contribution which will serve to speed our common objectives. May you have a highly productive and rewarding session.

National Conference on Social Welfare Distinguished Service Awards

THE NATIONAL CONFERENCE ON SOCIAL WELFARE AWARDS were established by Executive Committee action in 1954 to accomplish a twofold purpose by calling attention to the significant social problems of the times, and by recognition of the outstanding achievements of individuals or organizations in helping to solve them. The first Award was presented at the 1955 Annual Forum in San Francisco.

Conditions of the Awards and procedures for selection of recipients adopted by the Executive Committee specified that awards would be given only when outstanding candidates were submitted; that up to three awards might be given in any one year in recognition of outstanding contributions in administration, research, practice, or, in exceptional cases, for long and sustained achievement in the advancement of social welfare, but not solely for long service; and that recipients need not be members of the Conference or of the social work profession.

Final selection of recipients is made by the National Board of the Conference from nominations and supporting background material submitted by the members.

Awards for 1971 were presented by Margaret E. Berry, President of the National Conference on Social Welfare, to Sam S. Grais and Dorothy I. Height at the General Session on Monday, May 17, 1971.

NATIONAL CONFERENCE ON SOCIAL WELFARE
DISTINGUISHED SERVICE AWARDS 1955–1971

1955 EDITH M. BAKER, Washington, D.C.
FEDELE F. FAURI, Ann Arbor, Mich.
ELIZABETH WICKENDEN, New York

1956 TIAC (Temporary Inter-Association Council) PLANNING COMMITTEE,
New York

1957 THE REVEREND MARTIN LUTHER KING, JR., Montgomery, Ala.
WILBUR J. COHEN, Ann Arbor, Mich.

1958 THE HONORABLE JOHN E. FOGARTY, Rhode Island
LEONARD W. MAYO, New York

1959 ELISABETH SHIRLEY ENOCHS, Washington, D.C.
OLLIE A. RANDALL, New York

1960 LOULA DUNN, Chicago
RALPH BLANCHARD, New York
HELEN HALL, New York

1961 THE HONORABLE AIME J. FORAND, Rhode Island

1962 THE ATLANTA *Constitution,* Ralph McGill and Jack Nelson, Atlanta,
Ga.
JOSEPH P. ANDERSON, New York
CHARLOTTE TOWLE, Chicago

1963 HARRIETT M. BARTLETT, Cambridge, Mass.
ERNEST JOHN BOHN, Cleveland
FLORENCE G. HELLER, Glencoe, Ill.
Special Award: Television Documentary, "The Battle of Newburgh,"
IRVING GITLIN and the NATIONAL BROADCASTING COMPANY, New York
Special Citation (posthumous): ANNA ELEANOR ROOSEVELT, "First
Lady of the World"

1964 DR. ROBERT M. FELIX, Bethesda, Md.
Special Citation (posthumous): JOHN FITZGERALD KENNEDY, "Man of
Destiny"

1965 JAMES V. BENNETT, Washington, D.C.
SIDNEY HOLLANDER, Baltimore, Md.
CORA KASIUS, New York

1966 REPRESENTATIVE WILBUR D. MILLS, Ark.

1967 THE HONORABLE HUBERT H. HUMPHREY, Washington, D.C.
PLANNED PARENTHOOD–WORLD POPULATION
Special Awards (posthumous):
RUTH M. WILLIAMS, New York
HOWARD F. GUSTAFSON, Indianapolis

1968 LOMA MOYER ALLEN, Rochester, N.Y.
KENNETH BANCROFT CLARK, New York

1969 THE HONORABLE ELMER L. ANDERSEN, St. Paul, Minn.
HARRY L. LURIE, New York
IDA C. MERRIAM, Washington, D.C.

1970 No awards were presented

1971 Sam S. Grais, St. Paul, Minn.
Dorothy I. Height, New York

Contents

Abstracts

ALFORD, ROBERT R.
"The Political Economy of the American Health System"
The real crisis in our health system is its institutional structure which creates and sustains the power of self-interested "professional monopolies" (doctors and researchers) and "corporate rationalizers" (institutional administrators). Reform efforts of liberal intellectuals, political reformers, and community health advocates lack the power to generate interest in an integrated system and are inevitably frustrated by the market-oriented groups dominating the planning and control of core institutions.

BERRY, MARGARET E.
"The People, Yes: Social Progress out of Group Protest"
Our concept of democracy, born of hope and aspiration, is the inevitable arena for protest and struggle. Individuals and groups of oppressed minorities, inspired by self-interest, have risen against oppression and exploitation to demand their rights by direct action in defense of human rights over property rights. Protest alone cannot bring change. This comes from aroused social conscience—a coalition of forces—demanding protection of rights in a society free from prejudice and fear.

BROWN, BERTRAM S., M.D.
"Community Mental Health: the View from Fund City"
Success of our national health plan in delivering comprehensive, efficient, and economical health services and assuring users of convenient access to facilities at prepaid contract prices demands cooperative advocacy and concerted effort by professions, community, and citizens. Mutual collaboration between health maintenance organizations and community health plans now established in nationwide centers is essential to the ideal of responsiveness to human needs through teamwork for health and welfare.

BUTTRICK, SHIRLEY M.
"Innovative Ideas in Social Service Delivery"
A definition of social services and their objectives in measurable terms is imperative to successful plans for separation of services from

income-maintenance programs. Accepted functions of social policy—
to redistribute income, power, and prestige and to integrate service
systems through community-based, family-oriented programs—is unrealistic without basic knowledge of problems of resource allocation,
funding, accountability systems, and the planning process and its
application to change.

GILLIGAN, JOHN J.
"A Federal Public Welfare Policy—a Governor's Appraisal"
The current welfare policy is based on assumptions that our profit
motive is irreplaceable; that subsidies to industry provide jobs to
workers; that its programs, from revenue sharing to welfare reform,
will restore the freedom and dignity of the individual. Instead, it
perpetuates poverty's vicious cycle by ignoring the principle that
economic necessities are a basic freedom to be protected and de-
fended as are our political rights.

KATZ, ARTHUR J.
"Clients' Participation in Institutional Change"
Head Start as a part of the Office of Economic Opportunity Community Action program has an ideological commitment to institutional change and child development. Its relationship to children
and their families and its broad objective to "improve human conditions of the poor through change in community institutions"
provide built-in assurance of consumer involvement in policy determination and development of grass-roots support for change in
public education, health, and welfare.

LARA-BRAUD, JORGE
"The Southwest: Aspirations of the Mexican Americans"
Efforts to Americanize Mexican Americans were based on the
mistaken assumption that they would shed the cultural trappings of
their ancestry in favor of the national way of life. The results have
forged a new people blending the best of both legacies in a bilingual,
binational community capable of becoming the most suitable bridge
to genuine Pan-Americanism and the most effective mediator in the
conflict between black and white.

LEE, HOWARD N.
"Political Activism for Social Work"
As nonaggressive critics of social ills, social workers have failed to
influence political decisions or to shape public policy. In promoting
a reordering of priorities and a welfare program with built-in income
capable of breaking the poverty cycle, adequate social services, and

guaranteed educational benefits the profession must use the schools
of social work to gain knowledge of political processes and its professional organization to win political action.

LINOWITZ, SOL M.
"An Alternate Social Policy for Federal Budgeting"
If society is to survive the corrosive combination of institutional
paralysis, individual powerlessness, and citizen Balkanization, our
"reordering of national priorities" must be translated into substantive policy change defined in terms of public resources and federal
budget. The National Urban Coalition's "counterbudget" proposes
a solution to our threatening economic and social problems through
substantial reduction of military spending, suggested new revenues,
elimination of federal tax inequities, and anticipated economic
growth.

LLOYD, GARY A., AND JOHN MICHAEL DALEY, JR.
"Community Control of Health and Welfare Programs"
Community control as the decision-making power of community
participation can work only when the group has authority to initiate
and implement action. Success will depend on its ability to influence
resource distribution, professionals and bureaucracies, pluralism, and
the good of the individual or group in the public interest. As participatory democracy, its doubtful challenge to power elites, its cost and
inefficiency, are factors contributing to its lack of success.

OLAN, RABBI LEVI A.
"Aspirations for Ethnic Minorities"
We have tried to create one nation from diversity by Americanization
of immigrants determined to retain their ethnic traditions, by melting pot fusion of Old World peoples into a new type, and, more
recently, by cultural pluralism, accepting ethnic contributions into
our total culture. In a pluralistic society, danger lies in the interfer-
ence of group attitudes and minorities demanding group identity
often opposed to our national interest.

PATLAN, JUAN J.
"The Model Cities Program: II. A Mexican American View"
San Antonio's Model Cities program could be expected to fail. Its
staff and citizen participants, without authority, were defeated by
local politics. Planning, without balanced approach to barrio problems, brought no home rehabilitation, minimal single-home construction, and scattered multiple units unacceptable to barrio residents.
Recommended substitute is a Community Development Corporation

directly responsible to residents and able to provide opportunities and capital for development of their skills and resources.

RANGEL, CHARLES B.
"Making the Political Process Respond to Human Needs"
The politician sees welfare in terms of rising costs and the poor as part of a system failing to meet their needs. Organized opposition of the poor defeated the 1969 Family Assistance Plan proposed as revolutionary social reform. The new FAP, as welfare reform, fails to alleviate poverty, is discriminatory against blacks, and includes potential increased costs to states, job requirements, and cutbacks in medical and hospital payments.

DE RODRÍGUEZ, LIGIA VÁZQUEZ
"Needs and Aspirations of the Puerto Rican People"
Primary concern among Puerto Ricans is political status: independence, statehood, or commonwealth. Problems, in order of priority, are drugs, unemployment, delinquency, medical services, poverty, public services, education. Their values place social prestige above money and resist investment of island capital in industrialization but deplore U.S. domination of production and capital. Ideals stress native cultural traditions, accenting family unity, home ownership, language, and religion.

RYAN, WILLIAM
"The Social Welfare Client: Blaming the Victim"
Current social reforms, our rehabilitative service programs, devised in righteous humanitarianism prescribe revision of the attitudes, character defects, and culture of the victim—not the social injustices of his surroundings. "Blaming the victim" is a compromise ideology reconciling self-interest with humanitarianism applied to most social problems. Malignancies of poverty, race, and urban decay are seen as defects justifying change in their victims—not the society.

WARREN, ROLAND L.
"The Model Cities Program: I. An Assessment"
Model Cities strategy for improving the quality of urban life was based on the faulty assumption that social problems, rooted in deficiencies of individuals, can be corrected by remedial social services. Evaluation in terms of comprehensiveness, concentration, and citizen participation indicates modest success in improved social services and cities' planning competence, and dramatic success, justifying the whole venture, in citizen participation under impossible circumstances.

WOODCOCK, LEONARD

"The Health Care System; a Critique and a Legislative Proposal"
A health security program embracing the entire range of services—
prevention, treatment, and rehabilitation—centered in group practice health maintenance organizations is proposed as a solution to
our obsolete health care system. Medical care would be left to private
practice under federal standards for service and practice with federal
financing through general revenues and social security mechanisms
at no increased costs over our system which fails both consumer and
provider.

THE SOCIAL WELFARE FORUM, 1971

The People, Yes: Social Progress out of Group Protest

MARGARET E. BERRY

This country was born out of hopes and aspirations—hopes of debtors for freedom from bondage, hopes of free thinkers, of entrepreneurs. We have been a great arena in which diverse individuals and groups have been pushing, tumbling, accommodating, striving. This struggle has given us a vitality, a strength, an exuberance, shaping a nation which is unique, one which has great generosity and at the same time one that can be capable of arrogant and uncaring acts.

Our nation was born in protest, in indignation against an oppressor. Waves of protest, large and small, have come steadily throughout its history, all of them the expressions of indignant people, pushed beyond endurance, asserting against forces of exploitation and privilege their own value and dignity.

Many of these acts of protest have been spontaneous and isolated. There was Shays's short-lived rebellion in 1786, when 1,000 Massachusetts farmers fought to close the courts, stopping mortgage foreclosures. There was Dorr's Rebellion in 1842, when Governor Dorr of Rhode Island led 234 men in storming the Providence armory arsenal, trying to establish his right to govern under a new constitution giving expanded suffrage.

Many of these acts have flowed together, into great streams of change, bringing new life and growth to concepts of democracy. One great stream represented the agrarian revolt, the stand of small farmers against the unseen forces which robbed them of the fruits of their hard labor. Gradually, they saw that their poverty was tied to the railroads, which were subsidized by public money and thus could control freight rates, grain ele-

vators, storage fees, grading of produce. And so, in the great
Populist revolt, farmers' alliances developed for mutual aid and
political reform. Their rising protest resulted in the People's
party by 1891. They wanted only a chance to work, and a fair
reward for their labor. They blamed manufacturers, moneylend-
ers, railroads, and middlemen for their plight. They could no
longer escape to a new frontier, so they turned to government to
redress their grievances, to control the selfish tendencies of those
who exploited.

Out of their own self-interest, the People's party worked for a
fair ballot, direct democracy, woman suffrage, possibility of
referenda—all kinds of political reforms which in time came to
pass, and which we hold today as our unquestioned right in a
democratic government.

The heritage of agricultural protest persists. We think of the
Southern Tenant Farmers Union, an attempt to meet the appalling conditions affecting Mexican Americans, "Okies," and
"Arkies" in the terrible Dust Bowl days; of the Farm Holiday
Association of the 1930s when organized farmers in the Mid-
west kept bankers from foreclosing mortgages; of Cesar Chavez,
who continues in this great tradition.

Another great stream in history is that of the labor movement,
grown from dozens of isolated struggles against exploitation and
from successive economic catastrophes. People eventually refuse
to go hungry. In the panic of 1837, the flour merchants were
accused of hoarding, and warehouses were attacked. In contemporary accounts this was interpreted as revolution.

A more organized effort against hunger came through union-
ism, the rise of workingmen's societies from 1820 on, a period
when poverty was overwhelming. People struggled then, as now,
against the widely held belief that "all can find work; that the
poor by industry and prudence may support themselves com-
fortably; that sufferings arise from idleness and dissipation, and
that public assistance fosters dependence." [1] The workingmen's
societies, in their own self-interest, sought free education for all.

---

[1] Arthur M. Schlesinger, Jr., *The Age of Jackson* (New York: Little, Brown &
Co., 1953), p. 133.

They saw the prisons filled with debtors—in 1830 five sixths of the people in prison were there for debts of under $20—and they worked for the abolition of imprisonment for debt. They fought for less expensive legal charges, for an equal tax on property, and for curbing the power of banks. They made the first attempt at a broad alliance through the General Trades Union, in 1833. And then, in the way we always have of labeling the new and challenging as "foreign doctrine," labor organizers were denounced as "levelers" and anarchists, as atheists and foreigners, their union considered unlawful and mischievous.

The litany of the labor movement includes shameful chapters when direct action was met by extreme repression and violence. The general railway strike of 1877 came when railroads had responded to a recession by making widespread job and wage cuts. A religious periodical commented that "rioters were worse than mad dogs."

Many of us heard of the self-reliance and incredible bravery of the cotton and hosiery mill workers in the Piedmont, whose misery in 1929 held them firm against starvation, eviction, and state troopers. Some of us remember 1932, when 3,000 despairing workers marched to demand jobs, an end to discrimination against employment of Negroes, free coal, company assumption of mortgage payments, and for those partially employed, at least 50 percent of their former wage level. An unarmed crowd, which kept marching when ordered to stop at the Dearborn city limits, was assaulted by tear gas, fire hoses, and gunfire. The freezing day ended with three killed and fifty wounded.

We knew of the struggle of the West Virginia mine workers, trapped in a dying industry. The armed crews of locomotives fired into the defenseless tent colonies of evicted workers. We were horrified by the Memorial Day massacre of 1937, when 1,500 strikers, striving to establish the union in Little Steel plants, marched to the Republic plant in Chicago, protesting the use of strikebreakers. The peaceful march ended with ten men shot, six of them in the back, and fifty-eight wounded. Movies of the incredible brutality were suppressed until they were shown to a Senate investigating committee.

And so the streams of protest have flowed through our history. Along with these are other efforts: the too-little-known revolts of the slaves; the struggles of the reviled and ridiculed suffragettes; the dedication of the abolitionists; the depression-born Bonus Army of 1932, its 15,000 veterans routed from Washington by General MacArthur on orders of President Hoover, their makeshift shelters left in smoldering ruins; Cox's Army of 12,000 Pennsylvanians gathered in 1932 by Father James Cox, a Pittsburgh priest, who led them in trucks and cars to Washington, denouncing Mellon, banks, and the government.

This short recital is merely to remind us that in times of crisis, oppressed minorities—blacks, Mexican Americans, immigrants, women, workers, farmers—rise up and demand their rights by direct action. Often, direct action was the only means by which unpropertied, nonpowered, largely inarticulate groups could make their grievances known. These popular protest movements were sparked by immediate, pressing, and personal grievances, by individual and group self-interest. Invariably, however, their policies and programs included goals which, when secured, enlarged democracy for all Americans. By gaining their own rights, they enlarged welfare and justice generally for the whole of our society.

Three things seem to be generally characteristic of all these efforts. First, the actions of the protesters shocked the defenders of the status quo. People tended to see in each specific challenge a threat to tear down the whole society.

Secondly, the protests have usually had to do with an assertion of human rights over property rights. People were moved by an urge for self-determination, to choose for themselves how to style their own lives. They fought against impersonal power. Arthur Schlesinger, Jr., calls Jacksonian democracy the attempt of the "producing" classes to unite against the movement to make the rich richer, to resist the concentration of wealth in a single class. He concludes:

The judgment of American liberalism has been that it was best for the whole society, including the capitalists, that their power be constantly checked and limited by the humble members of society

[and] that every great crisis in American history has produced a leader adequate to the occasion from the ranks of those who believed vigorously and seriously in liberty, democracy, and the common man.[2]

A third consistent factor has been the turning to government as the ultimate instrument for protection of, or enlargement of, human rights, and for equalization of economic resources. Government has been seen as the protector against selfish interests. Understanding this function of government, groups have necessarily turned to political action and sought political power.

All this history has a contemporary ring, for protests continue to be part of the American tradition. We all gain from the individual acts of assertion; we are all indebted to Mrs. Rosa Parks who, on one particular day, was too tired, or too proud, to walk to the back of the bus. We are all indebted to the whole Freedom movement. We were deeply moved by the Vietnam veterans who camped out in Washington, condemning a brutalizing and immoral war, and holding the nation to account for requiring meaningless human sacrifice. We see the National Welfare Rights Organization protesting in its own way the indignities visited on the poor, and working on the national legislative scene for a truly adequate income for every American family.

The National Conference on Social Welfare has been both arena and target in the last three years for groups asserting their selfhood and their goals. This is part of a useful historical process which has led to ultimate gain for the whole of society. Protest alone has not brought the change, although it has aroused the conscience of others. The eventual basic change has come about as a result of a coalition of technicians, managers, doctors, lawyers, social workers, housewives, businessmen—all those forces who work out, compromise, and negotiate, if necessary, the tedious details.

The Annual Forum gives us an opportunity to apply ourselves to the unfinished business of American democracy, the human aspirations which, if they are to be realized, require the

2 *Ibid.*, p. 521.

reordering of our national priorities. We need an early end to the overkill of Vietnam. We need to give up spending $15 billion a year for the one-time use of disposable packaging materials, and $1.4 billion for those throwaway cans and bottles. We need to use our resources to build thousands of homes, especially for low-income people. We need expanded education. We need theaters and music in every city. We need medical care for all. We need to put into immediate effect the Full Employment Act, which declares as national policy that everyone who wants to work should have a job. We need an adequate annual income for every citizen. We need a commitment to use a small part of our wealth to protect human life as part of our country's richness, just as we subsidize airlines, and unused acreage, and roads, and the defense industry, and upper-income housing. We need only a will-to-share so that our riches, great but not limitless, are divided more equitably. Yet in 1970, for the first time since 1961, the proportion of poor people increased by 5 percent.

Social welfare is a broad field. Its agencies have varied styles. Some deliver services; others embody ideologies or values; some constantly search for improvement and reform. Within these agencies are the employed workers. Each one should consider the significance of his own work. Is he, in truth, a "welfare colonialist," part of a bureaucracy which crushes rather than nurtures self-development and personal realization? This question will require painful objectivity and thoughtful response. Is he employed in a way consistent with his beliefs, where being an advocate or an activist is his special way of helping? He is fortunate. Is he employed as a helper, not himself leading, but through professional self-discipline enabling others—individuals, families, groups—to determine their own purposes, and helping strengthen them to move toward their own goals? This is the essence of the professional self. This is a discipline which no other profession has even attempted.

We live in troubled times which need the "prophets" who goad us by calling for justice and holding us to absolute standards. But let us not belittle or flagellate those who carry out the "priestly" functions, who counsel, strengthen, listen without judging, who by holding their own needs in check, by being "disinterested helpers," enable others to grow and achieve their own aspirations. We need both the priests and the prophets. Our common goal is a society free from prejudice and fear where we can care for each other as members of one human family.

The Southwest: Aspirations of the Mexican Americans

JORGE LARA-BRAUD

Most representative of the Southwest are the Mexican Americans, while the Southwest is the most cosmopolitan region of the nation. No other area of the United States encompasses a wider diversity of races, religions, and national origins. California, Colorado, Arizona, New Mexico, and Texas together contain some of the largest groups of American Indians, the largest concentration of Orientals in the continental United States, some three million blacks, large numbers of Koreans, Polynesians, Indonesians, Hawaiians, and Asian Indians, and, of course, Mexican Americans in excess of six million.

Against this background the experience of Mexican Americans takes on the character of an authentic saga. Theirs is the only community that has managed to become American while keeping alive the language and traditions of those—Indians, Spaniards, and Mexicans—who first populated the Southwest. We are talking about four centuries of uninterrupted cultural replenishment. If length of residence and persistence of language and culture north of the Rio Grande are the criteria for seniority, the claims of Pilgrims, Puritans, Forty-Niners, Confederates, and their descendants are not really very impressive. Others, whose names were Bernal, Garza, González, Chávez, and Tijerina, were here first to welcome or resist them.

The saga cannot be romanticized. It is also a history of exhausting resistance against the invasion from the north. "Invasion" is not an improper term. The Texas War of Independence of 1836 and the war against Mexico in 1846–48 were classical military operations to legitimize previous or future invasions. Proud descendants on both sides do well to pay tribute to their gallant heroes. But no amount of patriotic homage can erase the ugly fact that military conquest further legitimized for the next century the illusion of superiority of the race, creed, and language of the conqueror.

The record abounds with examples of decent, compassionate Anglos who in the name of decency and compassion attempted to erase any expression of Mexicanhood on the grounds that its perpetuation would be detrimental to Mexican Americans and menacing to Anglo-Americans. The church literature of white Anglo-Saxon Protestants and Catholics from the time of the war against Mexico until the 1930s is the most telling chronicle of how even the best intentions missed the mark. The common assumption was that Mexican Americans themselves would want to abandon their foreign ways once they were introduced to the richness of the "national" way of life.

Social service institutions in this country first grew out of the initiative and support by churches. Thus, the shape of social services to this day is largely determined by concepts held by of priests, ministers, rabbis, and women's missionary societies. To vent hostility on long-dead, honorable people for their mistaken notions is not an honorable exercise. To recognize their contribution where they were wise, and even more to challenge their legacy where they were patently wrong, is somehow to do honor to them and to ourselves.

Mexican Americans have been challenging their would-be redeemers for more than a century. The reason is simple. The attempt to Americanize them resulted in denying them both Mexicanhood and Americanhood. Following the war of 1846–48, halfhearted efforts were put forth to develop bilingual forms of institutional life, including, as in New Mexico, legislative procedures in Spanish and English. The large influx of English-speaking settlers into the newly acquired American territories swamped the land with large numbers of near-illiterates who considered it accomplishment enough to understand each other in colorful variants of English. By the end of the nineteenth century, Spanish was generally looked upon with disdain, and the people who spoke it with condescension or disgust.

Meanwhile, in theory, a Mexican American could shed the cultural trappings of his parents and grandparents, including the language, and qualify as a full-fledged American. That turned out to be a cruel illusion. Rare has been the citizen of Mexican extraction who has been accepted as a true equal by his fellow citizens of Northern European extraction. More often than not that accomplishment necessitates a fair skin, impeccable English, and exceptionally high credentials. There is, of course, a larger dimension of "formal" equality. It is the kind that one observes mostly in municipal, state, and federal bureaucracies. It is chiefly the result of minority group pressure for greater employment opportunities under civil rights legislation. The level of such equality seldom rises higher than middle-echelon positions. A Mexican American bureaucrat rubs elbows with his Anglo professional equal, but the relationship does not normally lead to any significant social interaction. In a thousand subtle ways the predominant society reminds the Mexican American success type that after all he has not quite measured up.

If the success types fare so modestly, one wonders what happens to those with less status. It is here that we touch on the most devastating aspects of measuring human accomplishment in terms of a white, Anglo-Saxon, American norm. Those who are different for reasons of color, language, or tradition will inevitably be regarded as less than persons. Practically every Mexican American has at one time or another heard from some honest Anglo the question, "If you are not going to be like us, why don't you go back to Mexico?" The implication is clear. If one does not change, or at least disguise his differences, he does not belong and he will be treated accordingly. What makes this situation even more tragic is that many decent Anglos are not even aware of their deep-rooted conditioning of disapproval for permanent "foreigners" in their midst. After all, is this not America, where the language is English, where the civilizer was white, where the heroes are Washington, Jefferson, Jackson, Houston, Lincoln, Wilson, and Kennedy? What is this business of Spanish, of Indian civilizations, of a band of nonwhites founding Los Angeles, and heroes with unpronounceable names like Cuauhtémoc, Hidalgo, Juárez, and Zapata?

This may sound academic. It is not. It is the very crux of the conflict of more than one century between Anglos and Mexican Americans. It is also the explanation of why there is a human disaster area in the Southwest whose name is Mexican American. If Anglos are real persons and non-Anglos less than persons, if human accomplishment is measured in terms of a white, Anglo-Saxon, American norm, then Mexican Americans can do with less education, less employment, less money, less food, less housing, less health, less justice, and less dignity. Let no one accuse us of demagoguery. Any statistical study will prove that except for the American Indian, no other community in this prosperous nation enjoys less of the requirements for well-being than Mexican Americans.

Against the background of these harsh realities, we are justified in attributing the character of saga to the historical experience of Mexican Americans. It is more than mere cultural survival. It is rather the forging of a new people, blending the best legacies of the Mexican and the American past. Its languages are Spanish, English, and a versatile new combination of the two. Because of its own diversity of colors, from blond to mulatto, it has developed powerful antibodies against the virus of racism. The Anglo racist is looked upon less and less as the enemy and more and more as a pathological relative whose therapy must not be delayed, lest his racial delusions cause more destruction to himself and his victims. Let us not, however, give the impression of self-righteousness.

The Mexican American is not more naturally noble than anyone else. He is fortunate in that he can draw on a binational heritage replete with historical accomplishments, exemplary patriots, and humanistic traditions. The convergence of Mexico and the United States across two centuries in the Southwest has greatly enlarged his vision of human possibilities. In the growing interaction between the United States and Latin America he is the most suitable human bridge for some sort of genuine Pan-Americanism. Since he is bilingual, the future is also with him. In thirty years English will be very much of a minority language in the hemisphere, outnumbered two to one in relation to native speakers of Spanish and Portuguese. A unilingual American will soon be an embarrassment to himself and his country. Most important of all for the well-being of the Southwest, the Mexican American can be the most effective mediator in the continuing conflict between black and white, since he encompasses the entire color spectrum that divides them.

With or without assistance the Mexican American will prevail. The question is whether he can also prevail with all his other American brothers. The example of many who are prosperous but empty should teach us that power at the expense of the powerlessness of others is criminal and ultimately detrimental to all. In the Southwest we have been given the most cosmopolitan human laboratory in the world to test the noble American dream of liberty and justice for all. Let the dream come true. Let the saga belong to all of us. Let us then make every expression of our corporate life mirror the rich human diversity of the region. Let us then be bilingual and multicultural in schools, legislatures, municipalities, courts, police, hospitals, draft boards, corporations, bureaucracies, welfare offices, and churches. It is worth the effort. If we succeed, our children and their children will call us blessed.

Needs and Aspirations of the Puerto Rican People

LIGIA VÁZQUEZ DE RODRÍGUEZ

In MAKING A SOBER APPRAISAL of the needs and aspirations of the Puerto Rican people the terms "needs" and "aspirations" need no definition. If there is to be an operative linkage between the two, services will have to be evolved which solve the need and make the aspiration come true. This possibility poses the inescapable exigency of devising the means to cope with the need while making viable the process which better corresponds to the people's aspirations, and to determine how people want the process to occur. In other words, an adequate solution must be found to the dilemma of what is, what is possible, and what is valuable.

The aspirations of the Puerto Ricans are similar to those of other people in the occidental world. In a recent study [1] Dr. Luis Nieves Falcón, Director of the Social Science Research Center, Department of Social Sciences of the University of Puerto Rico, interviewed 1,300 persons, representing the adult population of the island from both urban and rural areas. Certain salient findings are worth mentioning:

1. The study revealed a high grade of satisfaction with the present society. (Similar results were obtained by Tumin and Feldman in a study with public school teachers in Puerto Rico.[2]) Nieves Falcón states that in spite of this general attitude, there is a feeling of dissatisfaction, especially among middle-aged, low-

[1] Luis Nieves Falcón, *La Opinión Pública y las Aspiraciones de los Puertorriqueños* (Rio Piedras, Puerto Rico: Social Science Research Center, University of Puerto Rico, 1970).
[2] Melvin M. Tumin and Arnold Feldman, *Social Class and Social Change in Puerto Rico* (Princeton, N.J.: Princeton University Press, 1961), pp. 202–13.

income dwellers in poor marginal areas and public housing projects who have little schooling and are unemployed. A similar concern is beginning to spread among groups with more education and higher income.

2. Where there is personal satisfaction with the neighborhood, it is associated with private residence, schooling, income, and job.

3. The most important problems cited by the respondents to the open questions of the study were in order of priority: drugs, unemployment, delinquency, medical services, poverty, public services, and education. Housing, health, and overpopulation were mentioned by 5 percent, 3 percent and 2 percent respectively of the persons interviewed.

When a closed question was asked about this matter, the answers in order of rank were: need for more attention to the poor people, unemployment, political status, health, education, and housing. The author concludes that the most important problems were those associated with the economic development of the country and the resulting imbalance.

4. The needs of the Puerto Rican families were stated as follows:

TABLE I [a]

NEEDS OF THE PUERTO RICAN FAMILIES

Needs	Constitutes a Need	Does Not Constitute a Need	Do Not Know or No Answer
	Percent	Percent	Percent
Savings for the future	78	21	1
Better paid jobs	51	48	1
Medical attention (doctor-hospital)	47	52	1
Means for the education of children	46	51	3
Better houses	43	57	-
Governmental help	40	59	1
Opportunity to learn or study a job	39	60	1

Needs	Constitutes a Need	Does Not Constitute a Need	Do Not Know or No Answer
	Percent	Percent	Percent
More recreation	38	62	-
Automobile	36	64	-
Own house	36	64	-
More leisure time	33	66	1
Better food	31	68	1
Employment	30	70	-

ª *Ibid.,* p. 71.

5. The majority of the persons interviewed favored measures of high social content. The minority who were opposed were particularly concentrated in the more privileged groups. The issues mentioned were: regulation of medicine prices; reasonable fees for legal services; laws governing the profits withholdings of foreign industries; and the raising of taxes of the rich in order to help the poor.

6. More autonomy for the government of Puerto Rico was favored in relation to laws, army, salaries, political status, military bases, and so on.

7. The respondents evidenced a deep cultural conviction. The majority were against the English language becoming the official one of the Government of Puerto Rico and against the people ceasing to speak Spanish. They were in favor of the schools teaching more facts about the Puerto Rican people and believed that the television programs should include more information about Puerto Rican issues. They were also in favor of more laws to protect Puerto Rican artists so that they would have priority of employment in entertainment.

8. More than half of the interviewees supported public help to religious schools, mining control by a public agency and a plebiscite to decide whether the people want or do not want statehood. The majority objected to governmental intervention in the control of childbirth.

The aspirations mentioned in this and other studies are curtailed by serious needs and problems of the islanders. Puerto

Rico, an island of 3,423 square miles, has a population of 2,712,033—or about 800 per square mile, one of the world's highest population density rates. During the last three decades Puerto Rico has evolved from a severely underdeveloped country to an almost industrialized one. Few countries have undergone such a peaceful socioeconomic revolution.

The dramatic changes that have occurred in that short time have been evidenced in characteristics such as these:

1. A shifting in the economy from an agricultural to an industrial base
2. Urbanization
3. An increase in mobility and in communication media
4. A considerable increase in standards of living
5. A democratization of the political system
6. A tendency toward a more materialistic way of life
7. An increase in political autonomy from the United States
8. A considerable improvement in medical care and public health services
9. A considerable expansion of educational services and opportunities
10. An increase in material commodities approaching levels reached in the most modern societies.[3]

Professor Noriega de Santa discusses the strain effects of social changes in the Puerto Rican society [4] and summarizes the following points of tension affecting the social life of the island, as stated by Cunningham:

1. A traditional system of relations based on social class and family background for social status and an industrial system based on personal competition, initiative, and conspicuous consumption as a basis for status
2. High aspirations and low achievements
3. The value of dignity, pride, and honor and the increasing emphasis on material wealth and consumption

3 Henry Wells, *The Modernization of Puerto Rico* (Cambridge, Mass.: Harvard University Press, 1969), quoted by Professor Noriega de Santa.
4 Carmen Lydia Noriega de Santa, "The Family as a Social Welfare Institution in a Developing Country" (School of Social Work, University of Puerto Rico, Río Piedras, 1970).

4. The value system that reveres the *jíbaro* and that which reveres the successful entrepreneur

5. The present commitment to democracy and the traditional methods of power that prevailed in the colonial system.[5]

She adds that other sources of tension for the Puerto Rican people, or for some social segments in the Island, are represented by: the tremendous population explosion; the unequal distribution of economic benefits; cultural assimilation and its conflicts; sociopolitical relations within the federal system; the transcending issue of the need for an eventually "permanent" political status; and a feeling that through the weakening of traditional patterns of living in the Puerto Rican family, a loss of family unity and control is in process.

Despite these deep-seated concerns, high population density, lack of money, and scanty resources, the country strives to reach the goals set by the Government of Puerto Rico:

The ultimate goal of the people of Puerto Rico is to create a civilization of excellence. The individual—his freedom, opportunities, welfare, development and dignity—is the foremost concern in Puerto Rico. A civilization of excellence is one of equal opportunities where social justice flourishes.

. . . The basic goals to achieve this civilization are:

1. Full education, in quantity, quality and profundity

2. Maximum health

3. Home ownerhsip for each family

4. A balance in life between rural and urban areas and orderly development of the cities

5. An increasing proportion of the Puerto Rican economy in the hands of the Island's residents

6. Abolition of extreme poverty and its principal concomitant, unemployment.[6]

[5] See Ineke Cunningham, "An Inventory of Research in Puerto Rico Relevant to Social Change and Public Policy," in Millard Hansen, ed., *Social Change and Social Policy* (Río Piedras, Puerto Rico: Social Science Research Center, 1968), p. 47. Most of these points are cited by Cunningham as findings in Tumin and Feldman, *op. cit.*

[6] "A Summary of the Four Year Economic and Social Development Plan of Puerto Rico 1969–72" (San Juan, Puerto Rico: Planning Board of Puerto Rico, 1970), p. 1.

EDUCATION

The Government of Puerto Rico aspires to give universal education to all its people. During 1950–51 the total enrollment (first to twelve grades) in the public and private accredited schools represented 66 percent of the total population within the ages of six to eighteen; the figure was 83.2 percent during 1962–63 and 88.02 during 1969–70.[7]

Enrollment in the University of Puerto Rico (the only statal university), which included 6,308 students in 1940, increased to 26,540 in 1960 and is now 42,739. The total number of students in all five universities of the island, private and public, in August, 1970, was 64,704.[8] But there are severe deficiencies in the educational system. In 1964, 55 percent of all students were in double enrollment (three hours in school daily) or in the interlocking system (five continuous hours of school in one room under one teacher). In 1969, 65 percent of all elementary students were in full-time classes; 24 percent had five hours of classes daily; 4 percent had four hours; and 7 percent, three hours.[9] Seventy-nine percent of the double-enrollment students were concentrated in the rural zone. A powerful contributing factor to the school problems is the lack of teachers and of appropriate buildings. Although the government allots the largest percentage of its general budget to education, still the needs surpass the gains.

Furthermore, the Governor, Don Luis A. Ferré, states:

Our school system does not prepare our young people adequately to incorporate themselves to a civilization which every day requires more technical specialization.

Nor does this educational system develop in our youth an overall vision of life—which can give it a correct perspective of the high values of the spirit. . . .

7 Ismael Rodríguez Bou, "El Impacto de la Salud en el Desarrollo del Programa Educativo de Puerto Rico," Biannual Convention of the Public Health Association of Puerto Rico, San Juan, Puerto Rico, 1964, p. 16.
8 Information supplied by Mr. Roque Guzmán Jusino, Economic Advisor of the Higher Board of Education, University of Puerto Rico, Río Piedras.
9 Informe de Recursos Humanos al Gobernador 1970 (San Juan, Puerto Rico: 1971), Junta de Planificación, Estado Libre Asociado de Puerto Rico, p. 207.

We must give greater participation to our youth in the mechanism which orients its academic life and its political future. Our young people do not want any more paternalism. They want a democracy which opens its arms to include their participation in it as well.[10]

HEALTH

Puerto Rico has achieved significant improvement in all health aspects. The most important causes of death in 1940 were those associated with malnutrition and unsanitary conditions. Deaths from these ailments have decreased dramatically, and cancer and heart diseases are now the principal causes of death.

The mortality rate plunged from 20.9 per 1,000 inhabitants in 1940 to 6.4 in 1970. Infant mortality is still a serious concern; 138.5 per 1,000 inhabitants in 1937, it was a constant of 30 per 1,000 in 1970. In general, the life span has lengthened from 46 years in 1940 to 71 years in 1970.[11]

The average Puerto Rican is below the weight and height norms. Malnutrition continues to be one of the most common conditions of school children. Drug addiction is another grave evil, Puerto Rico being the third country of the world in drug abuse.[12] At the present time, the Permanent Commission for the Control of Drug Addiction is trying to cope with the problem by establishing prevention, treatment, and rehabilitation programs.

HOUSING [13]

In Puerto Rico, the family traditionally aspires to own its home. Kurt Back studied the problems of relocation in the island and found that four out of five people chose a house as their first answer to the question: "If you were to win the lottery, what would you buy first?" For most poor and moderate income Puerto Rican families, Back learned, the ideal house would be a single concrete building, with at least three bedrooms, a living-

---

10 Governor's Message to the Legislature of Puerto Rico, San Juan *Star*, January 15, 1970, pp. 20–22.

11 *Ibid.* and Rodríguez Bou, *op. cit.*

12 Stated by Dr. Roland Wingfield, conference about drug addiction, 1970.

13 For this section, the author is indebted to Mrs. Carmen Fidelina Quiñones de Rodríguez, "Housing Problems and Programs in Puerto Rico" (School of Social Work, University of Puerto Rico, 1971; mimeographed).

dining room, and a separate kitchen, with electricity and sanitary facilities, on a piece of land of their own.[14]

As the population increased and families continued to move to the urban areas, housing needs increased also. This posed a problem, because usually these famiiles go to a slum, where they either rent a house at a high price or build on public or submarginal land.

During the last few years, the creation of slums has come to the attention of the public through the newspapers. People are invading public land to build their houses, and they usually resist police intervention. The Slum Clearance Act approved in 1945 established that the construction of a squatter's house on public lands is a public offense, but people frequently test the validity of the act, which seems to be ineffective. Consequently, slums on public land have increased considerably, especially in the San Juan metropolitan area.

In a study which involved two public housing projects, it was found that the majority of the families came from different parts of the island to the San Juan metropolitan area in search of better living opportunities or a job. They settled in the lowermost urban confines, "as they had no house of their own, no money, no jobs, no income. No doubt, the only place to go without these primordial elements of modern life, is the slum, undesirable as it is." [15]

The 1960 Census of Housing indicated that of the 522,000 housing units in the slum, 44 percent were substandard, while 40 percent of the sound structures lacked some or all basic facilities.[16] According to the Urban Renewal and Housing Corporation, in 1970 the proportion (estimated at 27 percent) of the total housing classified as substandard in Puerto Rico was much higher than that in the United States. About two thirds of the inadequate urban dwellings are located in the three

14 Kurt W. Back, *Slums, Projects and People; Social Psychological Problems of Relocations in Puerto Rico* (Durham, N.C.: Duke University Press, 1962), p. 3.

15 Juan A. Roselló, M.D., Manuel Torres Aguiar, M.D., and Carmen Sylvia García, *Vista Hermosa Community Project*, Mental Health Program, School of Medicine (San Juan, Puerto Rico: University of Puerto Rico, 1967).

16 A Summary of the Four Year Economic and Social Development Plan for Puerto Rico, *op. cit.*, p. 33.

major centers of San Juan, Ponce, and Mayagüez. In spite of
the government's effort to produce adequate shelter for the poor,
the situation has remained almost unchanged during the last ten
years.

BALANCE BETWEEN RURAL AND URBAN AREAS AND ORDERLY
DEVELOPMENT OF THE CITIES [17]

Various studies in the United States have found that the inner
cities have the highest density of population. In Puerto Rico
the situation is no different. The 1970 census revealed that the
population of the standard metropolitan area of San Juan has increased 31.4 percent since 1960, while the population of Carolina, which is near San Juan, has increased more than two and
a half times. This high mobility to urban areas, although not
to such a high degree, is found in the three other metropolitan
areas of Ponce, Mayagüez, and Caguas. Many towns in the central part of the island have lost population, such as Ciales (15
percent), Utuado (12 percent), and Jayuya (10 percent).

INSULAR ECONOMY

There has been an apparent resistance by islanders to investing
capital in the industrialization programs. This has to do with the
differential traits of Puerto Rican and North American entrepreneurs. Cochran considers that the Puerto Ricans are more
inclined to prefer social prestige than money and are more de-
tached and indifferent to technology and science.[18]

The powerful capitalist enterprises tend to eliminate the
small, weak businesses belonging to islanders. At present, the
economy of the island is mainly in the hands of North American
owners, who thus control two of the factors of production—
resources and capital.

Puerto Rico has also a very peculiar situation which Lewis
describes:

It is a basically distributive entity characterized typically by the
proliferation of companies undertaking the sale and consumption of

[17] This section was written by Mrs. Carmen F. Quiñones de Rodríguez.
[18] Thomas C. Cochran, *El Hombre de Negocios Puertorriqueño* (Río Piedras,
Puerto Rico: Publicaciones del Centro de Investigaciones Sociales, 1961), p. 170.

goods produced in the United States economy. Its "new men" are clerks, managers, salesmen and advertising publicists rather than production technicians and their work largely concentrates upon sponsoring and catering to the new consumptions habits of the Puerto Rican buyer. The island is a busy distributive outlet for the stateside manufacturer.[19]

He further points out that there is a divorce between production and consumption. Being a commonwealth, the island depends to a large extent upon federal programs.

POVERTY

Puerto Rico has always had a most severe poverty problem. This was so before the North American occupation of the island in 1898, and Puerto Rico still has a dismal situation even after a rapid period of industrialization which has transformed the economy and the whole life pattern of the islanders. Although both death and birth rates have decreased significantly, the number of births still is four times that of deaths.[20] Moreover, the statistical projections reveal that the urban population will grow from 2.3 million to more than 3 million in the next twenty years and that the total population will double in that same period.[21] By the beginning of the twenty-first century, it has been estimated, Puerto Rico will have 5 million people and a population density of 1,600 inhabitants per square mile.[22] Another important factor that contributes to this somber picture is that in 1969, for the first time in ten years, inmigration exceeded emigration.[23]

The island economy has developed rapidly from $287 million in 1940 to more than $2,000 million in 1967; [24] in 1971 the gross national product is near $4 billion. During 1969–70 per

19 Gordon K. Lewis, *Puerto Rico, Freedom and Power in the Caribbean* (New York: Harper Torchbooks, 1963), p. 129.

20 "Disminuye Número de Muertes en Puerto Rico," *El Mundo*, June 6, 1969, p. 11*A*.

21 "Cree Población en Puerto Rico se Duplique en 20 Años," *El Mundo*, August 20, 1970, p. 4*B*.

22 "Informe del Consejo Asesor del Gobernador," *El Mundo*, November 27, 1969, p. 3*A*.

23 "Inmigración Supera a la Emigración," *El Mundo*, August 1, 1969.

24 Jenaro Baquero, "Magnitud y Características de la Inversión Exterior en Puerto Rico," *Revista de Ciencias Sociales*, VIII (1964), 7–8.

capita net annual income was $1,427. In 1960, one fourth of the families had annual incomes under $500 and 90.6 percent had incomes below $5,000.[25]

Additional statistics reveal that three fifths of all families on the island receive one fourth of the total income of Puerto Rico, while one fifth of all the families control more than half the total income.[26]

The population of Puerto Rico is predominantly young; 56.3 percent of all children are between the ages of 14 and 17, and 38.31 percent of the total population are under 14 years of age.[27] In 1970 the median age for the population was 21.38 years for women and 19.80 for men.[28] There are more women than men: 50.3 percent.[29] Fifty-three percent of the total population live in the urban zones, and it is estimated that 62.2 percent will live in the urban areas by 1980. In sum, "5.4 percent of the total population has the richness of the country, 45 percent has malnutrition and for every working person, there are 4.5 persons depending upon him, who are unemployed." [30] Thirteen percent of the population are unemployed, which includes one of every four persons between the ages of 18 and 24 who are actively seeking work.[31] Many more are underemployed or do not continue to look for a job after having lost all hopes of finding one.

The public assistance program, which is one of the main agencies trying to tackle the poverty problem, offers inadequate help. Although its criterion on poverty is stated as "families with a $3,000 year income or less for an average family of five members,[32] if help were given accordingly, more than 75 percent of the island's families would be included.

25 Data obtained from the 1960 U.S. Census of Population, Table 57.

26 Jorge Morales Yordán, "Desarrollo Político y Pobreza," seminar on the problem of poverty in Puerto Rico, School of Public Administration, University of Puerto Rico: 1970, p. 6.

27 *Informe de Recursos Humanos al Gobernador, op. cit.,* p. 6.

28 *Ibid.,* p. 7.

29 1960 U.S. Census of Population, Table 35, pp. 53–116.

30 Rosa C. Marín, "Revela Datos de Isla," *El Mundo,* April 22, 1970, p. 174.

31 Governor's Message to the Legislature, *op. cit.,* p. 20.

32 *Puerto Rico State Plan,* Services to Families and Children, Table V, A and B, Social Security Act, Regulation 220.6, Subscription 2.1, p. 8, effective April 1, 1970.

TABLE II ^a

AVERAGE MONTHLY PUBLIC ASSISTANCE PAYMENTS

Category	Puerto Rico	United States
Aged	$13.40	$74.75
Blind	13.30	102.05
Disabled	13.40	94.50
Children	9.10	47.20

ᵃ Statistics taken from "Average Monthly Assistance Money Payment per Recipient," *Welfare in Review,* VIII, No. 5 (1970), 35.

At present 78,694 cases, comprising 253,346 persons, are receiving public assistance.[33] Nearly one fifth of the total population are recipients of the federal food program.[34] From 1943, when the public assistance program was created, to 1970, average monthly payments have risen from $7.50 to $12.30. The cost of living has risen 64.7 percent in that same period of time.

The inadequate, ridiculous assistance payment given in Puerto Rico is due in part to the fact that the program has a ceiling imposed by the federal government which restrains the economic assignment. Yet, federal requirements are almost the same as those for the states. These federal impositions have curtailed the creativity of the agency in dealing with poverty and have turned the agency into a residual, obsolete one.

The Department of Health of Puerto Rico determined, after a careful study, that a family of four in Puerto Rico needs a minimum annual income of $5,702 in order to meet its basic needs.[35] This amount is higher than the required income for a family of four determined by the Department of Labor of the United States because prices in Puerto Rico are at least 15 percent to 20 percent higher than those in the states, due mainly to the high freight costs imposed by the mainland. Therefore, as

33 *Boletín Estadístico,* Departamento de Servicios Sociales, Estado Libre Asociado de Puerto Rico (San Juan: 1968–69) Table V, p. 16.
34 *Memorial Explicativo del Presupuesto de Gastos de Funcionamiento,* Departamento de Servicios Sociales, Estado Libre Asociado, San Juan, p. 7, sección B-5.
35 *Necesidades Básica del Puertorriqueño en el 1970,* División de Planificación, Investigación y Evaluación, Departamento de Salud (San Juan, Puerto Rico, 1970).

we have seen, 90 percent of the families of Puerto Rico have substandard incomes.

It is easy to perceive the gap between the needs and the aspirations of the Puerto Rican people. The situation stems in part from inadequate social planning:

Social planning was given a low priority from the very outset on the assumption that the amelioration of social problems would come about as the direct results of an increase in the Commonwealth economic base and the consequent rise in economic levels which that economic growth would provide.[36]

This statement explains why the Planning Board of Puerto Rico put so much emphasis on "data collection and trend analysis" and little attention was paid to the sociocultural and psychological consequences of the fierce transformation.[37] By virtue of its being inextricably bound to the economy of the United States, which impinges the demands of a powerful, domineering country upon a small, subordinate one, the situation is a most difficult one. Many programs are established on the island without due consideration of the needs and problems of the Puerto Ricans. And, solutions are difficult to devise because of the island's political status. Nevertheless, the Puerto Ricans are committed to find the right trail, and there is hope that it may be done.

[36] Center for New York City Affairs, *Improving the Capability for Social Planning in Puerto Rico* (New York: New School of Social Research: 1969), p. 2.
[37] *Loc. cit.*

Aspirations for Ethnic Minorities

RABBI LEVI A. OLAN

THE FORGING OF ONE NATION out of several ethnic, religious, and national groups has been the concern of America from the beginning. The European experience is different from that of the United States. With the rise of nationalism after 1800 and the Treaty of Versailles, social boundaries became more valid than political ones. Each subordinate people acclaimed the necessity of a common language, customs, historical experience, biological relatedness, and a separate, autonomous existence. There were "kin states." Hungary was a kin state to the Slovaks in Czechoslovakia. Germany was a kin state to the Sudeten Germans in Bohemia and Moravia. This led to secessionism, militancy, and, ultimately, war. The minority problem was a nationality problem.

In Europe incessant changes in political boundaries did not alter the essential nature of the minority problem. In fact, the more it changed, the more it remained the same. In America, this continuous change produced something else.

The first settlers in this country were "different" in Europe but homogeneous in America. It was these Englishmen who gave their stamp to the culture and institutions which became "American." It was they who gave to the young nation its leadership and language, law and philosophy, and religion. The nineteenth-century immigrants and those who followed were considered to be outsiders, with a definite minority status.

The Declaration of Independence declares only for individual liberty. It is silent on cultural pluralism. The American political and legal system recognizes no differences on grounds of race, religion, or national origin. It has remained characteristic of this nation to profess its faith in equality of opportunity for all.

Whether Mexican Americans, Negroes, Jews, and Catholics should maintain their identity is not a matter of formal concern. In fact, the founding fathers feared the alien ideas which immigrants would bring to the nation. Jefferson, a liberal on slavery and race, said: "They will infuse into [our legislation] their spirit, warp and bias its direction and render it a heterogeneous, incoherent, distracted mass."

Our democracy was founded as a "white" state. The Negro is excluded from the Constitution, which William Lloyd Garrison labeled "a pact with the devil." Those who point to the conflict between our ideals and our actions forget that we never had, as a nation, a commitment to the Negro. In the Constitution, a Negro slave is three fifths of a man for representation in the House of Representatives. The Constitution also authorized the federal government to return runaway slaves to their owners. Slaves were allowed in Washington's army only after the British offered to free them if they would fight for them. Lincoln said that he would settle the Civil War even if he could not free a single slave. Emancipation was merely a military expedient. "History points to two conclusions," writes Eli Ginzberg, "animosity, indifference, neglect toward the Negro in both North and South; and most Negro progress to date was made in the economic self-interest of the white community rather than through its active encouragement." [1]

The hard fact is that the basic institutions of America were not structured to include either immigrants or Negroes. Our "intractable" difficulty since 1880 has been to try to restructure them to make room for "outsiders."

IMMIGRANTS

Three different efforts have been made to create one nation out of the many diverse racial, religious, and national groups that settled in America: assimilation, the melting pot, and acceptance of cultural pluralism. The Civil War, followed by industrial expansion and westward settlement, created a need for immi-

---

[1] Eli Ginzberg, "The Negroes' Problem is the Whites," in Milton L. Barron, ed., *Minorities in a Changing World* (New York: Knopf, 1967), p. 351.

grants and produced a favorable climate for their reception. Swedes and Norwegians came from Northern and Western Europe. By 1880 they were the establishment, whose character was white, Anglo-Saxon, and Protestant—the WASP. The immigrants who followed came from Eastern and Southern Europe —Italians, Jews, Slavs, and Poles. The Western frontier was closing, forcing these newcomers to huddle in urban slums and to take their place on the lowest rung of the industrial ladder. Along with this came some ugly racism, the projection of the nativist-Aryan principle, and the American Protective Association to warn against the Pope taking over the United States.

Assimilation. The assimilation effort began. One educator told his colleagues: "Our task is to break up these groups or settlements, to assimilate them and amalgamate these people as a part of our American race, and to implant in their children, so far as can be done, the Anglo-Saxon conception of righteousness, law and order, and popular government." [2] A feverish effort to Americanize the immigrant reached its climax during the First World War. Even President Wilson, who spoke eloquently about self-determination for European nationals, wrote: "America does not consist of groups. A man who thinks of himself as belonging to a particular national group in America has not yet become an American." [3]

Industry became fearful of radical labor movements instigated by the new workers and the strikes which they engendered. A tremendous effort was made to adjust the "foreigners" to the WASP version of American society. The federal government, as well as state and local agencies, became involved. Evening classes were introduced to help assimilate them, that is, to teach them to conform. It all ended in frustration. In the 1920s came the policy of restricted immigration which proclaimed officially the inferiority and unassimilability of Eastern and Southern Europeans. The depression and the Second World War led to the McCarran-Walter Act of 1952 which placed the final seal upon these assumptions and upon the superiority of the Anglo-Saxon.

2 Ellwood P. Cubberley, *Changing Conceptions of Education* (Boston: Houghton Mifflin Co., 1909), p. 6.
3 Woodrow Wilson, quoted in Oscar Handlin, *The American People in the Twentieth Century* (Boston: Beacon Press, 1963), p. 121.

Assimilation had failed. The ghettos with their own churches, charities, and clubs established themselves as an answer to the exclusion which had been forced upon the immigrants. They learned to dwell apart, where they retained their ethnic traditions, published their own newspapers in their native language. They tended to become a minority, with second-class standing. Whatever acculturation occurred was without any intermingling on a primary group level. The country clubs became a feature of this situation. Myron Kaufmann describes a Jewish boy at Harvard who tries to be "one of them." [4] The answer was an invitation to "look me over but don't touch me." The Negro and the Mexican American did not receive even a polite invitation. Assimilation was a failure.

The melting pot. The second effort to resolve the problem of one nation and many ethnic, religious groups is known as the melting pot. Handlin defines this as one where "all could be absorbed and that all could contribute to an emerging national character." [5] Ralph Waldo Emerson wrote glowingly:

. . . in this continent—asylum of all nations—the energy of Irish, Germans, Swedes, Poles, and Cossacks, and all the European tribes— of the Africans and the Polynesians—will construct a new race, a new religion, a new state, a new literature, which will be as vigorous as the New Europe, which came out of the smelting pot of the Dark Ages, or that which earlier emerged from Pelasgic and Etruscan barbarism.[6]

It was the English-Jewish writer Israel Zangwill, in 1908, who dramatically spoke for this view in his play *The Melting Pot:* "America is God's crucible, the great melting pot where all races are melting and reforming . . . Germans and Frenchmen, Irishmen and Englishmen, Jews and Russians—into the crucible with you all! God is making the American." [7]

Even if the ideal is a desirable one, and there is grave doubt

4 Myron Kaufmann, *Remember Me to God* (Philadelphia: Lippincott, 1957), quoted in Joshua A. Fishman, "Childhood Indoctrination for Minority Group Membership," *Daedalus,* Spring, 1961.

5 Oscar Handlin, ed., *Immigration as a Factor in American History* (Englewood Cliffs, N. J.: Prentice-Hall, Inc., 1959) , p. 146.

6 Quoted in Introduction by Stuart P. Sherman to *Essays and Poems of Emerson* (New York, 1921), p. xxxiv.

7 Israel Zangwill, *The Melting Pot.* (New York: Macmillan, 1909), pp. 37, 199.

about it, it proved to be impossible of achievement. Theodore
Roosevelt could say that "the representations of Old World races
are being fused together into a new type," but this did not stop
him from maintaining that "the crucible into which all the new
types are melted into one was shaped from 1776 to 1789 and
our nationality was definitely fixed in all its essentials by the
men of Washington's day." [8]

The question is: who melts what? The Southern and Eastern
Europeans would be completely lost (melted) in this host
society, leaving no cultural trace at all. All except the Irish
Catholics and the German Jews prior to 1880 were absorbed
into the general white "sociological Protestant" sector of American life. Some of them may have a vague consciousness of immigrant ancestors. Milton Gordon suggests that what we have
achieved is not a "melting pot" but a "transmuting pot." All
the ingredients are transformed and assimilated into an ideal
Anglo-Saxon world. Protestant descendants of Germans and
Scandinavians can merge into the WASP society with relative
ease. Jews, Irish Catholics, Italian Catholics, and Polish Catholics cannot do so without a religious conversion or a "sociological
passing," neither one of which is attractive. Negroes, Indians,
Orientals, Mexican Americans, and Puerto Ricans are kept out
by racial barriers. America did not become the melting pot out
of which arose the new American. At best, it may be described as
a "multiple melting pot" for which a better name is "pluralism."

Cultural pluralism. Cultural pluralism was a fact before it was
proposed as a theory. People who came to this country settled
together if for no other reason than to be able to speak to one
another in the only language they knew. Some of them even
sought land from the government in order to live together.
Cultural pluralism existed here before idealists like Jane Addams
and John Dewey projected the idea of an America which was
more like a symphony than a melting pot. Dewey wrote:

I wish our teaching of American history in the public schools would
take more account of the great waves of migration by which our land
for three centuries has been continuously built up, and make every
pupil conscious of the rich breadth of our national make-up. When

[8] Quoted in Saveth, *op. cit.,* p. 121.

every pupil recognizes all the factors which have gone into our being, he will continue to prize and reverence that coming from his own past, and he will think of it as honored in being simply one factor in forming a whole nobler and finer than itself.[9]

It was Horace Kallen who spelled out the concept of cultural pluralism. He suggested that a man can change everything but his grandfather, and that he is related to his ethnic group involuntarily and indissolubly. But in all of this he saw a positive asset, since a man realizes himself and his potentialities through membership in his group: "It is the efficacious and natural habitat of his temperament . . . the center at which he stands, the point of his most intimate social reactions, therefore of his intensest emotional life." [10] Kallen claims that this is what the founding fathers meant both in the Declaration and in the Constitution. Equality meant difference; people are different from, but equal to, each other in their right to life, liberty, and the pursuit of happiness. He pointed to the positive values of pluralism, the valuable contributions of each ethnic group to the total culture of America. He saw the nation benefiting from the indirect "impact of diversities."

Structural pluralism. The present situation in America discloses the presence of structural pluralism with a minimum of cultural pluralism. The separate institutions of religion, philanthropy, and social clubs occupy an accepted position, and are probably here to stay for some time. The unique beliefs, values, and symbols of each separate group play a far lesser role. There is nothing in our democratic value complex that calls for these to be merged. Every citizen has the right to choose with whom to be intimate. This does not in any way justify discrimination in employment, housing, education, toilets, or marriage of races. It would help America if this pluralistic view were made a conscious part of life. People who choose to retain their ethnic affiliation are not "clannish."

There is a danger, however, inherent in a pluralistic society.

[9] John Dewey, "Nationalizing Education," in National Education Association of United States, Addresses and Proceedings of the Fifty Fourth Annual meeting, 1916, pp. 185–86.
[10] Horace M. Kallen, *Culture and Democracy in the United States* (New York: Boni and Liveright, 1924), p. 200.

It can become dysfunctional as attitudes of groups interfere with the operation of society itself. An emphasis upon racial, religious, or national background instead of competence and training as a basis for competition in an industrialized society is self-defeating. A warning example is the excessive emphasis on pluralism in the Netherlands. There is a built-in, low degree of prejudice in a modestly structured separation. Organizational separation according to church or race or nationality, as in the Boy Scouts or certain civic agencies, can become detrimental to the larger social purpose of a community.

The fact is that the problems of group adjustment are still with us. It is true that the noisy nativism of a generation ago has disappeared or is not visible. The day of large-scale white immigration is passed. We are now dealing with second-, third-, and even fourth-generation natives who were born in America. While there are still some adjustments to be made, the urgency is absent. We face a completely new situation in our effort to fashion one nation out of many groups. This time it is color which makes the difference.

Those who now critically challenge the profession of American democracy are natives; they have been living in this land for generations; and some of their ancestors were here before the white man stepped foot on it. They have been the suppressed minorities. They are now projecting their demands for equality as well as for the right to group identity. There is a common pattern in the experiences of the American Indian, the Mexican American, and the Negro.

AMERICAN INDIAN

In the case of the American Indian, our nation suffers severe guilt. The Indian wars which our history books describe in terms of manifest destiny are to the Indians nothing but foreign adventures to create an empire. The massacre at Sand Creek in 1864 [11] was an earlier My Lai. The American Congress devises policies and programs to get the Indians off their lands, and

11 See "Sand Creek Massacre" in Vine Deloria, Jr., ed., *Of Utmost Good Faith* (San Francisco: Straight Arrow Books, 1971), pp. 161–66.

into the great American dream. Vine Deloria, Jr., an American Indian, comments:

> Believe me, this is the last place we want to be. . . . the issue becomes how they can get us into the mainstream and make us as neurotic as middle-class whites. . . . Even though you'd call me a liberal Democrat, I've come to the point now where I'd vote for George Wallace if he has a good Indian program, one that would let us hold our land, and help us survive as a culture.[12]

In the last five years, the life of the white middle class ceased to be attractive. Indians of mixed blood who had toyed with the idea of assimilation into the Anglo-American way of life began to identify as full bloods. Deloria says: "White society is breaking down all around us. It can't offer people support anymore; even myths like the melting pot are dead. People are regrouping." [13] In fact, the Indian tribe rises as a model community for the whole American nation. In it the dignity of the individual is respected, and the identity of each person is sufficiently assured to save him from the alienation of the "lonely crowd." In a burst of ethnic pride the writer proposes: "For the white man to continue to exist he must adopt a total Indian way of life." [14]

The whites not only need a sense of personal dignity and identity, they must recapture a respect for nature and stop exploiting it. They need a new morality to replace the bankrupt moral code which treats its minorities so brutally. Indeed, the whole social fabric is coming apart in America, and tribalism is one way to rebuild it. We need to humanize life, and the Indian community is an example par excellence. The American Indian claims his right as an individual American and his right to live a separate community existence.

MEXICAN AMERICANS

The Mexican Americans are, by and large, Americans by early acquisition of territory in the West. The national creed would assimilate them as soon as they fully accept Anglo-American values and way of life. There is the "high type," so styled be-

---

12 An Interview with Vine Deloria, Jr., *Mademoiselle*, April, 1971.
13 *Ibid.*   14 *Ibid.*

cause of their occupational achievements and wealth (by good Anglo standards) and their command of Anglo-American ways. These people are accepted by service clubs, on committees of the United Fund, and on race relations commissions. There is a limited amount of social intercourse, even some intermarriage. They are, it seems, capable of assimilation but not of full acceptance. The "non-high type" is the victim of the assumption that he is inferior.

To the Anglo, the inferiority of the Mexican American appears to be self-evident. An Anglo-American woman polished it off by saying, "Mexicans are inferior because they are so typically Mexican." The stereotype works overtime: "Mexicans are all alike"; "a Mexican is a Mexican." They are described as dirty, drunkards, improvident, indolent, deceitful, of low morality, unpredictable, unrealistic, and hostile to Anglo-Americans. To the Anglo-American, all these "traits" justify a policy of exclusion and discrimination. At the same time, it is condescendingly agreed that Mexicans are musical, always ready for a fiesta, romantic, love flowers, and have a green thumb. This is a polite way of saying they are childlike and irresponsible, and therefore capable only of subordinate status.

The Mexican Americans remain separated by choice as well as by necessity. The majority, particularly the younger generation, share some of the characteristics of the Anglo culture. They accept its materialism as well as its medical beliefs, language, and courtship customs. Nevertheless, most of them retain a subtle aspect of their ethnic heritage. They are trying to live in the best of two worlds. They must acculturate to get ahead, but not to the point where power and weatlh are as dominant in their lives as in that of the Anglos. They want acceptance, equality, and group identity. They want these now.

NEGROES

Michael Harrington suggests that the "accumulated wisdom of the great European immigrant groups has become irrelevant; for it will not help the poor or the Negro." [15] This is what Louis

---

[15] Quoted by Nathan Glazer in "The Peoples of America" in Barron, ed., *op. cit.*, p. 142.

Lomax, James Baldwin, Nat Hentoff, and other supporters of Negro militancy are saying. There is a severe estrangement between other ethnic groups and the Negro. All whites appear to the militant Negroes to be like those who used them on their way up. The petty prejudices that still exist against the white immigrant are nothing like the hatred that the Negro meets. The virtues of a pluralistic society are for the Negro a hollow mockery. He sees in it the limitation of government power. Separate voluntary groups bound together by their own patterns of worship, education, social life, residential concentration, and even economic activity enhance the life of one group—becoming exclusive and discriminatory, from the viewpoint of the American Negro.

The "new" Negro was born in the Second World War. He began to move to the industrial North, thus altering the Negro population from regional, rural, and agricultural to national, urban, and industrial. He was becoming "American" in the demographic modes of the dominant white majority. A middle class began to appear. Almost a half million Negroes are now in colleges and professional schools, and the same number have incomes of about $8,000. The Negro has taken his place in the military service, and is supported by the steady enactment of antidiscriminatory legislation.

In the dilemma of the Negro the crucial issue of our national problem of the one and the many is very clear. On the one hand, he wants full acceptance into the larger society without any discrimination. On the other, he seeks to preserve his racial heritage and its structural separation. He brings into sharp focus the failure of America to explicate the problem of individual group interests in relation to national interests. In the national interest, it is important to work for the final liquidation of Negro separation in all areas of life—economic, social, cultural and residential. At the same time, the new mood of ethnic identity emphasizes Negro separation.

The situations of the American Indians, Mexican Americans, and Negroes—and Puerto Ricans and Jews—have some elements in common. They all share a conscious thrust toward civil rights, freedom, and equality for the individual regardless of color, creed, or national origin. They also disclose a common interest in the preservation of their group identity. As desegregation proceeds and integration advances will group loyalties become a resistant to the democratic process? There are some who claim that it will bring disunity among Americans. Group loyalties are desirable and even necessary for spiritual self-preservation and self-fulfillment, as well as a source of national enrichment. It is very important for us to know what we mean by "integration" in a pluralistic society.

Among the effects of freedom are the fluidity and mobility of the group, a condition which makes it difficult for separate groups to retain their members. The intermingling in the armed services and the open society that makes for intermarriage are not conducive to group loyalty. The individual is free to choose his associations, to identify or not to identify. When the group becomes aggressively rigid it can crush the individual no less than the general forces at work. There is a difference between desegregation and integration. In one case it is the preservation of the rights of the individual. This is a matter of laws and their proper enforcement. Integration, however, is more than a matter of the removal of prejudice as well as discrimination. It is more than just desegregation. It calls for an attitudinal change, removal of the fears, hatreds, suspicions, stereotypes, and superstitions. This is a program which, as Kenneth Clark tells us, "cannot come overnight. It requires education, and deals poignantly with the problems of changing men's minds." [16] Desegregation does not of itself bring integration, primary as it is. The government can and should desegregate with something more than all deliberate speed. The courts seem to be saying that, but the government cannot force integration.

Roscoe Pound says that there are "limits of effective legal action." The enactment and enforcement of law are important, but only as episodes in a process by which society, working through a number of institutions, manages to realize a given principle. He tells us that most laws are obeyed by most people:

[16] Kenneth B. Clark, "Desegregation: the Role of the Social Sciences," *Teachers College Record*, LXII No. 1, 16–17.

When men demand much of law, when they seek to devolve upon it the whole burden of social control, when they seek to make it do the work of church and home, the enforcement of law comes to involve many difficulties. . . . The purposes of the legal order are [then] not all on the surface, and it may be that many whose nature is by no means anti-social are out of accord with some or even with many of these purposes. . . . It is then we begin to hear complaints that laws are not enforced and the forgotten problem of the limitation upon effective legal action once more becomes acute.[17]

The fugitive slave law of 1850 and the Prohibition law are shining examples. The first was an immoral act, and the second tried to regulate conduct that is morally neutral.

The Civil Rights Act of 1964 is not like these. It is a just law which a majority may impose upon everyone. There is need for political and social leadership if we are to attain the end which the law seeks. Law of itself has some persuasive power. Now we must persuade the people of its morality, and convince a majority that it is right. America has a long way to go to achieve desegregation and integration. By laws, by enforcement of those laws, and by a crusade to persuade the peoples of the nation, we must move right on.

It is also important that we acknowledge that we are a pluralistic society, and that we explore the uses we can make of the situation. In a day of the "lonely crowd" and "alienated man" the group can help improve the quality of general life. The Negro is not responsible for crime, but the Negro community has an opportunity to help solve the problem in a way to which no white effort is comparable. In a society whose values are in grave question, the value systems of the American Indian as to the natural world, the Jew as to the family, and the Mexican American as to materialism are worthy of preservation. These values are better preserved in the ethnic groups and become a contribution to the general value system of the nation. In a day when man is in a desperate search to find his real self, the continuation of a pluralistic, ethnic, or religious community is a wholesome answer, although only a partial one.

Anthropologists tell us that minority groups disappear, ab-

17 Address before the Pennsylvania Bar Association, June 27, 1916.

sorbed by the dominant strain. Only when they are isolated, as are the Indians on the reservations, is there a chance for a group to survive. This may be true in the long run. For the present and the immediate future, ethnic groups in America are too strongly established to be suppressed. It is to be hoped that as we meet the demands of equality, freedom, and human rights for every individual, these groups will accept our complex society in which separation is neither required nor forbidden but is to be tolerated with sympathy.

The Social Welfare Client: Blaming the Victim

WILLIAM RYAN

THERE IS A PROCESS that I have named elsewhere "blaming the victim." [1] It is a process that goes on very frequently these days—in the minds of social scientists, of reform politicians, of liberal journalists, and of social welfare professionals. And it is a process, a set of ideas, that is dramatically damaging to the very people we are presumably most concerned about and most committed to help.

What is meant by "blaming the victim"?

Twenty years ago, Zero Mostel used to impersonate a Dixiecrat senator conducting an investigation on the origins of the Second World War. At the climax of the sketch, the senator boomed out, in an excruciating mixture of triumph and suspicion, "What was Pearl Harbor doing in the Pacific?"

Twenty years ago, we could laugh at Zero Mostel's caricature. In recent years, however, the victim is being blamed every day in the arena of social problems, public health, anti-poverty programs, and social welfare.

The miserable health care of the poor is explained away on the grounds that the victim has poor motivation, lacks health information, is "hard to reach," and delays in seeking proper medical care. By spotlighting the supposed characteristics of the victim, we are invited to ignore the fact that medical care in America is organized in a scandalously unjust manner, so that, in effect, good health and long life are auctioned off to the highest bidder.

The miseducated child in the slum school is said to contain

[1] William Ryan, *Blaming the Victim* (New York: Pantheon Books, 1971).

within himself the causes of his inability to read and write well. The shorthand phrase is "cultural deprivation," which conveys that the poor child carries a scanty pack of cultural baggage as he enters school. He does not know about books and magazines and newspapers, they say. They say that if he talks at all—an unlikely event since slum parents "don't talk to their children"—he certainly does not speak correctly. If one can manage to get him to sit in a chair, they say, he squirms and looks out the window. In a word, he is "disadvantaged" and "socially deprived," they say, and this, of course, accounts for his failure (*his* failure, they say) to learn much in school.

No one remembers to ask questions about the collapsing buildings and torn textbooks, the insensitive teachers, the blustering principals, the relentless segregation, the rigid administrator, the bigoted or cowardly members of the school board, the insulting history book, the stingy taxpayers. We are encouraged to confine our attention to the child and dwell on all his "defects." "Cultural deprivation" becomes an omnibus explanation for the educational disaster area known as the inner-city school.

Pointing to the supposedly deviant Negro family as the "fundamental weakness of the Negro community" is another way to blame the victim. "Negro family" too has become a shorthand phrase, with stereotyped connotations of matriarchy, fatherlessness, and pervasive illegitimacy. Growing up in the "crumbling" Negro family is supposed to account for most of the racial evils in America. Insiders, of course, know that this phrase is supposed to evoke images of growing up with a long-absent or never-present father, with bossy women ruling the roost, so that the children are irreparably damaged. This refers particularly to the poor, bewildered male children, whose psyches, it is supposed, are fatally wounded and who are never, alas, to learn the trick of becoming upright, downright, forthright All-American boys. By focusing our attention on the Negro family as the apparent cause of racial inequality, we are diverted, and racism, discrimination, segregation, and the powerlessness of the ghetto are subtly, but thoroughly, downgraded in importance.

An immediate question might be: "So what? What difference

does it make?" It makes a great deal of difference because this way of thinking has infected and thereby crippled the bulk of our social policy planning in recent decades.

Consider a recent event.

A number of mayors gathered in New York to bewail the state of our cities. Boston's mayor predicted that the deplorable condition of Brooklyn's slums might well foreshadow the decline of an entire civilization. It became clear rather quickly that the ingathering of mayors was for the purpose of beating the drum for more money to pursue what most of them would probably call "programs to reverse urban decay."

It sounded very dramatic and, indeed, very noble. Who is there to stand up and oppose "programs to reverse urban decay?" Indeed, who is there even to stand up and ask a hard question like, "Why has the health of cities been declining so precipitately during the very period that the programs advocated by the mayors have been flourishing?" We have had urban renewal and manpower training and compensatory education and antipoverty programs and community health centers and work-incentive programs for years.

I would suggest a fairly simple, if rather drastic, explanation: these programs, accepted unthinkingly as "progressive" efforts to rescue the cities are, in fact, nothing of the sort; they are mostly useless and occasionally injurious to the city and to those who live in the city. Further, the state of mind that impels the mayors to clamor for "more" is a direct reflection of "blaming the victim."

This is a cockeyed and dangerous way of thinking, principally because it provides the theoretical base for most of the ineffective "social reforms" of recent years, that have actually reformed nothing, have gone nowhere, and have had no effect on the problems they were supposed to cure. Each program of this nature, sooner or later, proves to be a massive flop. The program fails so miserably because the planners who dream it up misread the nature of the problem. They misread the problem so grossly because their analysis is distorted and their view foreshortened by the ideological process of "blaming the victim."

Careful analysis reveals that in virtually every one of our liberal reform programs the basic assumption is that there is something wrong with the victim, and the purpose of the program is to change him, to provide him with skills, with motivation, with information. These programs never aim at the structural reform of social institutions, such as the schools, the housing system, or the patterns of service delivery.

A major pharmaceutical manufacturer, as an act of humanitarian concern, has distributed copies of a large poster warning, "Lead paint can kill!" The poster, featuring a photograph of a charming little girl, goes on to explain that if children eat lead paint, it can poison them, they can develop serious symptoms, suffer permanent brain damage, even die.

The National Association for Retarded Children, in a television commercial, urges mothers to watch their children to keep them from eating chips of lead paint. The health department of a major American city has put out a coloring book that labels as neglectful and thoughtless the mother who does not keep her infant under constant surveillance to keep him from eating paint chips.

Now, no one would argue that it is not important to spread knowledge about the danger of eating paint. But to campaign against lead paint only in these terms is destructive and misleading and, in a sense, an effective way to support slum landlords who define the problem of lead poisoning in precisely these terms.

The cause of the poisoning is the lead in the paint on the walls of the apartment in which the children live. The presence of the lead is illegal. To use lead paint in a residence is illegal. To permit lead paint to be exposed in a residence is not only illegal, it is potentially criminal since most housing codes provide for criminal penalties. The general problem of lead poisoning, then, is more accurately analyzed as the result of a systematic program of lawbreaking by one interest group in the community, with the toleration and encouragement of the public authority charged with enforcing that law. To ignore these continued and repeated law violations, to ignore the fact that the supposed law enforcer actually cooperates in lawbreaking, and then to load a burden of guilt on the mother of a dead or dangerously ill child is an egregious distortion of reality. And to do so under the guise of public spirited and humanitarian service to the community is intolerable.

The righteous humanitarian concern displayed by the drug company with its poster, and the health department with its coloring book, is a genuine concern, and this is a typical feature of "blaming the victim." Also typical is the swerving away from the central target that requires systematic change and, instead, focusing on the individual affected. The ultimate effect is always to distract attention from the basic causes and to leave the primary social injustice untouched. Most telling, the proposed remedy for the problem is of course to work on the victim himself. Prescriptions are invariably conceived to revamp and revise the victim, never to change the surrounding circumstances. They want to change his attitudes, alter his values, fill in his cultural deficits, energize his apathetic soul, cure his character defects, train him and polish him and woo him from his savage ways.

Every important social problem—crime, mental illness, welfare, civil disorder, racial injustice—has been analyzed within the framework of blaming the victim, and in many cases, the analysis has led to the well-meaning but pointless programs that are frustrating, not only to the taxpayer who sees no gains from them, but also to the supposed beneficiaries who perceive no benefit. I say "well-meaning" deliberately, because it is important to recognize that people who blame the victim are not recognizable as racists or reactionaries in any ordinary sense. They include sympathetic social scientists with social consciences in good working order and liberal politicians with a genuine commitment to reform. They dissociate themselves from crude ideas like "survival of the fittest" or racial superiority. "The Negro is *not born* inferior," they shout apoplectically. "Force of circumstance," they explain in reasonable tones, "has made him inferior." They dismiss with self-righteous contempt any claims that the poor man in America is plainly unworthy or shiftless or enamored of idleness. No, they say, he is "caught in the cycle of poverty." He is trained to be poor by his culture and his family life, endowed by his environment (perhaps by his ignorant mother's outdated style of toilet training) with those unfortunately unpleasant characteristics that make him ineligible for a passport into the affluent society.

The old-fashioned conservative ideologies simply dismissed victims as inferior, genetically defective, or morally unfit: the emphasis was on the intrinsic, even hereditary, defect. The new ideology attributes defect and inadequacy to the malignant nature of poverty, injustice, slum life, and racial difficulties. The stigma that marks the victim and accounts for his condition is acquired, of social rather than genetic origin. But the stigma, the defect, the fatal difference is still located within the victim. With such an elegant formulation, the person who sees himself as a humanitarian can have it both ways. He can simultaneously concentrate his charitable interest on the defects of the victim, condemn the vague social and environmental stresses that produced the defect (some time ago), and ignore the continuing effect of victimizing social forces (right now). It is a brilliant ideology for justifying a perverse form of social action designed to change, not society, as one might expect, but rather society's victim.

The logical outcome of analyzing social problems in terms of the deficiencies of the victim is the development of programs aimed at correcting those deficiencies. The formula for action becomes extraordinarily simple: change the victim.

At the core of this way of thinking is the idea a number of individuals "have" the problem in question. As a person is said to "have" cancer, or to "have" a speech defect, others are thought to "have" poverty or to "have" a slum apartment or to "have" racial discrimination, as if it were his own burden or his own property rather than a deficiency in the total community, a social condition, quite independent from the individuals who are suffering from that social condition at any given moment. Those who supposedly "have" the problem are further defined as somehow different from the rest of us, which is a short step from saying that there is something wrong with them.

It is dangerous to see other persons as markedly different from ourselves. Different ones are seen as less competent, less skilled, less knowing—in short, less human. The ancient Greeks deduced from a single characteristic, a difference in language, that the barbarians—that is, the "babblers" who spoke a strange tongue —were wild, uncivilized, dangerous, rapacious, uneducated, lawless, and, indeed, scarcely more than animals. Automatically labeling strangers as savages, weird and inhuman creatures (thus explaining difference by exaggerating difference), not infrequently justifies mistreatment, enslavement, or even extermination of the different ones.

Blaming the victim depends on a similar process of identification (carried out, to be sure, in the most kindly, philanthropic, and intellectual manner) whereby the victim of social problems is identified as strange, different; in other words, as a barbarian, a savage. Discovering savages, then, is an essential component of, and prerequisite to, blaming the victim, and the art of savage discovery is a core skill that must be acquired by all aspiring victim blamers. They must learn how to demonstrate that the poor, the black, the ill, the jobless, the slum tenants, are different and strange. They must learn to conduct or interpret the research that shows how "these people" think in different forms, act in different patterns, cling to different values, seek different goals, and learn different truths.

The idea that social problems can be defined as a bunch of people who are different, who have something *wrong* with them, is illustrated vividly by the frightening thoughts that career around the minds of America whenever the subject of welfare is mentioned. These thoughts range from the malevolently savage —"They're lazy, they're cheaters, immoral, and we've got to do something about them, God damn them!"—to the uselessly paternalistic—"They're demoralized, they're deprived and apathetic, and we've got to do something about them, poor souls!" Both ideas rest on the belief that the person on welfare has somehow to be changed. Offering to "rehabilitate" them or to provide "social services" may sound more progressive and up-to-date and sympathetic, but it is only another version of blaming the victim.

Welfare is not, by any logical use of the term, a "problem"; in fact, it was invented as a *solution* to a problem—the problem of people having no income because they could not or should not work. When Nixon, Reagan, and Rockefeller talk about dealing with the welfare problem by putting people to work, they are, to speak plainly, talking as dishonest demagogues. They know perfectly well that the number of people getting assistance who are in any humane sense actually employable is very tiny; and of those employable and still unwilling to work, infinitesimal. It is almost as hypocritical to speak of training or rehabilitating the assistance recipient to make him employable.

To begin with, about half of all welfare recipients are school-age or preschool children. It seems unlikely that anyone is seriously proposing that we bring back child labor. The next largest group, about one fourth of the total, are the aged. Are they to come out of retirement and return to work? And the 10 percent who are blind or disabled—should we command them to take up their beds and hustle down to the employment office? Almost all the remainder of the group (and here we come to the real targets of the hypocrisy and demagoguery) are the mothers. These are the people Nixon is eager to have scrub floors and empty bedpans. One would hope that not even he would be prepared to pay the price of having the woman who is "encouraged" to empty bedpans leave her three-year-old at home until her seven-year-old gets back from school to act as a baby-sitter. The usual addition at this point is the idea that we will have a chain of government-supported day care centers to which the children will be sent. And if the mother does not want to trust her children to strangers? Presumably she will be "rehabilitated" into understanding that it is, after all, better to empty bedpans and leave her children with strangers than to stay home and let her children starve to death. And chances are she will, sooner or later, come to understand this central axiom of individual enterprise. However, that does not make it right to force mothers of small children to work for substandard wages.

Yet that is the point we come to when we insist on analyzing the problem from the point of view of blaming the victim. The real problem is the unavoidable fact that there are now millions of people, and there will be more, who cannot or should not work, and they do not need rehabilitation or social services. What they need is income. The problem—the scandal—of welfare, then, is not that it encourages poor people not to work, but that it guarantees that they remain poor.

It is much easier to understand the process of blaming the victim as a way of thinking than it is to understand the motivation for it. Why do victim blamers "blame the victim"? The development and application of this ideology, and of all the mythologies associated with it, are readily exposed by careful analysis as hostile acts directed against the disadvantaged, the distressed, the disinherited. It is class warfare in reverse. Yet those who are most fascinated and enchanted by this ideology tend to be progressive, humanitarian, and, in the best sense of the word, charitable persons. They would usually define themselves as moderates or liberals. Why do they pursue this dreadful war against the poor and the oppressed?

For me the answer can be formulated best in psychological terms. The highly charged psychological problem confronting this hypothetical progressive, charitable person is that of reconciling his own self-interest with his humanitarian impulses. This process of reconciliation is not worked out in a logical, rational, conscious way. It is a process that takes place far below the level of sharp consciousness, and the solution—blaming the victim—is arrived at subconsciously as a compromise that apparently satisfies both his self-interest and his charitable concerns.

Our potential victim blamers are in a dilemma. They cannot bring themselves to attack the system that has been so good to them, but they want so badly to be helpful to the victims of racism and economic injustice.

Their solution is a brilliant compromise. They turn their attention to the victim in his postvictimized state. They explain what is wrong with him in terms of social experiences in the past that have left wounds, defects, paralysis, and disability. Their first order of business is to bind up wounds, inject penicillin, administer morphine, and evacuate the wounded for rehabilitation.

They want to make the victim less vulnerable, send him back into battle with better weapons, thicker armor, a higher level of morale. In order to do so effectively, of course, they must analyze the victim carefully, dispassionately, objectively, scientifically, empathetically, mathematically, and hardheadedly, to see what made him so vulnerable in the first place.

The solution of the dilemma is to blame the victim. Those who accept this solution with a sigh of relief are inevitably blinding themselves to the basic causes of the problems. They are, most crucially, rejecting the possibility of blaming, not the victim, but themselves. They are all unconsciously passing judgments on themselves and bringing in a unanimous verdict of not guilty.

If one comes to believe that the culture of poverty produces persons fated to be poor, who can find any fault with our corporation-dominated economy? If the Negro family produces young men incapable of achieving equality, let us deal with that before we go on to the task of changing the pervasive racism that informs and shapes and distorts our every social institution. If an unsatisfactory resolution of one's Oedipus complex accounts for all emotional distress and mental disorder, then by all means let us attend to that and postpone worrying about the pounding, day-to-day stresses of life on the bottom rungs that drive so many to drink, dope, and madness.

The next big question is: how do we stop the process of blaming the victim? Three steps have to be taken. The first is inoculation, becoming sensitized to the general process so that we can recognize it in whatever form it may take. The second step is to analyze the social problems we are dealing with and the programs we are involved in to test their congruence. How well does the program fit the problem? Is there a real thrust toward social and institutional change, or does the program merely propose to alter the victim? The third step, if the program proves to be based on another version of blaming the victim, is to develop a new program designed to change or diminish the forces that are oppressing the victim.

The basic task is to learn to recognize the pattern, which is relatively easy to identify. Any kind of explanation, any kind of formulation of the cause of a given social problem, that locates the root causes in the characteristics of the victim is automatically under suspicion. There are very few, if any, social problems of any significant size and importance, affecting large numbers of persons, that can be logically explained as growing out of the qualities and characteristics of the persons who suffer from those problems.

Take the drug problem. How do we think about the problems of narcotics and youth? What do we see as the nature of the problem, as the cause of the problem? The most common formulation goes something like this: Many young people are alienated and anxious, distressed by the world they see about them. They are, because of the so-called "generation gap," separated to an unusual degree from the normal supports provided by parents, teachers, and other adults. They are struggling with overwhelming emotional problems of disillusion and identity, and finding relief and escape from their despair and anxiety in narcotics. This appears to be an admirably sympathetic, progressive, and humane formulation, and from it flow naturally the kinds of programs that are sprouting all over the country: drop-in centers, rap sessions, self-help groups, halfway houses and residential centers run for and by the kids, as well as new proposals such as separate high schools for youngsters who are on drugs. The generalized solution is: help the kids overcome their identity problems, their sense of alienation, their despair, and they will no longer need drugs.

This is an admirable point of view, in some ways, and at least partially correct—but this line of thought is another example of blaming the victim.

I suggest that adolescent emotional disorder is no more the cause of the drug problem than unresolved oral dependency is the cause of the cigarette problem. If there were no cigarettes, there would be no cigarette problem. If there were no drugs, there would be no drug problem. With all our humanitarian concern for the problems of addicts, we tend to ignore the fact that the narcotics traffic is a big and profitable business with active promotion and sales campaigns. Like other businesses, it is ruthlessly committed to an expanding market, the recruitment of new customers, and retention of the old. Unlike other businesses, it has become a plague on the land. The core of the narcotics problem, then, is the narcotics business, not the individual who has been hooked.

Check the logic of my argument. No one would claim that all or even most emotionally disturbed adolescents are heavy users of drugs. And I do not think anyone would claim that all or most heavy users of drugs are disturbed. True, there is a rather high correlation between the two, and I certainly would not argue that the problem of rehabilitating drug users is not primarily a problem of psychological treatment. Nevertheless, *all the rehabilitation of drug users that we can conceivably undertake will* not *solve the drug problem;* it will only wean away some of the customers of the drug business.

If a person's leg is broken in an automobile accident, no one would argue that a physician should not set the leg and treat the patient. But it is equally important for the physician to know very clearly that he is only setting a broken leg, he is *not* making a contribution to automotive safety.

The same principle applies to the drug problem. We must do everything we can to save the young people who are involved in drugs. Each of them represents enormous distress and suffering; each of them faces deep tragedy. But if we are to deal with the drug problem, we have to deal with the drug *business.* And we have to recognize that we are confronting a strong and evil and ruthless monopoly. But that is what we have to do, and I suggest that we start thinking about how we can persuade the local narcotics squads, the Attorney General, the Governor, the Congress, the Treasury Department, the FBI, the President—whomever we must persuade—that America is sick of having its young people destroyed by an evil, dirty business.

It is time to stop blaming the victim of ghetto schools. It is time to stop wasting the hundreds of millions we spend on "compensatory education" when, in fact, compensatory education and "cultural deprivation" are relatively minor issues. The task is to change the schools, not the kids.

The racial problem in America has nothing substantial to do with strengthening the Negro family. The Negro family is obviously a tough and resilient institution for its children to have survived three centuries of unending oppression. The solution of the racial problem remains what it always has been: end white racism and discrimination.

The health problems of the poor will not be solved by "outreach" programs or health education or even by some kind of second-class health insurance. These problems will be solved only when we and our government decide to take health and life off the auction block. The private enterprise system may well be a satisfactory method of distributing automobiles and cabbages; it is a barbaric way of delivering health care. If a man cannot afford a car, he has the option of taking a bus or walking. If he cannot afford a doctor, his only option is to suffer ill-health and, ultimately, to die before his time (eight to ten years before the man who can afford to pay the doctor's bill). That is too high a price to pay to preserve the physician's princely right to treat whom he pleases at whatever price the traffic will bear.

The welfare problem is neither mysterious nor abnormal. For a variety of understandable and predictable reasons, ranging from the fact that nowadays more people live to be old to the fact that more families break up in modern America, more and more millions of perfectly normal people will not be able to support themselves, and therefore the community at large will be obliged to support them. The only welfare question is: are we going to support them in dignity at a decent level of subsistence, or are we going to make them crawl, suffer, and starve?

I suggest that we should be at least as generous to those whom we currently insist on keeping poor as we are to the well-to-do whom we subsidize at a lavish rate with the "other welfare," welfare for the rich—the tax allowances, the oil depletion allowances, the airline subsidies, the tax-free bonds, the accelerated depreciation allowances. Is it not curious that we fret about weakening the moral fibre of the AFDC family in Mississippi that is getting less than $1,000 a year but have no concern about the effects on the character of Mississippi's Senator Eastland when we pay him tens of thousands of dollars a year for not planting cotton on his plantation? We are remarkably open-handed in subsidizing Seattle aircraft plants to the tune of close to a billion dollars for building some part of an SST; the public assistance budget for the whole state of Washington, however, which is considerably less than one fourth of that amount, is considered some kind of terrible problem.

There are problems, and then there are problems. If we come to understand the real nature of the serious problems we are facing—poverty, slum housing, educational failure, the health of the poor—we must quickly reach the conclusion that virtually all our "progressive" social programs of urban renewal, compensatory education, manpower training, work incentive welfare plans, and dozens of others, are useless and harmful. Once we reach that point, we may be ready at last to eliminate poverty from the life of America and to stop "blaming the victim".

An Alternate Social Policy
for Federal Budgeting

SOL M. LINOWITZ

WE ARE LIVING in difficult, anxious, uncertain times. The country seems pervaded by a profound discontent that has no parallel in our history. Blacks, blue-collar workers, young and old, city dwellers and suburbanites, the poor and the prosperous, husbands and housewives, businessmen and consumers— almost without exception, Americans feel themselves at the mercy of forces they cannot understand, of people and institutions they cannot influence.

In this most advanced and affluent of nations, as many as fourteen million people go to bed hungry every night. More than thirty million must try to survive under housing conditions that rats find ideal but human beings find unspeakably appalling. Millions, many of them children, suffer from malnutrition. And there is mounting evidence that links malnutrition with improper physical and mental development, learning difficulties, behavior problems, and unemployment.

The American who has taken to the suburbs also feels aggrieved. He finds that the "better" things get, the more he makes, the worse off he seems to be: taxes, inflation, traffic jams, pills that are not safe to take, streets that are not safe to walk, water that is not safe to drink, air that is not safe to breathe. He finds it hard to accept the fact that crime and the welfare rolls continue their rapid rise and poverty persists while more and more tax money is being absorbed by welfare, crime control, and poverty programs. He sees his tax burden getting bigger and the problems getting worse; and he cannot make any sense out of it all.

From the point of view of the individual citizen, this elusive thing called "the system" simply is not working. It does not seem to be working for anybody. And none of us knows how to get a handle on it or, indeed, if there is a handle. So we find ourselves with institutional paralysis on the one hand and individual powerlessness on the other: a crippling and corrosive combination that no society can indefinitely survive.

Most of our difficulties stem from the simple and central fact that more and more Americans are living closer and closer together, clustered in great urban complexes, drawn together in their destinies and in their daily lives into an increasingly intricate set of interdependencies. Yet our cities themselves are fragmented by the institutions and attitudes of another era.

So all the problems and pressures of our society converge to hit us where we live: in our cities. Our cities are helpless, handicapped and hamstrung by outmoded jurisdictional arrangements, inadequate financing, and often the absence of any authority to make even the most elementary decisions.

Probably the one weakness that most saps a city's energies and subverts its every serious effort to restore and restructure itself is the Balkanization of the citizenry itself into hostile camps along the lines of race, geography, class, income, occupation. If the riots and other unrest in our urban areas reveal anything, it is that urban America and our society as a whole are indeed afflicted by that "spirit of factionalism" that the founders of this country feared as the one most likely to bring down our democracy. As one commentator puts it:

In these times, our kinship is not so much with the year 2000 as with the year 1776. We are back to the basics of organizing a new society and providing for its governance . . . to the very basic questions about how our society and system are to function . . .

America has been for generation after generation of immigrants a land of promise. It still is, and 400,000 immigrants came to the United States in 1970. For most of us this is a land of fulfilled promises. But for the blacks and for other dispossessed people this has become a land of broken promises.

Thomas Jefferson wanted to write into the Constitution that

the slaves would be set free. His colleagues talked him out of it. There were only four million of "we, the people"—and one in four was a slave. So history moved on, and slavery remained. From 1790 through 1850 no President would mention the word "slavery" in his State of the Union messages. This was not because it was not important each year to the true state of the Union, but because it was supremely important to try to keep the situation cool.

But as President Lincoln said in the midst of the Civil War, "we cannot escape history." Either the institution of slavery or our democracy had to go. A man named John Brown appeared at Harpers Ferry. John Brown wanted to start a war, and so we were started on the road to all the dark and bloody battlefields of a terrible war.

Now look at how slowly history may move.

Over a century ago, in 1862, Lincoln signed the Emancipation Proclamation and freed some two million people. Sixty years later we dedicated the Lincoln Memorial. A small section of seats was provided for the meek and segregated blacks, so that they could attend this celebration of their freedom.

It was another two score years before Martin Luther King, Jr., would stand on the steps of the Memorial and tell us, "I have a dream." There were some 200,000 who heard him directly, and perhaps in our hearts all 200 million of us knew that he dreamed the same American dream as had Thomas Jefferson. And we should have learned that we cannot expect millions to sit in their separate sections and live on dreams forever. We should have known that we must at long last make our society and our system function as we have long dreamed they might.

To do this, we must begin to do first things first. We must begin to put our major concerns and commitments where our real problems are. We must at long last make sure that the allocation of our public resources is congruent with the nation's needs. We must, in other words, reorder our national priorities.

We are all aware that this call is not new. At its inception in the riot-torn summer of 1967, the National Urban Coalition expressed the conviction that reordered national priorities were a prerequisite to the achievement of its principal objectives: the restoration of America's deteriorating cities and the reunification of our divided society.

More than three years have elapsed since that declaration. Both the Johnson and the Nixon Administration have endorsed the demand for an open and systematic discussion of the nation's priorities. The great majority of public interest oragnizations in this country have reaffirmed those endorsements.

Very little has happened.

Instead of producing reordered priorities, this avalanche of talk produced more talk. Instead of becoming a guide to new public decision-making processes, the call for new priorities has become a fashionable cliché.

Everyone is quick to brandish the phrase "reorder national priorities" when pressed about his program for solving America's problems. No one has demonstrated how to translate this slogan into substantive public policy changes.

Why have we been unable to move beyond our rhetoric despite the obvious urgency of the situation?

The answer, I believe, lies in our repeated attempts to define national goals in the abstract rather than in terms of the public resources required to achieve those goals. We demand reordered priorities to provide more funds for income maintenance, education, health, housing, and the environment. Too frequently, however, we fail to apply this talk of new priorities to our single most important instrument for relating national goals to scarce public resources: the federal budget.

In 1970 the federal government spent more for space exploration than for health research, more on subsidies to farmers than on food stamps, more for Pentagon public relations than on ways to dispose of the garbage that is burying us. Defining national priorities without reference to the federal budget is like trying to interpret a constitution without reference to the institutions it governs. Nothing is left but platitudes, empty rhetoric which everyone accepts but which has no real meaning.

To escape this rhetorical dead end, the National Urban Coalition in 1970 embarked on a project never before attempted by a nongovernmental organization. We undertook to construct a complete alternative federal budget, offering careful estimates of the costs of recommended programs and the revenues needed to pay for them in the next five years.

In April of 1971, after nearly a year of intensive consultation with hundreds of experts throughout the country and lengthy deliberations among our own members, this alternative federal budget—or counterbudget, as it has come to be called—was completed. Our main purpose was to suggest how resources might be reallocated, both within the federal budget and between the private and public sectors, for a frontal attack on the nation's most urgent problems.

The results were both dramatic and encouraging. The counterbudget demonstrated that without significantly increasing the share of the nation's income devoted to federal spending the nation could:

1. Establish an income-maintenance program to raise all twenty-five million Americans currently trapped in poverty above the official poverty line by 1975

2. Put an immediate end to hunger with a food-stamp program covering all poor Americans

3. Set up a national health insurance system that would finance basic medical care for every American by 1975

4. Expand federal housing programs to attain a level of construction capable of replacing all substandard housing units in the United States by the end of the decade

5. Develop new educational programs in elementary and secondary schools by 1974 to insure that no American enters the labor market without the capacity for self-support

6. Devote considerably more federal funds to such long-neglected areas as crime prevention, day care, mass transit, and metropolitan development.

We discovered, in short, that by reallocating public resources within the context of the federal budget and the realities of the American economy, we could produce a set of public programs more responsive to the nation's needs than those now in operation. Allocation decisions were made by comparing the benefits to be gained from spending scarce public resources for various purposes. We sought to allocate funds for those programs which promised the largest benefits per dollar invested.

Hundreds of people, including the Coalition's Steering Committee, academic experts, and former government officials, participated at various points in this priority-setting process. Meetings were held with leaders representing business, labor, local governments, blacks, Mexican Americans, American Indians, white ethnics, religion, education, youth, women, local urban coalitions, and social welfare organizations. Finally, our alternative budget was sent to dozens of independent experts and consultants to assure that its recommendations were consistent with the probable shape of the nation's economy and labor markets in the next five years.

Based on the expert advice received, the Steering Committee decided that the nation's security and well-being would be most effectively advanced by a major shift in federal budget resources from nonessential portions of military and space programs into programs aimed at human and social development. More specifically, the counterbudget recommends reducing military spending from the present level of $74.5 billion a year to $50 billion a year, and investing this $24 billion saving—along with the fiscal dividend resulting from healthy growth of the economy —in new and expanded domestic federal programs for income maintenance, education, health, housing, law enforcement, and other purposes.

In preparing the defense proposals, we undertook an exhaustive analysis of enemy threats and resultant United States requirements in the 1970s. After consulting with many former top Defense Department officials and other military experts, we concluded that our present military forces are unnecessarily large in relation to the purposes they serve. Military expenditures could be responsibly reduced through improved management and operating efficiencies, through elimination of obsolete weapon systems, through a larger assumption by our allies in Europe and Asia of the costs of their own defense, and through rapid termination of our military involvement in Vietnam.

However, even after such a sizable allocation within the federal budget, additional revenue will be required if the budget is to become responsive to the economic and social problems that threaten the nation. We concluded that a federal budget capable of moving us a significant distance toward the attainment of major national goals would total $353 billion by 1976—$159 billion more than the expected federal revenues for the current fiscal year. We believe that this additional revenue can be obtained from the following sources:

1. Vigorous national economic growth which would produce additional tax revenues of $90 billion by 1976

This calculation assumes a rapid return to full employment and an average real annual increase in the gross national product of over 4 percent during the next five years.

2. Elimination of inequities in the federal tax system
3. Increased taxes for social security, railroad retirement, and unemployment, coupled with a new payroll tax for national health insurance, which would have a combined yield of approximately $42 million in 1976
4. Beginning in 1974, reimposition of the 10 percent federal surtax on personal and corporate income which, given our assumptions about economic growth, would yield about $18 billion by 1976.

We are under no illusions that this proposed tax increase would be popular, but the American people must face the hard fact that if they want more and better services, they must pay for them.

Creating comprehensive blueprints for meeting America's problems is an important first step toward reordering priorities. However, it is not enough. Ways must be found to translate proposed reallocations into actual changes in the federal budget. At present, several obstacles bar the way.

To begin with, there are serious flaws in the way the budget is shaped. The first is what might best be called the "let's-see-what-we-gave-them-last-year-and-give-them-a-little-more-this-year" approach. Encrusted in the fragmented committee system of Congress, this approach to each successive federal budget makes major reallocations by the legislative branch virtually impossible. Until Congress devises a way to consider the budget as a whole, it will be able to do little more than tinker with the bits and pieces handed to it by the Administration.

The second deficiency is the lack of public participation in th budget process. Both the executive branch's federal budget proposal and the Congress's appropriations response are written behind closed doors. The implication is that the public is either untrustworthy or insufficiently competent to have a voice in making such critical national choices.

We can no longer regard the federal budget as an arcane affair to be conducted in secret by a select few, for it determines the fate and future of our society. The National Urban Coalition believes that the Congress should hold full public hearings annually on the budget and on national priorities. We have indicated our willingness to present our counterbudget and to discuss its details before the full appropriations committees of the House and the Senate.

I ask social workers to join us in urging the Congress to transform the appropriations process into a genuine national effort to review our priorities. I ask you to join us in urging the Congress to hold public hearings on the budget as a whole and on various alternatives proposed by the President. I ask you to join us in offering carefully constructed proposals for reordering our priorities and insisting that they be considered in the process of formulating the budget.

It is time to come to grips with our full responsibilities as citizens of a democratic nation. It is time for us to regain control of our own destiny. And it is time to recognize that it costs greatly to be a great nation.

A Federal Public Welfare Policy—
a Governor's Appraisal

JOHN J. GILLIGAN

IN APRIL, 1971, the President of the United States delivered a speech on the subject of welfare to the Republican Governors Conference in Williamsburg, Virginia. His speech included statements that will make the task of developing a humane system of public assistance immeasurably more difficult.

All of us have seen and read, some have even conducted, studies on welfare recipients. We know that all studies—government or private—have shown that the overwhelming majority of those receiving public assistance are the very young and the very old—children and the aged. We know that the number of people who receive welfare payments and who are able to work is but a tiny fraction of all welfare recipients. We know, in short, that the malingering work force alleged to be hiding on the welfare rolls just does not exist.

We know from bitter experience that the erroneous belief that such a welfare work force does exist and needs only to be flushed out by cuts in assistance and harsh work requirements is a crippling blow to efforts to construct a humane system of public assistance. Yet despite what we know—and what Mr. Nixon surely must know—the President had this to say to the Republican governors:

> It is incredible that we have allowed a system of law under which one person can be penalized for doing an honest day's work and another can be rewarded for doing nothing at all.
>
> I do not think we can tolerate a system under which working people can be made to feel like fools by those who will not work.

Declaring that his intention was to "get the people off of welfare rolls," Mr. Nixon claimed that "the way to get them off, is to provide incentives and discentives, which will make them get off." Mr. Nixon then said: "I think those who refuse to register for work and accept work or training should be ineligible for welfare payments. We have written such a stipulation into our welfare reform proposal."

What has the President accomplished with such statements?

He has resurrected for public consumption the hoary myth that a major cause of our welfare problems lies in the free-loading propensities of welfare recipients, who prefer the easy check to a steady job.

He has placed the moral force of the highest office in this nation—the unifying symbol of the American body politic—in the service of a notion that not only blatantly distorts the facts, but perpetuates and reinforces that very degradation of America's helpless citizens that his program is supposed to eliminate.

In doing so Mr. Nixon has also presented to opponents of a decent welfare system an ideological club with which to batter realistic, constructive, public assistance policies and, indeed, even his own welfare program.

It is bad enough that the President is engaging in the kind of deceptive rhetoric that has so damaged the credibility of our national leaders in recent years. The real significance, however, of his statements—and their major fault—is that they point directly away from central problems facing this society. They give us no real understanding of the nature of American society and its industrial, technological character. They condemn those who are still earnestly trying to follow the President's leadership to an ideological strait jacket which, as Vice President Agnew's assaults on the peace movement did in November of 1970, attempts to bind them to the view that the moral, political, economic, and social problems of our society stem from a group of malcontents who would destroy our way of life.

Such a myopic view of American society by national leaders only further impedes an effective response to our problems. For if the diagnosis is wrong, the treatment will surely be wrong.

If the sad history of our involvement in Vietnam and the horrifying story of My Lai teach us one thing, it is that we do not really know what we are. We did not believe that we were capable of what we have in fact done—waged a war of devastation and mass killings.

What we have learned since 1961 is that we have much to learn about our society, about our attitudes toward others, and about ourselves. We are at present a confused, perplexed society.

It is tempting to console ourselves with a simplistic, self-righteous—and fanciful—view of our problems. The recognition of our confusion and uncertainty has already sparked commercial exploitation by a major auto maker, which is now selling its cars with the slogan: "Something to believe in."

It is precisely the inevitable confrontation of fancy with fact that has magnified so enormously our present troubles. We cannot afford, then, the resurrection of mythical conceptions, when their effect—because of their source, the President of the United States—is to foster contempt in place of compassion, and ignorance in place of understanding. We cannot afford it because then it becomes easy for us to do nothing.

If we cannot expect of our President the leadership, moral courage, and compassion that this nation so desperately needs, then we must demand it of ourselves. We must understand the realities of our society and the action and attitudes they require.

To begin with, this country has to face precisely what Mr. Nixon and Governor Ronald Reagan of California have deliberately avoided, namely, the incontrovertible evidence that 95 percent of those on welfare simply *cannot* work. No work incentive, no work requirement has even the slightest relevance to the aged, the disabled, and the children who together make up almost the entire list of welfare recipients. For these children and incapacitated adults, Mr. Nixon's rhetoric is a gratuitous slap in the face.

A small fraction—perhaps one in twenty—of welfare recipients is physically able to work: the vast majority of these people are mothers of small children.

Some of these mothers have school-age children. Given adequate day care facilities which do not exist now, some of these mothers could work.

A fraction of one percent of welfare recipients are ablebodied males who are not working.

To understand the situation of these physically able people we must understand the technological, industrial character of our economy. America is now, and for the foreseeable future will continue to be, a work-oriented society. Through work we make our most evident contribution to our common life and earn our daily sustenance. Everyone, therefore, should work, for the sake of society and of himself. Having said that, we have said little about the problem of work in modern American society.

For the overwhelming majority of Americans today, work means salaried employment in large organizations which vigorously promote technological innovation in the form of more sophisticated machinery and more efficient procedures. Rapid technological progress has brought staggering wealth to this society. It has also brought us mechanization and automation, trends which have in the past and will more rapidly in the future make obsolete the skills and training of ever larger numbers of unemployed workers.

The most dramatic example of the impact of technological progress on the work force is the transformation of American agriculture, where in the last few decades, mechanization and other technical advances have drastically reduced the need for labor. This drastic decline in rural employment opportunities has been largely responsible for the migration of some twenty million people from the farms to the cities since 1940.

Indeed, the root of our present welfare crisis lies precisely in the modernization of agriculture, which has thrown millions of rural Americans with few skills and little education into an urban economy where the market for such workers was rapidly vanishing.

Agriculture is only the most dramatic example of the impact on employment of technology. Mechanization and automation are now, at an accelerating pace, reaching into the ranks of skilled labor and even into the white-collar work force. Neither the skilled nor the white-collar worker is immune to the inroads of machines and computers.

Whether or not these trends necessarily mean an absolute decline in employment opportunities, it is clear that the accelerating obsolescence of workers' skills will mean more and longer periods of unemployment for our citizens as more and more jobs become victims of technological advance and the search for another job involves more training in higher skills. In this context the attempt to equate the lack of a job with a deficiency in character becomes increasingly futile and unrealistic.

Accompanying the rapid technological change in our economy has been a tremendous growth in the influence of the federal government over economic conditions. This influence is so great that the fiscal and monetary policies of the national government are now the most important determinants of the state of our economy. Indeed, it is now the recognized responsibility of the national government to maintain a stable economy. Even beyond that general responsibility, the U. S. Congress twenty-five years ago declared it to be the duty of the federal government to make sure that there was employment for every American able to work.

In light of these realities about our welfare recipients, the technological character of our economy, and the dominant role and responsibility of the federal government in maintaining a stable economy at full employment, it takes no special insight to see that the disaster of our present system of public assistance represents the failure of our national leadersnip.

If to satisfy some perverse craving we decided that we wanted to perpetuate and encourage poverty in the country, what would we do?

I think we would attempt to isolate a certain segment of the population from the economic and cultural mainstream.

We would concentrate them in certain restricted areas.

We would provide them just enough to survive, and no more.

We would mark them as outcasts and worthless people.

We would deny them participation in our social and political life.

We would teach them that the only way that they could get even basic necessities, never mind the amenities, was to steal them.

We would destroy their incentive to work by saying, "If you work, we will take away from you whatever your labor earns."

We would do these things for ten years and then say to them, "Now we expect you, after the way we treated you, to be upstanding, intelligent, hard-working, self-reliant, clean-living kids."

That is what we would do. And that is what we are doing today.

Would the Nixon approach change our present welfare system?

The speech that the President delivered at Williamsburg and the stiff work requirements of his program suggest that his central concern is battling a fictitious horde of "welfare chiselers." The assistance level he proposed—originally $1,600 for a family of four, now up to $2,400—is sufficient only to give the vicious cycle of poverty one more turn.

In 1948 Senator Robert Taft, Sr., the late "Mr. Republican," declared: "I believe we should make a deliberate effort to put a floor under the essential requirements of our lowest income families so that extreme hardship and poverty may be eliminated."

Neither $1,600 nor $2,400 will eliminate poverty from the lives of those who will have to survive on it. As a floor, Mr. Nixon's proposal is somewhere below the basement.

Is this the best we can do?

Mr. Nixon has deplored the enormous cost of welfare as part of a campaign to maintain economy in government. Even now, he keeps locked up some $12 billion that Congress has already appropriated for domestic programs. Yet at the same time he wants to give, by executive fiat, from $3 billion to $5 billion to corporations in 1971 through more generous tax-depreciation procedures. He says that this multibillion-dollar gift package is needed to prime the economy.

In his statements on welfare he ignores the fact that the welfare dollar is the fastest dollar in the country. While a corporation may save instead of spend Mr. Nixon's gift, a welfare recipient will go right out and buy the milk and meat and bread that are missing from the dinner table.

The billions in accelerated depreciation for industry are not the only example of the curious fiscal priorities of the Nixon Administration. Mr. Nixon's priorities in 1970 wasted one billion dollars of Ohio taxes alone in the rice fields of Vietnam. Now, in 1971, he offers $200 million in loans for Lockheed Aircraft yet only $11 million in revenue sharing for the city of Cleveland.

What justification is given for the Lockheed loans?

President Nixon defends them not by the profit motive that he claims is irreplaceable; not by the value of the planes Lockheed makes; but by the livelihoods of 25,000 Lockheed employees who are in danger of losing their jobs. Yet in the fall of 1970 President Nixon vetoed a public works appropriation bill that would have given jobs to unemployed workers across the country.

With four million Americans now unemployed due to Mr. Nixon's own economic policies, what is so special, so compelling, about Lockheed? Is Lockheed acceptable because it is private industry? If that is the criterion for receiving federal funds to make employment, I suggest that President Nixon would be better advised to use federal funds for more useful social purposes by paying Lockheed to run playgrounds in our cities and the Penn Central Railroad to operate day care centers for the welfare mothers he wants to put to work.

The warped sense of priorities so clearly demonstrated by President Nixon's spending policies are but further evidence of his inability or unwillingness to provide the consistent, constructive vision so sorely needed in our national leaders.

Mr. Nixon has spoken much, and with much emphasis, of the value of the individual in America. He has spoken much of his desire to restore the freedom and dignity of the individual in an age of large, centralized government. His programs, he claims, from revenue sharing to welfare reform, are designed to meet that need, to reduce the individual's dependence on, and thus enhance his freedom from, a bloated government bureaucracy.

It would be enough to point out the steady erosion of civil liberties during his Administration to see the contradictions in his position. We have only to consider his approval of mass arrest of citizens, his approval of wire tapping at the whim of a federal bureaucrat—a gross encroachment on individual rights—to see how confused is his concept of freedom.

Equally contradictory to his avowed principles is his position on welfare. While professing the intention to restore those on welfare to dignity and independence, Mr. Nixon offers a program with an income floor that is so low it can only perpetuate dependence and degradation. The deeper fault of his position is that he continues to foster the notion that the provision of basic economic needs is a gift from government to those who cannot provide for themselves— a gift that marks even the "truly deserving" poor as economic and social outcasts, dependent for their sustenance on a beneficent government.

Yet do we say that we are dependent on a government policy for our freedom of speech, freedom of the press, freedom from religious persecution, for the whole range of political freedoms we enjoy? Do we say that these freedoms are gifts of government? Of course not.

We believe that these political freedoms are rights of man. Government does not bestow these freedoms on individuals, but rather it protects them as inherent rights of these individuals.

We must as a society now recognize that the individual's freedom is denied not just by the steel shackles of preventive detention, but by the economic chains of poverty which bind men to dependence on government largesse. What Mr. Nixon has failed to see is that we must, then, establish the principle that the individual has a basic right to the economic necessities of life—a right that is not government's to give or take away, but only to protect and enforce.

In a complex national economy where technological innovation ignores political boundaries, and where employment opportunities are so dependent on the actions of the federal government, the full responsibility for safeguarding that right belongs to the national government. The government can enforce that right in three ways:

1. For an individual who cannot be expected to work, the federal government should provide an income not at the starvation level, but at a level which assures the minimum requirements of a decent life.

2. For an individual who could conceivably work but is not at present working, the federal government should create a job, either directly or through contracts with private industry.

It is a cruel hoax to require someone to take a job when there is no job available. If the government does not create a job for that person, then it should simply provide the same income that it provides for those who cannot work.

3. For an individual who works but does not earn enough to provide even the basic necessities, the government should provide the additional income he needs to meet his minimum requirements.

We know that the establishment of a minimum income as a right of the individual, fully protected by the federal government, requires a change in the attitude of many Americans— a change prompted by recognition of the changing economic and social conditions in America.

In Ohio we are making a determined effort to reorient our thinking on public assistance, to match our attitudes and actions to reality and to our vision of what our state and our nation can be.

We recognize that the rightful responsibility for public assistance programs belongs to the federal government. From every platform in the state I have urged the national government to assume the full costs of a reorganized, coordinated system of public assistance with uniform national standards.

We also determined that until Congress approves that proposal, Ohio will do, not the least, but the best it can to help its helpless citizens. At a time when many states are cutting back the services they provide for their citizens, our administration is proposing a very substantial expansion of state services. We have proposed increasing our expenditures for those on welfare by 117 percent over the last biennial budget, to bring to hundreds of thousands of Ohioans the dignity and decent living conditions so long denied them.

In proposing this increase, I challenged the state legislators to investigate Ohio's welfare files and find in a random selection of twenty-five cases more than one or two where anyone was for any reason receiving illegally any welfare payment. I said that if they could find those cases, I would wholeheartedly support their vote against the administration's welfare budget. Both legislators and newsmen have taken up that challenge, but no one has succeeded in meeting it.

Our administration is also determined to recognize now a welfare system which, in Ohio as in the other states, confronts the welfare recipient with a bewildering mass of fragmented services that would challenge the stamina and ingenuity of even the most seasoned veteran of bureaucratic procedures. We are trying to coordinate our services so that those who need them can get them as quickly and easily as possible.

We recognize that beyond the basic material necessities, a first-rate education is essential if our children—whatever their economic background—are to gain the knowledge and skills that they will need to lead productive lives of dignity and decency. We have proposed increasing state aid to education by over $800 million for the next biennium so that we can guarantee to every child in Ohio an equal opportunity for a quality education. In that proposal we have committed Ohio to special concern for those children whose poverty threatens a crippling blow to their chances for a decent life and a share in the abundance of America.

Our program includes special allocations for major increases in state support of education of disadvantaged youth. Our program also provides $250 per pupil, in addition to the regular state subsidy, to school districts—largely big city districts—with a specified number of AFDC children enrolled.

These proposals reflect our belief that the true measure of

a state and of a society is not a spotless war record, or a trillion-dollar economy, or first place in world aviation, but man's relation to man.

A government that has forgotten that, is a government that has forgotten its purposes and its people.

In Ohio we are trying to remember.

Political Activism for Social Work

HOWARD N. LEE

As HISTORIANS LOOK BACK on our socialization process and approach to problem-solving, they will find that although within the life span of a generation we have reached the moon, conquered many age-old crippling diseases, provided a vast majority of our citizens with a previously unimaginable standard of material welfare, we have only partially succeeded in finding a satisfactory technique for the delivery of social services.

This incredible flowering of our abilities has created the expectation that our social problems can be solved by application of the same visionary dynamism. We have learned to hope, for the first time in human experience, that a society can be constructed which is at once free of poverty, abundant in educational opportunity, tolerant of racial and ethnic diversity, and liberating for the human spirit.

The full potential for achieving the objectives of social and human renewal never before existed as it does today. At the same time, the very existence of that potential has created the expectation that these objectives can be quickly reached. Yet we who are among the "chronic hopers of the world" have learned also to temper optimism with realism. We have learned that it is easier to articulate problem dimensions than problem solutions. It is too easy to fall prey to the simple-minded theory that social problems will just disappear if the federal, state, and local governments throw in enough dollars and statute books. We should have learned also that the cruel and exaggerated rhetoric of unkept campaign promises can threaten the very creditability of government itself and destroy a society's stability.

About the time of John F. Kennedy's rise to power, Michael Harrington's *The Other America* was rising to popularity. This work exposed the ugliness of America and so embarrassingly projected the thorns that President Kennedy declared a war on poverty. The political system appeared to be prepared to support President Kennedy when he asked the country in his inaugural address of 1961 to "bear the burden of a long twilight struggle against the common enemies of man: tyranny, poverty, disease, and war itself." This was not the first time that words had been uttered or the hand of hope extended to the poor and depressed. In 1944, President Franklin D. Roosevelt had exhorted the country to accept a "second Bill of Rights under which a new basis of security and prosperity could be established for all, regardless of station, race, or creed."

Despite these high hopes and with all our resources and dedication, we seem only to have taken two turtle steps forward. Since 1961 administrations have been charged, pressured, begged, and called upon repeatedly to allocate the nation's funds in such a way that every person will have a decent portion of the country's wealth. Yet none has really been committed to this basic human cause which will do more than anything else to eliminate alienation from our national community and narrow the gap between what is said and what is done.

What is the problem? What are we waiting for? Why are we so embroiled in a controversy over making the welfare program adequate and workable? Why hasn't the war on poverty been won?

Some would say that the problem is not enough money, and they would be partially right. Expenditures and appropriations for solving social problems have always been low on the priority list. Poverty, by definition, means lack of money. Yet over the years we have somehow developed the mistaken idea that if we just give enough advice and services to the poor, they will quit being poor. This theory does not seem to be working. The time has come for us to realize, as have other nations, that doing nothing or not doing enough ultimately costs more.

Some others would say that insufficient and ill-trained manpower is the problem. They too would be partially right, for skilled manpower distributed throughout the spectrum of hu-

man service professions is, and will be for some time in the
future, a scarce commodity. Again, this must be related to our
national priority list. Funds have not been made available to
support educational efforts to train personnel to meet the manpower demands.

Still others would say that there is a lack of effective and
powerful political lobbying on state and federal levels. Without
question, lobby programs for social appropriations cannot compete with the better endowed lobby groups. I am not convinced that we should need to compete for political support in
this fashion. It seems to me that public officials should be the
most effective lobby for social appropriations and human service
programs. Although increased efforts must be made along these
lines, the total answer is not here.

There is a great deal of validity to each of these factors, but
there is something else that at this stage is more vital to our
success as a nation than anything else. I am speaking of the very
structure of our system and the innate capacity of our pluralistic
governmental institutions, at all levels, to respond in an orderly
and coordinated way by delivering good social services and
solving social problems. America is a technological and industrial giant, but she has not yet been able to deal adequately with
her human and social problems. While she boasts of a thriving
economy, more than seven million people on the welfare rolls
suffer some of the most demeaning indignities that can be in-
flicted through systematic persecution and control. While greater
emphasis is being placed on improved housing programs, more
and more welfare recipients are being crammed into the worst
housing in urban slum areas. While we are spending $500,000
on each enemy soldier killed in Vietnam, only $50.75 is appro-
priated for each person in the war on poverty. While we are
bailing Lockheed and Penn-Central out of their financial crises,
people are starving, and thousands of youth are denied an educational opportunity due to lack of scholarship funds.

This, then, raises the great question: where is the hidden crisis
in America? I believe it is in politics. Therefore, I think it
should be made clear to the American political leadership that

there must be a reordering of our national priorities. The same kind of commitment that has been generated in industrial and technological development must be generated to find solutions to our social problems by improving the mechanisms and the possibilities for delivering services.

But first we must end the war in Vietnam, which continues to drain away our national resources, economic, human, and spiritual. Then the resources that have been committed there must be turned to solving the problems of poverty, housing, hunger, education, and medical care here in America. This reversal will not come easily and will require a much deeper commitment from all of us, especially from our political leaders, who must realize that the system in its present form is failing everybody. Our deeds must begin to reflect our words.

I am thoroughly convinced that this will not happen without some conscious pressure from organizations such as the National Conference on Social Welfare, the National Association of Social Workers, and similar organizations which must make their presence felt in the political arena. I believe that now is the time for us to embark on a great new mission of reform, a task as noble and urgent as that which faced the founding fathers. We must redefine for our own age the meanings and functions of a governmental system and a society that is supposed to be structured to make the delivery of services quick and meaningful. Very few new values have emerged in the American political tradition. The ideals of liberty, equality, and justice have always been enshrined in our ethos. The question is how to realize them, and that is why issues of organization and procedure, and of the national allocation of power and responsibility are always at the heart of every political debate.

Those in political positions must be constantly reminded that a reform effort is needed now. In some areas, the present nonsystem is near breakdown. Many of our overlapping and cumbersome governmental and social institutions may have been suited to a past age, but their designs seem to be barriers to service delivery rather than accelerators. We need only to look at our system of justice and our system of welfare as two examples. Crises no longer occur one at a time; they occur simultaneously on many fronts. We know that our powers as a society are great, but until recent years we have never realized the power that lies in organizational unity. We also know, by the same token, that the human consequences of political error have been magnified beyond comprehension. No longer can we rely on the adage that the good Lord will look out for idiots and the United States of America. We must begin to realize that in order to deal fairly and squarely with the social problems of today it will take action and pressure, which require the involvement of individuals, institutions, associations, and organizations on practically every level of society.

The inevitable question, then, is: who shall lead? Social work should lead. To my mind, no profession is in a better position to develop a broad overview of the social needs, develop strategies for meeting them, and agitate for attention. As social workers, we must be concerned for those individuals and families who bear the brunt of deteriorating urban life and the unrest and violence it breeds. We must point up the deficiencies and inadequacies in our system of justice. We must demand a reordering of priorities on all levels. Social work must both contribute to the development, enactment, and implementation of sound, over-all social policies and assume specific responsibility for assuring access to community services of good quality. We should recognize that not only the lack of opportunities but also the inadequacies of essential community services have contributed to the perpetuation of poverty, frustration, and rebellion in many urban neighborhoods.

While law enforcement agencies must continue to have the ultimate responsibility for maintaining order, social workers must assume responsibility for determining the social causes of the breakdown of order. While military minds must plan strategies for wars, social workers must plan strategies for assisting the victims of war. While the legal minds should be the keepers of justice, social workers must insure that justice is done. In any event, the social work profession has a role to play and should be involved with planning bodies and citizens' groups on a continuing basis in efforts to reduce tension, identify human problems and needs, and facilitate communication across personal, ethnic, and organizational lines.

Unfortunately, we have not made our professional skills available in this fashion. We have been so committed to carrying on a traditional and conventional role that we have not only been pulled away from the center of action, but have had to deal with internal problems threatening to split the profession. No longer can we accept the system without question and become its caretakers. No longer can we adjust our knowledge to what the system demands of us or even train professionals to fit only into the systematic mold. Instead, we must concentrate more on ways to change the system to meet real human needs and contribute to human development. The real test of a profession is its ability to be relevant in dealing with the problems it has been granted sanction to remedy. Because both our relevancy and our competency have been questioned, we are usually the last profession consulted on matters pertaining to social policy formulation and the search for social problem solutions. Although there has been some progress in raising the status of social workers and gaining greater respectability for the profession, we still have quite a way to go and many internal professional changes to make before we can be ready to lead.

When the United States was largely a rural nation, it was important for a man to understand nature, to acquire the ability to survive in the woods, to develop the skills of his hands—and for social workers to be friendly visitors and do things in nice, quiet ways. It was even more important for social workers to learn about the process of social change, allowing it to evolve naturally, and to shy away from the political arena. Except for a few revolutionary rebels like Jane Addams, social workers were careful not to rock society too much. But things have changed; not only are more social workers as individuals moving into the political system, but our national organizations are becoming more aggressive, demanding a role in shaping social policy. Because of this we have not brought some things up to date. If the profession of social work is to survive and carve out a secure position in today's society, then I believe we must make at least three radical departures from our conventional social work education as we redevelop and redefine our mission and our relation to welfare.

1. We need honestly to evaluate our educational programs in a straightforward, unified, systematic way. We need to determine whether students are being prepared to deal effectively with social problems and facilitate social change or whether they are merely prepared to adjust to the system, thereby continuing the same social illnesses. I believe that we are still concentrating too much on preparing students to function within established social agencies rather than preparing them to move in new directions. It is imperative that social workers become better educated in the art of penetrating the system in order to have some impact on the decision-making process on all levels, especially in politics.

This means that we can no longer graduate generalists in social work. I do not believe that so long as our educational system centers on a generalized curriculum, we will be able to move to a higher level of competency, developing the body of knowledge we need and projecting the uniqueness that social work should possess. Therefore, I believe that we need an educational program that will graduate specialists who possess high-level skills. Because we live in an age of specialization and an era of information explosion, it seems unrealistic to expect social workers to master the techniques and skills needed to function professionally in mental health, educational, and correctional settings to mention only three. Fifteen to twenty years ago it was reasonable to expect a student to learn all that he needed to know to be an effective social worker in the general sense, but today that is impossible. I propose that we introduce a format that allows a student to become well-learned in the special area in which he wishes to function as well as in the field of social work itself. I further propose that the entire two years be dedicated to course work and that a third year be added as a year of internship. I know that this suggestion is controversial and raises many questions, but I believe that unless we are willing to move in this direction our professional foundation will continue to be weak.

2. There is no doubt in my mind that social work is handicapped by being wedded to the concept of welfare. Welfare, historically, has too often meant protective caretaking of the non-able-bodied, yet the concepts of caretaking and rehabilitation are too limited by definition. It is not just people who are deprived, ill, and unskilled; our social, economic, and political structures are also sick, dysfunctional, deprived, and in need of rehabilitation. If social work is to be more responsive to human crises, it must operate from a concept sufficiently broad to embrace the range of front-line institutional functions that are required to produce and to maintain a socially productive man in a humanized society.

3. Because our situation is different from that which social work has faced before, our mission too must be redefined and our image must be changed. In many respects we can find the grounds for that mission expressed in the statements of many of our colleagues, in programs being carried on by certain schools of social work, and in the work of a few practitioners. This does not necessarily mean that we should sacrifice clinical practice. It simply means that we should broaden our professional base. I am convinced that we must become builders of new human social systems that respond to people, systems tailor-made to emphasize people as persons, and the constructors of "bridges" so that we can reach and communicate with people on all levels and across all lines. Further, we must become renovators of human relations, human dignity, and the human spirit, and architects of social development and socialization.

Social work must take the leadership in involving other human service organizations, placing social problems on the public agenda, and pressing to keep them there until the American public and its political leaders grapple creatively and effectively with them.

Putting ideals into practice is a complicated task. If the social work profession is serious about wanting to be responsive to the human condition, it must recognize a few basic requirements in addition to the radical changes I have discussed. First, action to humanize requires doing something oneself, whether the "self" is an individual or a corporate body, such as a staff, NASW chapter, board, or organization. It further requires influencing others: fellow professionals, welfare councils, city councils, county commissioners, state legislatures. The process of humanization requires a commitment both to individual action and to social action.

Second, humanization requires placing human values above other values, including professional values. Social work cannot succeed in humanizing the community if, when the going gets tough, it turns its back on humane ideals.

I believe firmly that if Americans wake up and make up their minds, we can stop all the suffering of millions of people. We can solve most of our social problems and take away the destructive influences that tend to create hopelessness and unrest. If we are really committed we can make it possible for millions of Americans to have a chance to be real men and women and for children to grow up to be healthy adults. If we are honest we will no longer sit silently by. I call upon social work as a profession, to enter into the mainstream of society and the political system and help America to achieve its ideals and to insure that every child who stands before the flag and recites "with liberty and justice for all" can fulfill the ideals of the Declaration of Independence: "We hold these truths to be self-evident, that all men are created equal." We must advance this ideal without hesitation and with great vigor.

If we put first things first, if we reorder our priorities, if we put people ahead of ABM's, manned Mars landings, advanced military and defense techniques, and continuation of the war in Vietnam, we can easily get the job done. The moral and necessary formula for our survival is not "live and let live" but "live and make it possible for others to live."

A similar sense of urgency and mutual dependence was expressed by an author writing about mental retardation. Why, she asked, has a grass-roots movement to combat this handicapping condition at last developed such momentum? Answering her own question, in words I would like to appropriate as my own, she replied:

It is because the world is very much with us today. We know, many of us perhaps only subconsciously, that if our way of life is to survive, every individual, be he handicapped or whole, be he rich or poor, be he black or white, be he educated or uneducated, or be he healthy or unhealthy, every individual must be counted as an individual and accorded his place in the sun.

It seems to me that this is appropriate in relation to the urgency of reordering our priorities to meet the needs of people through politics and social work. Every individual must be accorded not only his place in the sun, but access to those supportive services that will assist him in moving to take that place in the sun. Therefore, in the last analysis, it is to that end that we must bend our effort toward not only reforming, but toward reforming our systems and our structures and our institutions and our political methods in order to insure that we reach that man. There is no task more challenging and no cause more worthy of our concern, our commitment, and our action as we are propelled toward a new social work.

Making the Political Process Respond to Human Needs

CHARLES B. RANGEL

THIS IS A TIME when there is a crisis in virtually every sphere of domestic and foreign policy. Not the least of these is the "welfare" crisis.

But the welfare crisis means different things to different people. President Nixon, Chairman of the House Ways and Means Committee Wilbur Mills, and others continually speak of their own brand of the "welfare crisis." By the "welfare crisis," they mean the rising welfare costs, especially in the Aid to Families with Dependent Children (AFDC) category.

The fact of the matter is that for poor people, welfare, until recently, has always been a crisis. Welfare has never actually met their real needs. Only through piecemeal victories—victories such as outlawing the "man-in-the-house" rule, abolishing residency requirements, upping the percentage of need in AFDC, and abolishing the NOLEO requirement—have poor people been able to change the welfare system to make it more responsive to their real needs.

Mr. Nixon's and Mr. Mills's crisis—that is, the pinch that welfare is putting on our state treasuries—has largely come about because poor people are finally making some progress in solving their crisis.

All this rhetoric about a crisis has put the nation in the mood for reform. Unfortunately, it seems that we are going to opt for short-term palliatives at the expense of long-term reform. The present welfare system is being portrayed as the "bad guy" and the Administration-backed Mills plan is being labeled as the "good guy."

Realizing the seriousness of the problem, the Congressional

Black Caucus met with the President on March 25 of this year. We asked him to do three things: (1) replace the present system with a realistic guaranteed adequate income system; (2) eliminate degrading administrative practices; and (3) overhaul the food stamp program pending implementation of the new welfare reform measures.

First, the President said that he opposes a guaranteed adequate income because it would cost too much and would mean a substantial reallocation of funds. He said that if it were financed out of income tax revenues, it would require imposing a 58 percent surtax on the income of many individuals and corporations. He was speaking of an income level set at $6,500 for a family of four.

Second, he said that the Administration's welfare plan does in fact maximize self-respect in work opportunities because it would provide over 200,000 public service jobs at $1.60 an hour. He neglected to say that the bulk of those AFDC mothers would not be working in these jobs but in other jobs where they would earn substantially less. He also said that the "suitable" work requirement would mean that no one would have to work where there is a health or safety risk. However, the Mills bill he has subsequently endorsed has dropped this requirement.

Third, in responding to our request to overhaul the food stamp program, Mr. Nixon stated that the new food stamp purchase schedules provide that people with no or very little income will get their stamps free. He failed to mention, however, that according to his own Assistant Secretary of Agriculture, over 350,000 people in one- and two-person households with incomes above $160 and $210 a month respectively who are currently on food stamps will be cut off. Not only that, but another 1,750,000 participants will find that food stamps will be costing them more.

As you can see from this double talk, welfare reform has entered the political arena as big politics. On the one hand we have the Nixon-Reagan-Mills image of the problem:

1. State and local treasuries are being drained to the last dime because welfare rolls are skyrocketing.

2. The rolls are soaring because millions of people on welfare are loafers unwilling to get off their behinds and do a little work.

3. The nation's work ethic is crumbling because those now working at low-wage menial jobs are deciding that they are suckers and are dropping out of the work force.

On the other hand, we have the poor people. There are 12.8 million of them on welfare. Over 10.2 million of them are either children, aged, blind, or totally disabled. In other words, they cannot work. That leaves 2.6 million adults. Over 765,000 of these 2.6 million adults are already working or actively seeking work. That leaves only a little over 1.8 million people. According to the Department of Health, Education, and Welfare (HEW), most of these people are mothers who are needed at home full-time or mothers who have no marketable skills.

You will remember how the Nixon portrayal of the welfare crisis bred the Family Assistance Plan (FAP) in 1969. The Administration went to considerable lengths to disguise the true effect of the plan by parading it as a revolutionary social reform. In fact, Patrick Moynihan was positively effusive on the subject. President Nixon himself hailed it as the most progressive piece of social legislation since the Social Security Act. To be perfectly candid, a number of liberal groups were persuaded to support FAP, or at least to remain neutral, by the argument that it offered the only clear chance to establish the principle of a guaranteed income.

Yet despite these blandishments, FAP failed to be enacted. The reason it failed is that poor people organized and went in small groups to the liberal senators on the Senate Finance Committee and exposed the bankruptcy of the plan. As the 91st Congress ended, FAP remained stalled in committee.

But, like a bad penny, it turned up again. Only this time it turned up without any of its liberal flourishes. The old soft soap had gone.

Out of the window went the possibility of a guaranteed minimum income. It had been a noble thought, but the President publicly disavowed it, saying that it had nothing to do with welfare reform or the Administration proposal. He even equated it with Communism.

On May 19, 1971, the day after the House Ways and Means Committee reported out the bill, H.R. 1, the President endorsed the bill despite changes the committee wrote into it. Let us look at what the Administration is so excited about.

By now the litany must be familiar. I think, however, that it is important to go over it briefly to resolve any doubts concerning the merits of the legislation.

1. H.R. 1 would do very little to alleviate poverty in this country.

Its basic grant level of $2,400 for a family of four is some $1,350 less than the government's own official poverty line and some $4,100 below the Bureau of Labor Statistics' adequate-income line.

2. Nine out of ten welfare families may possibly be worse off than they are today.

The $2,400 level is above the present payment levels for only 10 percent of the welfare families: those in Alabama, Arkansas, Louisiana, Mississippi, and South Carolina. All others could be cut back unless the states supplemented with their own state funds in order to maintain current levels.

3. If states should increase payments above the current grant in cash and food stamps combined, they would have to pay the entire cost of these increases up to the level of their 1971 calendar year expenditures.

Because most states spend more on welfare now than they want to, they will keep the savings and not pass them on as cost-of-living increases. In fact, no state would be required to maintain its present payment levels. They could cut back to the federal $2,400 level and not spend anything on welfare. This means that it would be much easier for states to cut benefits than under the present system, which requires that a state percentage reduction be approvad by HEW. Thus, states would be encouraged to reduce welfare benefit levels.

4. The cost-of-living increases that states have been providing under the present welfare system would be abandoned. Under current law, cost-of-living increases are required although some states after making them, in effect cancel them out with across-the-board budget cuts. Nevertheless, on balance, the majority

of families under current law have benefited, something they would not similarly do under FAP.

5. Families with children would receive only half as much as the aged, blind, and disabled. Two aged people would receive the same amount as a family of four.

6. The plan discriminates against blacks. About three fourths of the aged, disabled, and blind people on welfare are white. However, more than half of the AFDC recipients are black. Since an AFDC family of four would receive the same as an aged couple, the AFDC families, largely black, would get proportionately half as much as the people in the other welfare categories who are largely white. By perpetuating the categorical approach to assistance, H.R. 1 enshrines in federal law all the worst inequities of the current system.

7. Welfare people may be referred to nearly any type of job. The only language in the bill on the "suitability" of the job says that recipients do not have to be forced to break a strike. The provisions which said that no one would be forced to take a job endangering health and safety or one that is too far from home have been removed.

8. Jobs for welfare recipients are not readily available. The 1969 HEW study of AFDC reports that 20 percent of the welfare mothers are in the labor market. Of these, 67 percent are already working. About 33 percent are unemployed—looking for work but unable to find it. Governor Ronald Reagan of California wrote to some 309,000 employers in the state asking each to hire one welfare recipient. Some 13,000 employers responded. They reported only 337 jobs, and only 26 were eventually filled in the follow-up.

9. Welfare people would have to reapply every two years. Although recipients are to accurately report their income every three months, according to the bill, they would have to apply every two years all over again. This would mean more paperwork, for caseworkers and more hardship for clients.

10. The advisory committees make no provision for inclusion of welfare people themselves. The advisory committees to evaluate the program would be composed of representatives of business, labor, and the government. The poor are not mentioned.

11. After the thirtieth day in the hospital, a welfare person would have to pay $7.50 a day; after the sixtieth day, he would have to pay $15 a day. The longer a person is ill, the lower his ability to pay becomes. Also, certain recipients may have to pay part of their hospital bills, something which they may be unable to do.

12. Services covered by Medicaid may be cut back. Rather than paying for the additional cost of the Medicaid program, the federal government would allow states to reduce the services provided. Under the Administration bill states would not be required to spend more on Medicaid than they presently do.

13. There is no job protection provision in the bill for welfare workers. Unless there is a high natural turnover rate for welfare employees, some social workers may be without jobs when the program is federalized.

If any social workers have in the past supported FAD because it seemed to establish the principle of guaranteed income, or because it simply seemed better than nothing, if any of you are thinking of supporting FAP now, or are exercising anything less than full and vigorous opposition to it, if any of you have any doubts at all, then, before you do anything else, READ THE BILL.

Read it carefully, read it closely, read it for yourselves.

Do not rely on the newspapers, do not rely on HEW, and surely, do not rely on the White House. Do not even rely on me. Read the bill.

For in the bill itself are all the arguments sufficient to its defeat.

FAP is *not* better than nothing; it is worse than anything we could have imagined.

Remember: now, as always, the greatest threat to progressive change is simple ignorance.

Once we clearly understand what the issues are, once we clearly understand what FAP is, and what it will do to poor people, I am confident that we can, together, defeat it.

Make no mistake about it: we *must* defeat FAP. We must defeat it resoundingly. We must defeat it now. Because until we do, until the bill is dead, we cannot even begin to achieve genuine welfare reform.

The Political Economy of the American Health System[1]

ROBERT R. ALFORD

THE WORD "CRISIS" is frequently used to describe the state of the American health system. Yet it is probable that the situation is better in 1971 than it has been at any time in our history. But the mood in 1971 is one of challenge to American institutions, on the grounds that they are failing. The Vietnam war cannot be ended; money cannot be diverted from space and war to pollution, health, and education; unemployment is higher than ever among blacks and youth; Congress seems frozen in old postures of defense of law and order; a conservative majority dominates the Supreme Court; the President is facing ever new credibility gaps on both domestic and foreign issues.

The challenges come from many sides: from the antiwar movement; from the demand for community representation and control of vital services; from the drive of students for some voice in the content and structure of their education; and from new groups of militants within professional associations. These tendencies are found in health as well as in other fields of vital human services.

But it is important to maintain perspective. Our major institutions continue to function in the same way as they have for many years, and no significant movement for change exists:

[1] This paper was prepared under a grant to the Center for Policy Research from the National Center for Health Research and Development, National Institute of Mental Health, U. S. Department of Health, Education, and Welfare. Although the paper generalizes from the literature and from a case study of New York City, it should be regarded as a set of "outrageous hypotheses," in the spirit of Robert S. Lynd's classic *Knowledge for What?* (Princeton, N.J.: Princeton University Press, 1939), rather than as a theory inferred from reliable empirical findings.

movements to change decisions—withdrawal from the war, for example—yes, but not movements to change institutions, which effectively resist and accommodate to pressures for change.

With respect to health institutions, qualified observers have commented on the similarity between the 1932 analysis by the Committee on the Costs of Medical Care [2] and reports issued thirty-five or more years later. Dr. Sumner Rosen, an economist on the staff of the Institute of Public Administration in New York City, has said that "the catalogue of problems drawn up almost forty years ago strongly resembles the latest list—inadequate services, insufficient funds, understaffed hospitals. Virtually nothing has changed." [3]

Nor does knowledge exist about how the present system works or what alternatives might be feasible. The 1967 Report of the National Advisory Commission on Health Manpower concludes that "there is a serious lack of the consistent and comprehensive statistical information that is required for rational analysis and planning, despite a surfeit of numbers about health." [4] The research director of the Kaiser Foundation Hospitals in Portland, Oregon, commenting on the lack of significant change between 1933 and 1967, adds that although many "conferences and papers" in thirty-five years have pointed out the need for adequate medical care research, we still do not have "comprehensive, coordinated, and reliable research, systematically carried on to help solve the many complex problems in the organization of health care services." [5]

ASSUMPTIONS ABOUT THE HEALTH CARE SYSTEM

The basic characteristics of the system may be summarized as follows, with special reference to New York City:

2 *Medical Care for the American People,* the final report of the Committee on the Costs of Medical Care, adopted October 31, 1932 (reprinted, by the U. S. Department of Health, Education, and Welfare, 1970).

3 Sumner N. Rosen, "Change and Resistance to Change," *Social Policy,* I, No. 5 (1971), 4.

4 *Report of the National Advisory Commission on Health Manpower;* 2 vols. (Washington, D.C.: Government Printing Office, 1967), I, 4.

5 Merwyn R. Greenlick, "Imperatives of Health Services Research," *Health Services Research,* IV (1969), 259.

1. *The input characteristics.* New York City has more and more diverse health care producing units than almost any other city in the United States if not the world. Private expenditures on health care per capita are higher than in most other cities in the country, as are city, state, and federal expenditures per capita for health care services.

The quality and concentration of well-trained doctors is higher than in most other cities.

2. *The output characteristics.* Health care is largely inaccessible, with long waiting times, complicated referrals to specialists, and a poor distribution of doctors. The population has little knowledge of where to get proper care.

The mortality rate is higher than in other countries which invest less in facilities and manpower.

Health care is expensive for patients in all categories. Medicare and Medicaid subsidize high and rising incomes of doctors, costly and unnecessary hospital care, and private insurance companies.

Since medical training stresses rare and high-technology diseases and operations, not enough general practitioners are trained.

The institutions of health care are mainly responsive to the well-paying private patient with an easily diagnosed disease or operation requiring short-term hopsitalization. Although the poor patient in a municipal hospital is likely to require even *more* care, he receives less and a poorer quality.

It is extremely difficult to find health care which is neither highly specialized nor the most cursory emergency treatment. The number and availability of general practitioners, providing primary care for an entire family over a period of time and acting as a liaison with more specialized services, has declined enormously.

3. *The basic structural units.* The great complexity and heterogeneity of the system must be emphasized.

Although doctors possess a professional monopoly over health care, they lack the appropriate knowledge and also even the power to treat patients adequately, given the hospital-based technology of modern health care. Laws and institutions are designed, however, to preserve their monopoly and guarantee high and rising incomes.

Medical schools restrict the production of doctors and train students either to treat high-technology, low-frequency diseases and operations, or for research.

Hospitals provide one class of care to those who pay and another to those who do not. They emphasize expensive, short-term care rather than emergency or ambulatory care in order to attract research and teaching-oriented staff.

The drug and equipment industry makes superprofits in the absence of any public or private (through insurance plans) controls.

Government enters the situation only to furnish nearly unrestricted financing of both "public" and "private" providers or, as in the case of New York City, to run underfinanced, understaffed hospitals.

Research and planning units may be either government or private, although usually they are publicly funded. Biomedical research absorbs most of the funds devoted to this area rather than social research on the health delivery system, although many observers believe that the major health problems are caused primarily by "environmental" factors (poor food, housing, sanitation, and other conditions closely related to income) and by problems of the organization of the delivery system. So-called health "planning" is confined to developing data on vital statistics, population characteristics, and internal program data for specific health care producing units, and does not gather or analyze data about the interrelations of the various organizations comprising the health system.

Community groups are usually unorganized and helpless consumers, but sometimes are militantly led by spokesmen for comprehensive, accessible, and inexpensive care.

4. *Basic operating characteristics.* These produce the kind of care summarized above, by the structural units defined above.

The actual services performed are less important than the income, prestige, and power to be gained by those who direct or head a health care producing unit.

The entire system is "public" in character; the public-private line is fictitious and serves key ideological functions. Even "private" organizations, such as voluntary hospitals, are legally chartered, and "private" organizations and services are largely funded directly through taxation or through contracts with public agencies.

The major powers of policy-making are located in "private" hands, through self-perpetuating boards, a symbolic representation of the "consumer" or "community" or "public" on boards, or a selection of officials by yet another agency which itself is dominated by "private" groups.

Increasing demands for health care are responded to by a tremendous number and variety of producers, each seeking to claim a portion of the market. Simultaneously, however, because of the publicly defined character and funding of the services, there is a demand for coordination and planning, which results in ever-increasing networks or layers of bureaucracy and staff, attempting to rationalize, on some basis of cost-effectiveness, the system which has now been outlined.

The federal government has been seen as a major force in reforming this system. Yet, federal activity has also intensified the problems. Government agencies are not independent forces for the public interest, regulating, coordinating, mediating, planning. Instead, government agencies are likely to become instruments for one or another part of the private sector. The Small Business Administration, for example, has been used on a number of occasions by one group of hospital interests to finance expansion, even while the Hill-Burton agency has been financing the expansion of another near-by hospital.[6]

The analyses by officials in a position to know are a devastating critique of the pluralism of the health producers industry. This is true at all levels—city, state, and federal, and for both public and private sectors.

At the federal level, according to Dr. James A. Shannon, former Director of the National Institutes of Health, health programs are a "broadly decentralized" and "highly fragmented" set

[6] *Federal Role in Health,* report of the Committee on Government Operations, United States Senate, made by its Subcommittee on Executive Reorganization and Government Research, 91st Congress, 2d Session, Report No. 92–809 (Washington, D.C.: Government Printing Office, 1970), pp. 25–26.

of "patchwork" activities that "make it difficult to consider broad issues in a coherent manner." These activities touch on every problem of health care and delivery "without dealing decisively with any one," he said.

Federal programs have "come into being sequentially as unbearable defects have been uncovered" in private health care systems, rather than as "elements in a complete and unified system." During the Johnson Administration alone the Congress enacted 51 pieces of health legislation that provided for some 400 "discrete" authorities. The establishing of comprehensive health planning programs and regional medical programs in 1966 is another case in point. According to Dr. Shannon, elements of these two programs are in direct conflict with each other.[7] The same process is visible at the city and state levels.

The main consequences of Medicare and Medicaid were the same. As a prominent medical sociologist says:

Whatever the merits of Medicare and Medicaid, they impressively illustrate that to increase substantially investments in health care without altering the framework in which services are delivered will only exacerbate the inefficiencies and absurdities of the current organization of medical care in America.[8]

TYPES OF REFORM AND THE MAJOR INTEREST GROUPS

The overwhelming fact about the various reforms of the health system that have been implemented or proposed—more money, more subsidy of insurance, more manpower, more demonstration projects, more clinics—is that they are absorbed into a system which is enormously resistant to change. The reforms which are suggested are sponsored by different elements in the health system and advantage one or another element, but do not seriously damage any interests. This pluralistic balancing of costs and benefits successfully defends the funding, powers, and resources of the producing institutions against any basic structural change.

Pressures for change come largely from two types of reformers.

[7] *Ibid.,* p. 31.
[8] David Mechanic, review of *The American Health Empire: Power, Profits, and Politics,* by Barbara and John Ehrenreich, and *The Quality of Mercy,* by Selig Greenberg, *Science,* May 14, 1971, pp. 701–3.

The first, whom I shall call the "market reformers," would expand the diversity of facilities available, the number of doctors, the competition between health facilities, and the quantity and quality of private insurance. Their assumption is that the basic task for the public sector is to underwrite medical bills for the poor, and that there should be maximum free choice among various health care producers. Consumers are assumed to be able to evaluate good and bad services, and thus market pressure will drive out the incompetent, excessively high-priced, or duplicated service, the inaccessible physician, clinic, or hospital. The market reformers wish to preserve the control of the physician over his practice, over the hospital, over his fees, and simply wish to open up the medical schools to meet the demand for doctors, to give patients more choice among doctors, clinics, and hospitals, and to make that choice a real one by providing public subsidies for medical costs.

These assumptions are questioned by the "bureaucratic reformers." They stress the importance of the hospital as the key location and organizer of health services, and wish to subordinate—in extreme cases—individual doctors to the control of hospital medical boards and administrators. The bureaucratic reformers are principally concerned with the coordination of fragmented services, the institution of planning, and the extension of public funding. Their assumption is that the technology of modern health care is essentially social or collective in character, requiring a complex division of labor between ambulatory and in-hospital care, primary practitioners and specialists, personal care, and advanced chemical and electronic treatments.

Neither of these strategies of reform is likely to work. Each type of reform stresses certain core functions in the health system, and regards others as secondary. But both neglect the way in which the groups representing those functions come to develop vital interests which sustain the present system and vitiate attempts at reform.

For the market reformers, supplying trained physicians, innovating through biomedical and technological research, and maintaining competition between diverse health care producers are the main functions to be maintained. They view the hospitals, medical schools, and public health agencies as only the organizational framework which sustains the primary functions of professional and research work. However, these types of work become buttressed through institutional mechanisms which guarantee professional control, and come to constitute powerful interest groups which I shall call the "professional monopolists."

For the bureaucratic reformers, the hospitals, medical schools, and public health agencies at all governmental levels perform the core functions of organizing, financing, and distributing health care. Hospitals are seen ideally as the center of networks of associated clinics and neighborhood health centers, providing comprehensive and coordinated care to an entire local population. The bureaucratic reformers view physicians and medical researchers as performing crucial work, but properly as subordinated and differentiated parts of a complex delivery system, integrated by bureaucracies, notably the hospital. But these large-scale organizations also become powerful interest groups, which I shall call the "corporate rationalizers."

A third type of reformer—the "system reformer"—is relatively unimportant in the American context as yet although plans for the ideal health system described in the literature would constitute a virtual revolutionary transformation if implemented. Free, accessible health care which equalizes the quality and quantity of treatment available both to the well-to-do and to the poor is not envisioned by any program of reform now being presented to the American public. Yet, the vision of comprehensive health care available to all implicitly underlies the activities of a third interest group which is not properly "in" the health system at all: the "community health advocates."

The key interests of each set of groups and their interrelated activities account for both the expansion of health-care-providing units at the bottom of the system and the elaboration of planning and coordinating bureaucratic machinery at the top.

The professional monopolists. The professional monopolists are mainly physicians, specialists, and health research workers in medical schools and universities, who usually have an advanced degree and also a position—either an entrepreneurial one guaranteed by law and custom or an official one defined by the hierarchy of statuses within an organization—which entitles them to monoply over certain kinds of work. Their incomes are derived from private practice or from foundations, governments, and universities, but they are essentially entrepreneurs, able to exploit organizational resources for their personal and professional interests. They can be called "monopolistic" because they have complete control over the conditions of their work, buttressed by the traditions of their professions and/or institutions, and because usually there is no other way to show effectiveness except through a demonstration grant, research project, or contract to them, or by contracting with them to perform their professional services. Frequently a clinic or health center will be set up which, although providing services, is established mainly for other purposes of the persons who hold power (not always or even usually the operating staff): research, training, professional aggrandizement, power within their "home" institutions, the prestige of extending their professional empire, and so forth.

The major consequence of the activity of the professional monopolists is a continuous proliferation of programs and projects which are established in a wide variety of ways, under many auspices, and with many sources of funding, and which undoubtedly in most cases provide real services of some kind. The reason it is so difficult to describe or explain how these work is that the professional monopolists who set them up attempt to provide a symbolic screen of legitimacy while maintaining power in their own hands through various organizational devices. A continuous flow of symbols will reassure the funding or allegedly controlling publics or constituencies about the functions being performed, while the individuals or groups which have a special interest in the income, prestige, or power generated by the agency are benefiting from its allocations of resources.

Thus, the symbolic screen will put off attempts at control or supervision, by making them difficult as well as less likely (because the nominally superior agency will be reassured). It is almost impossible to plan or coordinate or integrate the activities of the myriad projects and programs because important interests of the individuals and groups which establish and maintain them contradict the goals of those who wish to coordinate, plan, and integrate all of the functions implied or defined by the master symbols of the project: its title, the funding agency's contract with it, its annual report, and so on.

The corporate rationalizers. The corporate rationalizers are typically persons in top positions in a "health" organization: hospital administrators, medical school directors, public health officials, directors of city health agencies, heads of quasi-public insurance (Blue Cross), state and federal health officials. These individuals and groups are concerned with breaking the power of the professional monopolists. Their ideology, although not their interests, stresses a rational, efficient, cost-conscious, coordinated health care delivery system. They see the medical division of labor as arbitrary and anachronistic in view of modern hospital-based technology. The more successful they are in unifying functions, powers, and resources under a single glorifying symbol ("medical center"; "comprehensive health planning"), the greater their incomes are likely to be and the higher their community and professional prestige. Thus, there are ample incentives for these individuals to attempt to expand the powers of their home institution or organization.

Sometimes the corporate rationalizers ally themselves with the professional monopolists within their own institutions, as a way of gathering more financial resources and legitimacy, and also as a way of bringing more and more health care units into their domain, even if not under their control. But usually it is in the interests of the corporate rationalizers to attempt to control the conditions of work, the division of labor, and the salaries of their employees, in view of the exigencies of funding, the need to adopt technical and organizational innovations without the built-in resistances of professional (or union, for that matter) jurisdictions over tools and tasks. They, therefore, attempt to convert professionals, mainly physicians, into employees, and in a variety of ways to circumscribe their power in the hospital.

Although great size and resources are equated with capability and performance, in order to legitimate extending the domain of control of the corporate rationalizers, there is little evidence that even the internal structure of the giant hospital complexes is planned, integrated, and coordinated for the effective delivery of health services to a given target population, let alone the system as a whole. The establishment of "outreach" neighborhood health centers by a medical center is advertised as a progressive and rational development because it is seen as a step toward coordination and integration. But if the supposed coordinating mechanisms—ambulance services, referrals, communications of records and patient information—are little better than if the two organizations were not linked together, then the extension of control by the corporate rationalizers does not result in better, more comprehensive care.

Even if the target of the corporate rationalizers' activity is to coordinate and integrate single giant organizations into a cohesive whole, the successful instituting of such bureaucratic controls means that planning and coordination of the larger health system become *more* difficult. Generating enough power successfully to integrate a portion of it means, almost by definition, that this part is now insulated from outside influence, and can successfully resist being integrated into a still larger system.

The rhetoric of the corporate rationalizers conceals this consequence by assuming that social or political mechanisms exist which can unify and integrate the entire system. But such mechanisms do not exist in government or anywhere else. The mere passage of legislation establishing "comprehensive health planning" or "regional medical programs," which sets up new agencies supposedly to engage in regional planning, does not provide them with the necessary power and resources. If this is the case, then the act of creating another agency further fragments the system. Historically, a series of laws have responded to pressures for reform by establishing a series of agencies, none of which has sufficient power to do its job. Few of these are abolished, and subsequent legislation incorporates the previous agencies into the list of those to be "coordinated," thereby further complicating the system. The resources made available to these agencies frequently become part of the budgets controlled by the corporate rationalizers, charged with carrying out planning and coordination. Such expansion, as already indicated, carries direct rewards for the top officials.

A major consequence of the activity of the corporate rationalizers is a constant expansion of the functions, powers, and resources of their organizations. One organizational device for doing that is to institute a bureaucratic stratum designed to coordinate and integrate, as well as evaluate, the component units. Unfortunately, this new stratum cannot carry out this function because it is a staff operation with little power and is usually the instrument of one particular leadership faction within the organization. Thus, their recommendations frequently fail to carry enough weight to be implemented. Also the planning or research staff tends to be drawn, because of lack of any other source of personnel, from the ranks of the professional monopolists, who have little stake in truly rationalizing the operation and see the planning or research functions partly as instruments for their own personal and professional ends. Where the goals of the professional monopolists within the organization and the sponsoring faction of the corporate rationalizers coincide, an effective staff function will be performed; in that case, the committed and motivated staff will usually come into conflict with a powerful element in the top officialdom of the organization—either another group of professional monopolists whose toes they are stepping on, or a faction among the corporate rationalizers.

Thus, the net effect of the activities of the corporate rationalizers is to complicate and elaborate the bureaucratic structure. The relationship between them and the professional monopolists is symbolic in that the ever-increasing elaboration of the bureaucratic structure depends for its justification upon the expansion of health care providing units at the bottom. No group involved has a stake in the coordination and integration of the entire system toward the major goal of easily accessible, inexpensive, and high-quality health care.

The community health advocates. The third major interest group, the community health advocates, comprise liberal reformers in the political parties, various community control groups, in both the black and the white communities, some intellectuals, and some supporters within the city and other government bureaucracies and the medical schools. Because they are not part of the network of health institutions and agencies, they are free to demand more and better health services, and also some voice in the decisions and policies which might affect health care in the city.

The difficulty is that they are likely to fail. If their demands are focused upon a particular program or need, the response is likely to be the establishment of a particular kind of program or clinic—drug, alcoholism, mental health. The professional monopolists will seize upon the demand as an opportunity to legitimate their efforts to establish another project or program. While some tangible services to some people may be the outcome, the over-all result is the expansion and proliferation of still more highly specialized clinics, demonstration projects, or health centers, which confuse people trying to find care, are highly expensive in both staff and administrative costs, and thus lead to a further elaboration of the overriding bureaucratic structure.

If the demands of community health advocates are directed toward reorganizing the health system, then the activities of the corporate rationalizers are legitimated. New planning committees and new coordinating councils will be set up, with representation from the community groups, with the avowed goal of rationalizing the system. But the community representatives do not have the information necessary to play an important political role—they do not know the levers of power, the interests at stake, the actual nature of the operating institutions—and do not have the political resources necessary to acquire that information, since they are only minority members of advisory committees. The presence of community health advocates on one or another committee or council is a sign of legitimacy being claimed either by a set of professional monopolists or corporate rationalizers, or sometimes both, in their battle for resources and power.

Thus, the major consequence of the activity of community health advocates is to provide further legitimacy for the expansion both of specific research or service units controlled by professional monopolists, and the expansion of the layers of bureaucratic staff intended to provide coordination and planning under the control of the corporate rationalizers. Given the enormous discrepancy between the output of actual health services and their claims, there will be a continuous supply of persons from community groups ready to serve as community health advocates. However, persons who have played that role for some time will quickly become discouraged and leave, or will be coopted into the official network of health institutions and organizations. Other persons will arise from community organizations to replace them, for a wide variety of motives: prestige as a community representative; a chance to mingle with high city and other officials and community leaders; possibly a chance for a better job or a political career.

Given the original diversity of health producers and the personal and organizational stakes of the interdependent, although conflicting, network of professional monopolists and corporate rationalizers, the demands of the community health advocates are almost inevitably frustrated. In fact, the system as a whole, as a result of their activities, moves in a direction exactly opposite to that which they envision. Costs go up, as a result of the establishment of new, expensive programs. The accessibility of care goes down, as a result of the proliferation of specialized, high-technology, research- or teaching-oriented health care units.

CONSEQUENCES FOR HEALTH RESEARCH

Although the community health advocates have a real stake in accurate information on the quality and quantity of services and their cost and also information on a structure of controls which would be responsive to community health needs, they have no resources with which to command that information. The main information which the system generates is internal management information which provides the corporate rationalizers with some means of assessing the efficiency of their own organization or institution, and research data useful for professional and scientific problems but not for assessment of outputs and the performance of the organization. But outside groups cannot easily obtain that information to analyze for their own purposes, since it can be used to show the ways in which the various parts of the organizations fail to achieve their ostensible goals, advertised far and wide in the efforts to achieve more funds. Even if obtained, the information is not easily aggregated with information from other sources to estimate the causal relationships between the inputs of money and manpower from one organization to another, and the outputs of tangible health services. The professional monopolists, who tend to be strategically located in data-gathering and -processing positions, also have no incentive to release information to outside groups who may challenge their power to define their own work.

Thus, while obeisance may be made to information gathering and data processing, these symbolic claims again serve to screen the absence of the basic data which could be used to measure the specific quantity and quality of services. For the same reasons, the data do not exist which could allow the study of the health system as a whole. Almost no studies have been done which take as problematic the structure of health care providing institutions—their funding, control, relationships to each other, and impact on the quality and quantity of services. Most studies of the delivery system focus on the utilization of health services by income, occupational, and ethnic groups, on the socialization of physicians and nurses, or on the impact of the internal organization of a hospital upon patient care. While all of these studies can be justified on their own terms, they do not touch the core problem of the structure of the *producing* institutions, but focus instead either on the *consumers* of health care, or upon a specific institutional, organizational, or professional context in which a particular kind of care is provided. Such a paucity of studies is no accident; such studies would challenge the primary interests of both the professional monopolists and the corporate rationalizers in maintaining the structure of health institutions as they now exist.

CONCLUSIONS

The "crisis" of the American health system is *not* a result of the necessary competition of diverse interests, groups, and providers in a pluralistic and competitive health economy, nor is it a result of bureaucratic inefficiencies, to be corrected by yet more layers of administration established by government policy. Rather, the conflicts between the professional monopolists—seeking to erect barriers to protect their control over research, teaching, and care—and the corporate rationalizers—seeking to extend their control over the organization of services—account for many of the aspects of the American health system.

These conflicts stem, in turn, from a fundamental contradiction in modern health care between the social character of the technology of health care and the private appropriation of the power and resources involved. Health care, from the point of view of the most advanced technology, is a complex division of labor, requiring highly specialized knowledge at some points, routine screening at others. The integration of all aspects of the health care system—preventive care, outpatient checkups, routine treatment for specific minor illnesses, specialized treatment for rare diseases requiring expensive machines, long-term care for chronic conditions—would require the generation of the kind of social power which does not yet exist in America. The power necessary to create such an integrated system has been appropriated by various discrete interest groups and preserves existing allocations of social values and resources. Government is not an independent power standing above and beyond the competing interest groups.

The upper middle class is not as seriously affected by the cost, inadequacy, and low quality of care as are the poor because most of these families can afford a physician's care and thus have access through him to reasonably high-quality medical and hospital care. Many potential liberal reformers are not likely to protest or become active in their own interests, but out of a spirit of *noblesse oblige*. However, they are most likely to perceive the world as the corporate rationalizers do, with positive and progressive change to be achieved either by pouring in more money (usually federal), establishing new units to meet unfulfilled needs, or establishing new mechanisms for planning and coordinating the system as a whole. These "remedies," far from succeeding, serve only to exacerbate the problem.

Periodic crises are precipitated by one or another interest group in an attempt to arouse support for its goals, although media exposure which defines a crisis usually has nothing to do with any change in the basic performance of the health system. Most crises, notably those in the last ten years in New York City, have been precipitated by elements among the corporate rationalizers. The series of investigations by private, city, and state agencies from 1960 to 1970 stress the fragmentation and lack of coordination of the system, a sure sign of the goal of corporate rationalization—as are the various reorganizations of the hospitals carried out in the last decade. But none of the reforms has touched the basic power of the private sector and its institutions.

A few crises have been precipitated by community groups moving outside the established framework of representation and influence to take disruptive, militant action. These have produced specific responses, usually as new programs or still more "representation," taking the forms already described.

The real crisis involves the institutional and class structure which creates and sustains the power of the professional monopolists and the corporate rationalizers. This power is legal, political, economic, and cultural, and therefore any serious challenge will require the emergence of a social and political movement which rejects the legitimacy of established institutions and strikes at their roots. Such a movement is not yet in sight.

The Health Care System; a Critique and a Legislative Proposal[1]

LEONARD WOODCOCK

As we engage in the struggle for full civil rights for all, for adequate housing, improvement of the environment, full job opportunities, and welfare reform, we carry on the mission of strengthening America so perceptively understood by Walter Reuther. Today, perhaps the most pressing domestic issue is the health care crisis facing our nation. Almost two years ago President Nixon said that in the absence of administrative and legislative action, the medical care system would break down within two or three years, with consequences affecting millions throughout the United States.

By the President's timetable and by that of most informed observers, time is about to run out. Our outdated health care system bears a resemblance to the Model T automobile. In its day, that venerable machine had utility, dependability, versatility, endurance, and economy. It accounted for one half of all car sales and opened up mass production. But time took its toll. By the mid-1920s it began to lose ground. Its once innovative engineering features were obsolete and noncompetitive. Henry Ford, however, remained adamant in his refusal to replace the T until its demise became inevitable in 1927, after nineteen years of production.[2]

We have continued to rely for too long a time on a health care vehicle long obsolete. Today, insurers simply pay out dollars to poorly managed hospitals and dollar-oriented doctors. Physicians and other health workers are in short supply, and our medical

1 Paper delivered at session held in tribute to the late Walter Reuther, President, International Union, United Automobile Workers.
2 Allan Nevins and Frank Ernest Hill, *Ford: Expansion and Challenge: 1915–1933* (New York: Charles Scribner's Sons, 1957), p. 409–36.

schools face bankruptcy. The ghetto poor and the rural farm
resident find doctors and hospitals scarce. Even the well-to-do
have trouble getting access to proper care. The best health insurance plans meet only 40 percent to 50 percent of medical bills,
and a long-term disability may wipe out the patient or his
family. The poor get second-class medicine, and the elderly find
that Medicare falls about 50 percent short of covering their
health bills.

In mid-1971, this Model T medical system chugs and sputters
along, hitting on only three cylinders, an obsolete vehicle from
the standpoint of consumers and providers alike. The obsolescence of America's health care system and the crisis of health are
best described by their impact on people:

A Detroit member of the United Automobile Workers (UAW)
was forced to retire prematurely when the firm where she worked
closed its doors. Her net pension of $23.64 ($46.96 less the Blue
Cross–Blue Shield premium) has dwindled to thirty-six cents per
month as a result of a doubling of her self-paid Blue Cross–Blue
Shield premium between 1966 and 1970.

Claire Townsend, director of Ralph Nader's task force working in
and investigating the appalling conditions in nursing homes, concludes: ". . . instead of coming up with a crusader's wish to help
the nursing home problem, I came out last night vowing to commit
suicide before I get old." [3]

The lawsuit against Los Angeles County–University of Southern
California Medical Center was joined by all 80 residents of the
center, charging that patients are being treated in "unsafe, inadequate and unlawful facilities" and that treatment is "a public
nuisance and a serious threat to public health." [4]

A Detroit patient died in a hospital within eight and a half hours
of suffering a heart attack. His bill totaled $1,644.80.[5]

A tour of communities by the President and President-elect of the
American Public Health Association left them "shocked and still

3 Claire Townsend, *Nursing Homes for the Aged: the Agony of One Million
Americans,* Task Force report on nursing homes (Washington, D.C.: Center for
Study of Responsive Law, 1970), p. 97.
4 John G. Rogers, "Angry Young Doctors Are Rebelling," *Parade,* February
21, 1971, p. 4.
5 "Contact 10," Detroit *News,* February 25, 1971, p. 1B.

reeling. Circumstances that only can be called health brutality pervade the lives of millions of American people who live in communities that seemed designed to break the human spirit." In particular, they cite the case of a fifty-three-year-old American Indian from Montana, a veteran of the Second World War, raising seven children on a modest pension and what he can salvage from a junkyard. He is too poor to buy food stamps or to return to the hospital for post-cancer treatment which he has needed for nine years. Were he to return to the hospital, his children would not have food in his absence.[6]

The tragic state of health care in America can also be viewed in more impersonal but nonetheless shocking terms when one focuses on the broken down parts of our health care vehicle.

The social work profession joined organized labor and other progressive forces in the difficult but successful fight to achieve national health insurance for the elderly. Social workers and we who represent some 250,000 UAW retirees know how heavily they rely upon Medicare. In addition, the Congress passed a Medicaid program which gave more promise than performance in providing health services to the medically indigent. This too, social workers understand, for many of the state welfare departments administer the Medicaid programs.

Medicare benefits provide only limited health protection. Even this protection is hedged by patient cost sharing. Since Medicare began, deductibles and co-payments toward hospital and nursing home expenses under Medicare have risen 50 percent, and the monthly premium that Medicare subscribers pay to help finance their medical-surgical benefits will have risen 87 percent by July, 1971. Medicare subscribers must meet these rising charges from relatively fixed social security and (in some instances) private pension benefits. But they must also reach into their pockets, or turn to Medicaid in order to pay the 53.3 percent of their total health expenditures not covered by Medicare.[7] Medicare has also been beset by costs which greatly exceeded

6 Lester Breslow, M.D., "The Urgency of Social Action for Health," *American Journal of Public Health*, LX (1970), 13.

7 Barbara S. Cooper, "Medical Care Outlays for Aged and Non-aged Persons, 1966–1969," Social Security Administration Research and Statistics Note No. 7, June 18, 1970, p. 1.

actuarial projections, allegations of unnecessary treatment by
physicians, slipshod administration by the fiscal intermediaries
running the program, and nonreporting to the tax collector of
Medicare income by providers.[8]

The state Medicaid programs, which offer health protection to
the poor and to the medically indigent (including some Medicare clients), have proved to be increasingly ineffective. Beset by
the same criticisms leveled at Medicare, Medicaid has also failed
to realize its potential in providing coverage to the needy. In
1966 it was estimated that as many as 35 million needy persons
would be covered under Medicaid when it became fully operational; today, there are forty-eight states participating, but according to Health, Education and Welfare Secretary, Elliott
Richardson, "only one-third of the estimated poverty population
received services under this program in 1970 and only 133,000
of an estimated 750,000 women and infants in low-income circumstances receive comprehensive maternity and infant care." [9]

The troubles of Medicare and Medicaid are reflections of a
major crisis in all health care which is now widely recognized.
We need to be clear about the five major causes of the mess in
which we find ourselves. We will not achieve good health care
for all Americans unless we deal with each of these five and deal
with them more or less simultaneously.

1. *Runaway health care costs.* For fifteen years health costs
have been increasing at twice the general cost of living. We now
spend nearly $70 billion a year for health care purposes—7 per-
cent of our entire gross national product (GNP).[10] Compared to
fifteen years ago, the average auto worker gives up five times as
much to buy health insurance that is limited in coverage, and

8 "Medicare and Medicaid: Problems, Issues and Alternatives," report of the
staff of the Committee on Finance, United States Senate, 1970, pp. 3–27.

9 Fred H. Steininger, Director of Family Services, Welfare Administration,
"The New Medical Assistance Program," Bergen County (N.J.) Medical Society,
1966, p. 2; testimony of Secretary Elliott L. Richardson, before the U.S. Senate
Labor and Public Welfare Committee Health Subcommittee. February 22, 1971,
page 4.

10 Dorothy P. Rice and Barbara S. Cooper, "National Health Expenditures,
1929–70, "*Social Security Bulletin,* XXXIV, No. 1 (1971), 3.

under the present system there is no end in sight for these steeply rising costs. The insistence of the major automobile companies that UAW members assume the added cost of health insurance premiums was an important factor in causing the lengthy strike at the General Motors Corporation in 1970.

2. *National shortages of health manpower.* Dr. Roger O. Egeberg, Assistant Secretary of the Department of Health, Education, and Welfare, estimates that America needs 50,000 new physicians and tens of thousands of social workers, nurses and other allied health personnel to meet the nation's minimum needs. If present policies continue, the manpower gap will continue to widen. The situation threatens to deteriorate further as the crisis in funding medical education grows.

3. *Inadequate availability and delivery of health care.* The majority of physicians function in a "cottage type" industry. Most Americans receive their medical care by the cumbersome fee-for-service method with individual visits to general practitioners, separate visits to physicians practicing more than thirty medical specialties, and added trips for ancillary care. Rural and poverty areas are health poor. While the Detroit region as a whole has one doctor for every 792 people, planners of an east side medical center found only 15 physicians in an area containing some 200,000 people.[11] The Michigan Health Council lists 134 small Michigan communities as needing doctors.[12]

4. *Poor quality health care.* The quality of care ranges from superb to horrid, and we lack adequate controls for assurance of the high quality which our medical-scientific knowledge gives the American people a right to expect. The gap between what the health sciences are capable of offering and what our people are receiving continues to widen. The wealthiest nation in the world, with a GNP which has reached the one-trillion-dollar mark, lags far behind many industrialized nations in key measures of a nation's health.

[11] Dolores Katz, "Study Finds City's Doctor Shortage Getting Worse," Detroit *Free Press,* December 21, 1970, p. 8A.
[12] Dolores Katz, "Towns Hope Loans Will Attract Doctors," Detroit *Free Press,* March 21, 1971, p. 3A.

5. *Bias in favor of health providers and insurers.* Our system of medical care functions better for those who provide health care services, and for those who insure its costs, than for those who use the services. It needs to be restructured to serve both equally and adequately.

The private health insurance industry, which organized labor was instrumental in creating and expanding, has unfortunately proved completely unable to do the job for which it was created. Although private health insurance covered over 175 million Americans in 1969, this extensive coverage met only 24 percent of personal health care expenditures. Thus 26.7 million persons had no private health insurance in 1969, and the policies of those who were covered failed to meet more than one fourth of personal health care expenditures.[13]

Private health insurance has failed Americans in other ways. By focusing almost exclusively on sickness it cannot even be appropriately defined as "health" insurance. Benefits for ambulatory care, as opposed to costly in-hospital care, are deemphasized, and benefits for preventive care are practically nonexistent. The carriers have also failed to implement cost or quality controls. Their benefit programs are concerned solely with the exchange and protection of dollars, not with the provision of health care services.

There are today in excess of 1,800 private health insurance carriers with 1,800 separate and competing sales forces, with substantial advertising budgets, with duplicate administration, with hundreds of policy variations, with multitudinous forms, and elaborate coordination agreements to prevent double payments to subscribers. This proliferation results in an annual waste estimated at $1.1 billion in unnecessary expenditures. Those who shed crocodile tears about the dangers of bureaucratic costs of publicly supported programs might well look to "what hath been wrought" on the consumer by our private system.

Despite these obvious shortcomings, the Nixon Administration

[13] Marjorie Smith Mueller, "Private Health Insurance in 1969: a Review," *Social Security Bulletin,* XXXIV, No. 2 (1971), 18; *Source Book of Health Insurance Data, 1970* (New York: Health Insurance Institute, 1971), p. 15.

in February, 1971, advanced a series of proposals which would perpetuate the waste and inefficiency in the present private health insurance system and almost certainly guarantee a continuation of the inflation that has been fostered by the private insurance mechanism. The Administration's National Health Insurance Partnership Act provides for a totally unwarranted windfall to the private insurance industry under the guise of maintaining a free enterprise mechanism that Adam Smith himself would never have endorsed.

The basic reason for the unacceptability of the major features of these proposals is that they do not deal realistically with the situation. Facing a monumental problem which requires reorganization of health care delivery and financing, the Administration has come up with what Secretary Richardson described as "the right size patch." Among the many gaps in the program is limited preventive care and the complete absence of coverage for mental health services, dental services, prescription drugs, and a number of other services recognized as essential to comprehensive care. It is appalling that in 1971 serious proposals would ignore these major health needs.

The Administration's patches perpetuate a separate but less equal system of medical care for the poor. Rather than simplifying problems, they add to their complexity by piling new program proposal on new program proposal. They offer far fewer coverages than many Americans now have and they so hedge these benefits with cost sharing (the bane of Medicare subscribers), that only the economically secure and organizationally nimble could get through the barriers to obtain the kind of early preventive and diagnostic care so essential to good health.

Others have offered their panacea for the complex panoply of health problems. "Medicredit," introduced at the behest of the American Medical Association, would simply permit an expansion of voluntary health insurance through issuance of government health insurance certificates (which bear a striking resemblance to food stamps) for the indigent and income tax credits to offset health insurance premiums paid by the more affluent. Senator Russell Long has introduced a catastrophic health insurance program which provides coverage for the population under age sixty-five commencing in mid-illness, an approach which appeals to the cost-conscious, but hardly to the sick. "Healthcare," the creation of the Health Insurance Association of America, divides the population into three classes based on job or income status. Employers would be compelled to offer basic coverage to workers and their families; individuals would be "encouraged" to buy individual health insurance; government funds would provide private insurance pooling for the "uninsurable."

These four piecemeal approaches are not the new vehicles we need. Each would continue the inefficient and ineffective private health insurance system. Each guarantees that Americans would have separate but unequal benefits through categorical approaches depending on income, employment status, age, and so on. They provide little in the way of incentives for reorganizing medical practice so as better to serve both health consumers and health providers. Each ignores the rising voice that consumers demand in influencing health policy and administration. They place little reliance on the tested and proven social security mechanism for financing and administering benefits. In summary, their adoption would do little to moderate health inflation, make health services more efficient, or improve the health security of the American people.

Two years ago, the Committee for National Health Insurance, founded by Walter Reuther, began to develop a health security program which would deal with all major causes of the crisis. Dr. Michael DeBakey and Mrs. Mary Lasker are vice chairmen. The late Whitney M. Young, Jr., was also a vice chairman and active member. The social work profession is represented by Melvin A. Glasser, of the UAW; James Brindle, President of New York's Health Insurance Plan; and Charles Schottland, President of Brandeis University. Other members include outstanding Americans from both political parties and all walks of life.

In establishing the mandate of the committee, we did not propose to borrow a national health insurance system from any other nation. No nation has a system that would meet the unique needs of this country. We stated our confidence that we have in America the ingenuity and the social inventiveness needed to create a distinctively American system of national health insurance, one that would harmonize the best features of the present system, with maximum freedom of choice for both providers and consumers of health care services. Working from this mandate, a knowledgeable and expert technical committee succeeded in developing a thorough and complete program, which was introduced in bill form during the first session of the ninety-second Congress.

The Health Security bill of 1971, H.R. 22 and 23, was introduced by Representatives Martha Griffiths and James Corman, and is supported by more than a hundred other House members. The bill is S. 3 in the Senate and was introduced by Senator Edward Kennedy, and supported by William Saxbe, John Sherman Cooper, and twenty-three other senators.

It is a plan for an improved system for the efficient delivery and financing of high-quality, continuous, comprehensive health services for all in our nation. It is a plan to assure financial security against the costs of serious illness which can come unpredictably and devastatingly to any family. Most important, it is a single plan. It is not a piecemeal approach. It is not a hodgepodge, providing limited benefits to certain groups and leaving others out altogether. It is not oddments of ideas developed to accommodate special interests rather than the public interest. And it is a plan whose operation can be readily understood and utilized by the American people.

Health Security is not an insurance program; it is a health program. The insurance companies operate insurance plans. They are interested in limiting their risks and liabilities. We are interested in revitalizing the health care system.

The bill would provide the framework for a living program, adaptable to emerging technology and delivery mechanisms. It does not propose nationalized or socialized medicine. It does not propose that the federal government take over the nation's resources for providing medical care—the hospitals, or the physicians, dentists, nurses, and other personnel; nor would it arbitrarily compel the health professionals to reorganize and coordinate their fragmented services into a more efficient and less costly system. It leaves the furnishing of medical care in the private sector, with wide choices and elections for patterns of practice carefully preserved.

Thus, if the Health Security bill is described as "nationalized" or "monolithic," as some are doing, it should be clear that these words fairly apply to the basic, supportive financing; they do *not* apply to the continuing private provision of medical care which preserves free choice, alternatives, and voluntary actions of many kinds. Through this partnership of national governmental financing and private provision of the services supported by that system of financing, the Health Security bill offers a sound foundation upon which this nation can build a modern medical care system. Its cornerstone is the recognition in official national policy that access to the best available health care is a fundamental right in a progressive society. Further, the bill contains practical provisions to translate this promised right into reality.

All persons legally resident in the United States would be eligible for the benefits of Health Security. Eligibility would require neither an individual contribution history nor any means test.

With five modest limitations, the benefits are intended to embrace the entire range of personal health services, including prevention and early detection of disease, treatment of illness, and physical rehabilitation. There are no restrictions on needed services, no cut-off points, no coinsurance, no deductibles, and no waiting periods. The program provides full coverage for physicians' services, hospital services, and coverage for optometry services, podiatry services, and devices, appliances, and equipment.

The principal limitations are:

1. Dental care: restricted to children through age fifteen at the outset, with the covered age group increasing thereafter until persons through age twenty-five are included; eligibility permanent once it has been established

2. Skilled nursing home care: limited to 120 days per benefit period

3. Psychiatric hospitalization: limited to forty-five consecutive days of active treatment during a benefit period

4. Psychiatric consultations: limited to twenty visits during a benefit period

5. Drugs: outside an organized patient care program, only those which are necessary for treatment of chronic diseases or conditions which require costly drug therapy.

We believe that the ancillary health professions will be more fully and meaningfully utilized through the program's emphasis upon financial and other incentives to encourage the team practice of health care delivery. Social work is prominent among the professional services covered by Health Security when offered as part of institutional services or when furnished through health maintenance organizations.

A special feature of Health Security provides for a Resources Development Fund. A fixed percentage of over-all program funds, ultimately reaching $2 billion per annum, would be earmarked and used to strengthen the nation's resources of health personnel and facilities and upgrade the system for the delivery of care. This fund would provide for educational training, programs for new kinds of health personnel, especially for those disadvantaged by poverty or membership in minority groups. It would also provide financial support for needed health personnel and facilities in both urban and rural shortage areas.

While Health Security would continue to pay physicians in private practice on a fee-for-service or other basis, health maintenance organizations (HMOs) would receive first claim to Health Security funds, thus providing a powerful incentive for physicians to opt for such organized forms of practice as opposed to solo practice. Physicians would be able to pool their expenses and overhead and have available a wide range of ancillary and specialist assistance, thus freeing them to spend more time with patients. HMOs are a proven means for providing near-total, economical health care. They operate on the philosophy that keeping people well is far better and more efficient than treating them only after they get sick. By focusing on regular check-ups and out-of-hospital treatment, such plans are able to cut hospitalization by one-third to one-half. Detroit's Community Health Association subscribers, for example, use half as many hospital days per 1,000 members as those who receive their care under Michigan Blue Cross: 544 days versus 1,059 days.[14]

Another measure of the effectiveness of group practice plans is shown by a report on the Federal Employees Health Benefits Program. Federal employees have the choice of five types of health plans. The most recent report reveals that subscribers enrolled under group practice plans had only half as many appendectomies as those enrolled in the fee-for-service system, one-third as many tonsillectomies and adenoidectomies, and half as many operations for gynecological complaints.[15]

All services covered under the Health Security bill would be financed on a budgeted basis. Advance budgeting would, we believe, restrain the steeply rising costs and provide a method of allocating funds among categories of covered services. Through this process, the program could support a range of basic and auxiliary services and modify the undue emphasis on high-cost services and facilities.

By a system of regional allocation of funds, annual budgetary review, approval of institutional service expenditures, and financial reviews and controls on service costs, this program would provide the means for effecting important health cost controls.

The financial provisions for the Health Security program carry out the declared purpose to provide adequate and assured financing. The system would operate on an annual budget basis, providing nationally an amount of money equal to what is being spent for the covered services. Thus, budget provision and control would put an end to open-end escalating costs.

Today, health funds come from public expenditures, which represent about 40 percent of the total; from private health insurance premiums paid by employers, employees, and indi-

14 Community Health Association, Research and Planning Division, Detroit; Michigan Hospital Service Annual Report, 1970.
15 "The Federal Employees' Health Benefits Program: Seventh Term (1967) Coverage and Utilization" (Washington, D.C.: Group Health Association of America, 1970).

viduals; and from out-of-pocket expenditures. Under our program, one half of the needed funds would be derived from general revenues and half from earmarked social security taxes. The precise allocation among these various sources is endlessly arguable. However, the use of the several sources is, we believe, completely sound. Since the earmarked income would go into a permanently appropriated trust fund, as in the social security insurance programs, the functional operations would have secure and stable financing.

There has been more confusion and misrepresentation, intentional and otherwise, about the cost of the comprehensive Health Security than perhaps any other feature of the program. This is unfortunate, for in the great debate which is taking place the primary issue should be how best to get health services to all our people.

Therefore, let me put the cost proposition simply. Our fiscal experts have put into the *Congressional Record* evidence to support our view that with Health Security, with proper financing and quality controls, it would be possible to provide comprehensive health services to all the American people at no more cost than the nation is now spending for the fragmented services which most Americans receive while many receive no services at all. Furthermore, the estimates of a 13 percent inflation factor in health care costs would at least be halved in the first years of our program and reduced even further in subsequent years as the reorganization of services became fully effective.

There is no magic about the proposition that it is possible to provide more and better services to more people with the same amount of funds we spend in any given year. The savings effected through elimination of waste and duplication and through the development of a reorganized and more rational delivery system provide the keys to the new economies.

The financial and administrative arrangements of the entire program are designed to move the medical care system toward organized programs of health services, utilizing teams of professional, technical, and supporting personnel. Earmarked funds would support the most rapid practicable development toward this goal. State statutes which restrict or impede the development of group practice programs would be superseded by provisions of the program.

A key principle of the Health Security bill would guarantee new options in the delivery of health services. We believe that both the doctor and the patient should be free to choose an organized health services plan as an alternative to solo service. In either case, there should be freedom of choice to select a doctor, or accept a patient.

The bill includes significant provisions to safeguard quality of care. It would establish national standards for participating individuals and institutions. Independent practitioners would be eligible to participate upon meeting licensure and continuing education requirements. Provision is made for professional review and competent peer judgments to assure a level of service delivery compatible with good medical standards.

Health Security takes note of the rising voice of consumerism, and gives health "power to the people" as opposed to leaving health economic decisions solely to practitioners. Consumers would be assured a meaningful role at every administrative and decision-making level. A National Health Security Advisory Council, with a majority of consumer members would work closely with the proposed Health Security Board in establishing national policy, standards, and operating procedures. In addition, consumer organizations would be given technical and financial assistance to establish their own comprehensive health care programs.

Rather than increasing the mountain of paperwork, as some critics have suggested, the proposed program would reduce it. Under Health Security there would be one administering agency and one set of simplified forms. Both patients and practitioners would welcome the change.

The American people recognize that health care is in crisis. But this is a crisis era—housing, poverty, the cities, the environment, education, the question of individual and collective accountability for an unjust war. While not intending to simplify the vast undertaking necessary to make our health system more rational and responsive, I nonetheless suggest that health care reform is one of America's more manageable problems. The danger is that America will be enticed to adopt spot-weld approaches, and that our health problems will multiply, not diminish. We need a new model, not merely a used car polished and painted so that the exterior appearance disguises the mechanical malfunctions within. Nothing less than Health Security, which deals not only with financing but with reorganization of the entire system through which health care services are delivered, will suffice.

Decisive action on national health insurance will doubtless be a political reality, if not in 1971 then most certainly in 1972. In the coming months, we will hear of a bewildering variety of legislative proposals from every point along the political spectrum. I ask that we apply the following five tests to these several proposals. In the absence of an affirmative answer to each, I suggest that we reject such proposals as being inadequate to the task at hand.

1. Is it universal in covering all people and comprehensive in benefits offered?

2. Will it bring about fundamental changes in the delivery system?

3. Will it include effective cost and quality controls?

4. Will it make significant changes in the health manpower situation?

5. Will it eradicate the system of separate but less than equal health care in this country?

Social work should feel right at home in the debate on the need to change our health care system. Many of the same arguments, indeed made by many of the same people, were heard in the early 1930s as they informed America that the passage of social security legislation would be "the death knell of the American free enterprise system as we know it." Social workers recognized these and similar soothsayers of doom and dismay for what they truly were: protectors of their self-interests and the status quo.

The fight that social workers helped wage to give priority to the needs of people in the 1930s is a shining beacon in tribute to their profession and the social action which is a part of it. I urge the profession today to cast new light on the road to human progress by joining actively and vigorously the advocates of Health Security for all Americans.

Community Mental Health: the View from Fund City

BERTRAM S. BROWN, M.D.

W<small>HAT</small> <small>ARE</small> <small>THE</small> <small>ISSUES</small> and problems of community mental health? What do we do about them?

There are a host and a range of complex issues and problems: decentralization, regionalization, consolidation, reorganization of health and welfare services, health maintenance organizations, and a wealth and welter of plans and proposals for health and welfare services.

Let us dive into this deluge of issues and examine them. They are far from being as fearful as they sound. Decentralization and regionalization, for example, simply mean placing responsibility for program operations and decisions at the level closest to the public consistent with effective and responsible performance. Thus, decision-making is placed as closely as possible to those directly responsible for the delivery of services. With respect to community health services, of course, this is desirable and necessary to the achievement of adequate quality and range.

Dr. Vernon Wilson, Administrator of the Health Services and Mental Health Administration, puts it well:

In our view, decentralization, or the turning over of more program activity to the states and regions, does not diminish the national contribution. Rather, it adds new dimensions to our work and that of regional, state, and local structures. From a motivational point of view, this involvement will be helpful for planning, implementing, and carrying out community projects targeted to community problems, whether the community is local, county, district, or state-wide.[1]

[1] Address before the Surgeon General's Annual Conference of the State and Territorial Mental Health Authorities, 1970.

Pertinent also is the broad scene of health services reorganization and consolidation and plans for building a national health strategy. Looming in these plans are the health insurance maintenance organizations (HMOs). In any event, they form an important part of the total pattern of burgeoning or potential actions which face community mental health and the health and welfare professions.

The idea of HMOs, of course, is not complicated on the face of it: to bring together a range of medical services in a single organization so that a patient is assured of convenient access to all of them, and to provide needed services for a fixed contract fee paid in advance by all subscribers.

Although the shape and substance of HMOs are yet to be determined fully, what we know or sense about them is of prime import to community mental health and to community mental health centers in particular. There are a number of significant issues or questions of relationships that arise vis-à-vis HMOs and community health. Major among them is the question of what is or will be the availability of mental health services through the HMOs.

Conceptually, the HMO seeks to encourage the delivery of comprehensive, efficient, and economical health services. But the question is unanswerable at this stage as to the comprehensiveness of mental health services, which is the goal of community mental health and psychiatry. To insure this comprehensiveness, it is imperative that mental health services be included within the HMO framework, or in any other structures that are adopted. At present, HMOs are not necessarily proposed or expectably emerging as realistic alternatives to community mental health centers.

Nor do HMOs and community mental health services appear to be mutually exclusive; they are, in fact, complementary. The community mental health center is an especially effective resource which can interact with, and relate to, HMOs as well as to other health care organizations. Such relationships could take various forms.

Community mental health centers, for instance, might emerge

as components of HMOs with responsibilities for providing mental health services. Or the centers might themselves serve as HMOs, contracting out for other health and medical services. Individual centers might serve a number of HMOs in a given area. The exact nature of the relationships will depend in part on the evolving concept of the HMO and the flexibility and imagination with which it is implemented.

We in mental health are in the main proud of the innovativeness and imaginative concepts and activities which have characterized the community mental health movement both locally and nationally. None would want these bold new approaches, which are of high promise and performance, to be mired or lost in a welter of rigid and unprogressive health service structures.

Given the extent of unmet needs and the fact that the HMOs may not be capable of providing a significantly essential amount of mental health services, at least for the foreseeable future, it would seem that mutual collaboration between HMOs and community mental health provides the most realistic basis for continued progress. It is our belief, moreover, that we should view the HMO concept and other emerging proposals for improving and consolidating health services as opportunities rather than merely as threats to our categorical existence. We are not so much concerned with the business of psychiatric pride and mental health's search for identity and equal partnership on the health and welfare team as we are with the real needs and problems of the community's mental health.

I must emphasize that there is concern for, and recognition in the federal government, in Congress, and in the Administration of, the importance of community mental health in the total welfare of the national community. Again I say that we do have the opportunity and options, if we put forward and develop sound and strong community mental health proposals, to win support of both appointed and elected representatives of government, local, county, and state, as well as federal. This support at all levels of government, as well as that of private organizations and the public generally, is a necessity if we are to continue to progress and to show more gains than losses in mental health.

Looking at mental health today, we can see both gains and losses. The gains include:

1. The resident population in state and county mental hospitals has continued to decline for the fifteenth consecutive year, and there is striking evidence of other community mental health gains.

2. The number and services of community mental health centers continue to increase.

3. Proper use of appropriate drugs is proving a valuable treatment tool.

4. Research in basic mental health fields and the behavioral sciences is producing clinical benefits. The awarding of the Nobel prize to Dr. Julius Axelrod of the National Institute of Mental Health (NIMH) for brain function research is one example. The studies of brain function and biochemistry helped lead to major clinical benefits in such as areas as the development of drugs and the more rational use of psychoactive compounds.

There are losses:

1. Schizophrenia, a major cause of disabling mental disorders, continues to defy and elude us.

2. Severe manpower shortages hamper almost every mental health program in America.

3. Financial strictures become more and more binding, while the problems of mental illness, alcoholism, drug abuse, suicide, and violence seem to multiply.

4. The cost of mental illness mounts (now some $21 billion a year), organizational complexities increase, and facilities are hard pressed to meet even critical or stopgap needs.

Nevertheless, we need not despair. Hope and help are in our hands. There are trends toward cooperative advocacy and program priorities.

Cooperative advocacy has many faces, opportunities, and uses in mental health. In a sense, it is decentralization and the involvement of citizens and community groups in decision-making. Cooperative advocacy means working together with each level from local to national, making decisions, and sharing problems, investments, and benefits.

In sum, the trend over the next decade is seen as one of increasing state and local participation in many kinds of decision-making appropriate to their levels of operation. We envision the federal role as one of decreasing paternalism with a growing peer-colleague partnership. In the future, a major challenge and opportunity for federal, state, and local mental health colleagues is that of greater profit sharing. More and better ways can and should be found, for example, whereby the federal agency can share not only funds but especially the results of research, training, and demonstration projects.

Similarly, more and better means can and should be developed through which state and local communities can properly share in the investment of funds for mental health, both in contributing and in receiving funds. Priorities will also play a large part in all our roles over the coming years, because we may never have enough investments to furnish funds for new as well as continuing programs.

The first great need from our perspective was brought sharply in focus by the convincing evidence of the necessity for attention to the mental health of children in this country. It was determined to make it a number 1 priority to fill in the gaps in services for mentally ill children, in activities to prevent illness and foster child mental health, and in programs for adolescents and others brought to state institutions and juvenile delinquency correction systems.

As a second major priority, we are focusing NIMH resources on the mental health aspects of problems of minority groups. With the strong support of Secretary Richardson of the Department of Health, Education, and Welfare, a center for the study of minority group mental health problems has been set up at the NIMH. It is the operating nucleus of activity dealing with concerns affecting minority groups, and a number of new projects involving Chicanos and Indians are already beginning.

As our third priority, we are turning new light upon the field of behavioral sciences and what they can mean for mental health. The NIMH has a mandate in this field and has contributed to the growth and use of the behavioral sciences over the past twenty years. We have provided opportunities for biological, psychological, and social scientists to conduct research in brain function, personality structure, dynamics and development, family interaction, small-group processes, and intergroup relations in communities undergoing rapid culture change. We have conducted and supported these and other kinds of related research through both our extramural, or grants, programs and our intramural programs of research by NIMH staff scientists. This work is worthwhile and significant, but the behavioral sciences can contribute even more to solutions of mental health problems.

Now, if we mean what we say when we state priorities like these and line them up as items in the NIMH budget, additional help, expanded resources, and widespread support will have to be found. This again is what we call cooperative advocacy. It is also a selling job, once we find a pocket of resources that might be opened up in a collaborative venture. The mental health community has already had some experience in doing this. We just need to do more of the same thing, find new cooperative avenues, and do the work better.

What many people said or felt could not be done has been done. There is a nationwide network of mental health centers. It is far from meeting all the goals as yet, but that it exists at all, that it is a vital and growing thing, is truly the major achievement of this part of our century for mental health.

What we in mental health are saying in all of this is at once simple and complex. It is simple in that it is a plea for partnership and our pledge to a truly shared enterprise. It is complex in that the challenge to commitment for better mental health and the working out of partnership agreements mean a change of consciousness away from indifference or passive cooperation and toward activism and positive collaboration. This is multilevel as to people and structures and multidimensional as to the substantive problems with which we deal.

Whatever consciousness we now have, or acquire as we live and grow, will be the right kind for each of us if we keep before us the shining goal of every health program worth its salt: the ideal of being responsive to human needs. I do not mean being stimulated by, or reacting only to, laws, protests, regulations, statistics, financing, political considerations, or whatever. I mean simply that we are going to succeed if we respond to the needs of people as human beings, not mere statistics, bodies, votes, or funds.

This kind of consciousness and responsiveness is the keystone to building community mental health today and for as many tomorrows ahead as we can see. This kind of consciousness and responsiveness is an imperative and is the same, in principle and in practice, whether viewed from the national perspective, from that of the local community, or from that of each individual engaged in health and welfare work.

Innovative Ideas in Social Service Delivery[1]

SHIRLEY M. BUTTRICK

THERE IS A THEORY in physical chemistry called the Heisenburg Uncertainty Principle. Briefly, this states that you can never locate an electron because the only means of mapping it are position and direction. In order to determine the position you have to alter the direction, and in order to determine the direction you have to alter the position. Loosely applied to the social service world, I take this to mean that once you discover where you are, you are not there any more.

For some time now we have been told that the social services are in ferment. Yet there is a new urgency to the statement. From writers of different persuasion, concerns have surfaced about the usefulness and organization of our public social welfare services.[2] This concern has increased in magnitude as the climate and funding for social welfare programs have become more stringent, and as the separation of the services from income-maintenance programs approaches the long-hoped-for reality.

Faced with planning for the separated public service agency and finally "freed" from the jungle of paper and eligibility considerations, we arrive with no clear definition of the services, formulations of goals, or ways of measuring outcomes. The social services thus stand alone, tied down within their own system or lack of one.

There is widespread agreement that insufficient attention has

1 The views expressed are those of the author and do not reflect the views of the Community Services Administration, HEW.
2 "Public social welfare services" as used here refer to the public assistance titles of the Social Security Act (Titles I, IV, X, XIV, XVI) and are what remain after the income-maintenance function is lifted out.

been directed toward developing conceptions of services. This has hampered evaluation efforts and, in turn, the development of a national social service system. There is further agreement on the need to define social services and to specify their objectives in measurable terms. The usual global statement of goals has made reasonable discriminations difficult, or else has illustrated a commitment to a single strategy, such as the promotion of economic objectives, with its predictable failure.[3]

Some have argued against funding a set of activities which are so poorly defined and for which benefit measurements remain so primitive. They have interpreted the maximizing of choice to mean the availability of cash (or credit card or voucher) to the consumer in order that he may register his choice in the market place, backed by effective demand. Yet this approach, while timely and imaginative, has limited usefulness. The lack of needed resources and the anticipated inadequate money provision represent at least two such limitations.[4]

DEFINITIONS AND GOALS

The problem of definitions and goals is not new. Many learned groups have wrestled with it.[5] What is being asked now is: What

[3] Martin Rein, "Social Services and Economic Independence," in *The Planning and Delivery of Social Services* (Washington, D.C.: National League of Cities, 1969), pp. 70–71.
[4] Shirley M. Buttrick, "On Choice and Services," *Social Service Review*, XLIV (1970), 427–33.
[5] The term "social services" as most commonly used refers to those services rendered to individuals or families under community auspices. This bears some resemblance to the definitions adopted by a United Nations working group in 1959 and to European usage. The latter includes health, education, housing, and income maintenance; programs that in the United States are studied and planned independently. Social services are distinguished from social welfare, but the boundaries are vague. Martin Rein stresses the commonality of the services in that they link individuals to other services, are concerned with the capacity to consume, extend the level of living for disadvantaged groups, serve as proxies for cash, and are sometimes used as levers for change. See U.S. Department of Health, Education, and Welfare, *Services for People*, Report of the Task Force on Organization of Social Services, 1961, pp. 4–8; Martin Rein, *op. cit.*, pp. 54–56. For an excellent discussion and summary of the developing definitions of social welfare see Herman D. Stein, "Issues in the Contribution of Social Welfare Research to National Development," preliminary draft prepared for the International Symposium on Social Welfare Research, Washington, D.C., 1971, pp. 1–5.

services should the federal government fund and why? On the basis of what results? Toward what ends? For whom? What, given the infiniteness of human needs and the resource allocation problem, should be provided for in a separated public social service agency?

Some feel that the desired specificity constitutes a veiled attack on the social services. The amounts expended on the social services as a percentage of the gross national product are not significant. One searches in vain through the Seebohm Report for a definition of services and measurable outcomes.[6] Yet this omission did not prevent England from undertaking an extensive reorganization of the personal services.

Still, the specifying of objectives can be enormously useful. Even with limited funds, program choices must be made, priorities set, and a mix of services undertaken. A viable role must proceed with the clarification of social objectives.

In spite of the demonstrable failures in tying social services to the goal of promoting economic independence, this view continues to dominate—at a time when we have come to believe that the services have relatively little to contribute to reducing poverty, dependency, and unemployment, all of which require national policies, commitments, and the reordering of priorities. While a great many services can be subsumed under the accepted goals of self-support and self-care (which includes the emergency and protective functions), the over-all direction of the social services is still seen as being in support of manpower and work-related goals.

The desire to obtain more money for the services has often meant the acceptance of inappropriate missions, with the expectation that the money could somehow be used to good advantage. When the day of reckoning comes, there turns out to be little relationship between the promise and the performance. Even though this strategy has backfired, social welfare personnel may follow it again in the belief that "more" is better than "less" and that something labeled a service is "good."

[6] Frederick Seebohm, *Report of the Committee on Local Authority and Allied Personal Service* (London: Her Majesty's Stationery Office, 1969).

Perhaps the time has come to assert that the specific function of social policy is the redistribution of personal social services and societal resources in favor of the bottom percentage of our society. If so, priority should be given to providing concrete services and protection that insure entitlement, and to representing the individual and his family in obtaining the resources. If the goal of the social services is "to redistribute income, power, and prestige under the assumption that there will be a better society when the disparities . . . are leveled," [7] then the difficult job of refining these objectives, determining the mix of services and resources, and evaluating results should begin. Yet this is not the stuff from which measurement of results is easily obtained, or the purpose for which administrations may wish to fund.

Universality and selectivity. The accepted principle (at least in theory) is that services should be provided to all who need them without regard to income. Like a latter-day Gresham's law, it is believed (and the facts lend credence) that poor services tend to drive out the good, and that services directed toward the poor tend to be poor services. For many, a separated service system was thought to be the beginning realization of a public system which would be appropriate in type and range, reflect the need of all population groups, be sufficient in amount for a given purpose (lest the priority criteria carry undesirable consequences), provide statutory assurance of rights, and insure access.[8] This is the philosophy which guided the Seebohm Commission; namely, the provision of a community-based and family-oriented service which would be available to all. The new social service department in England was to go beyond "discovery and rescue of social casualties." It was to enable the greatest possible number of individuals to give and receive service for the well-being of the community.

It is questionable how realistic this is for our country now. At the same time that the need for universality in provision is stated, it is immediately modified through the introduction of priorities for special needy groups and income classes. What is

---

[7] Rein, *op. cit.*, pp. 72–78.   [8] *Ibid.*, p. 78.

often termed a universal system tends to be used selectively by those whose incomes fall below a certain level.[9] The widening chasm between the poor and the nonpoor, the issue of racism, and the lack of commitment for the public services have provided a ready mix for failure. The question has developed whether public policy, outside of social insurance, has embraced or ever will embrace universalism in social welfare.[10] Nor does it seem possible to reconcile the tensions which exist between those programs designed to foster social cohesion and those programs whose primary goal is to minimize inequalities of opportunity and condition. Unfortunately, little attention has been devoted to the trade-offs that are involved in these conflicting goals. Titmuss has heightened awareness of this problem by asserting that the real challenge lies in learning how to discriminate selectively without stigma in favor of those whose needs are the greatest.[11]

Because universalism remains so elusive, the question becomes one of whether there is another way to achieve the same purpose. It is here that experimentation utilizing new forms of organization (consumer corporations and cooperatives), along with systematic use of purchase of services, is needed. Credit cards, voucher systems, and purchase of services offer considerable potential for change and have the marked advantage of insuring the use of the same system for all. However, no discussion of the issues around universal and selective provision is meaningful without an examination of the level and sufficiency of that provision.

SERVICE DELIVERY SYSTEMS

Ours has been a tendency to develop programs around consensus on solving particular problems. Social welfare programs have followed the political logic of what will be accepted, with little policy prescription or commitment to a national social policy.

9 Sanford Kravitz, "Issues Related to the Delivery of Social Welfare Services," (unpublished paper), p. 27.

10 "Universal" is used as the opposite of "selective," which here means restricting services to those who qualify under some form of income test.

11 George Hoshino, "Britain's Debate on Universal or Selective Social Services: Lessons for Americans," *Social Service Review*, XLIII (1969), 245–58; Buttrick *op. cit.*, p. 428.

The result has not been beneficial for conceptual clarity. Suggested ways for organizing the social services have ended up as a potpourri of principles, service "laundry lists," fields of service, problem classification, methods and targets for interventive strategies.

To a large extent, programs have emerged in response to the special pleading of identifiable interest groups, and an impressive catalogue of special-purpose programs now exists. In the process, barriers to communication, jurisdictional jealousies, and structural rigidities have been created.

Categorical and comprehensive approaches. Historically, "categorical" referred to the selecting out of special groups, such as children and the aged, from the "common pool of destitution" in order to accord such groups preferential treatment. "Comprehensive" approaches were understood to mean that *all* people in need (of money, of a service) would be accorded that amenity regardless of special status. However, as each categorical interest has staked out its claim it has sought to bring the full array of services to bear on the problem for its constituency. The tendency of each categorical program to expand to become comprehensive is a fact of organizational life.[12] It results in duplication, inefficiencies, and overspecialization. It facilitates the proverbial "passing of the buck" for the consumer (or the ducking of certain problems altogether). Coordination, as a possible solution, has turned out to be highly ineffective, especially since there has been no point of final or higher interventive authority.

In some quarters, the view prevails, that the present emphasis on services integration not only is unimportant, but may actually avoid the need for more fundamental changes.[13] Attention to the delivery of services without corresponding attention to the production of the services is also questioned.[14] Complicating the

12 Richard Titmuss, *Commitment to Welfare* (New York: Pantheon Press, 1968), p. 135.
13 This is referred to as "Richardson's Law," at the Department of Health, Education, and Welfare.
14 "Services integration" refers to a process and a technique for the delivery of service which responds in a holistic way to human social service needs in community settings. It has been described by Sid Gardner as an objective and a way of thinking which decategorizes the approach to problem-solving. Four

decision of where and how to go is the lack of empirical evidence with respect to whether or not services integration makes a real difference.

Still, the thrust to rationalize the assorted service programs is very strong. It derives from a collection of experiences that suggest that those who require the services of any of the programs may also need the benefit of others. It derives from a desire to bring together the diverse categorical systems to make it easier for the consumer to get what he needs. It derives from the practical wisdom that a service system dealing with the full range of an individual's or family's need is more effective than one geared to provide single-purpose treatment. It derives from the belief that multiple and overlapping programs, each with its own funding formula, administrative structure, rules and techniques, is not useful to the consumer. In fact, enormous energy gets expended solely on system maintenance. However, it has become clear that the categorical character of program legislation prevents specialized services from linking together easily and logically. More and more it is believed that the federal government should be able to facilitate services integration when special purpose systems want it.

Even if there were a consensus that services integration was the desired direction in which to go, the constraints against integrating (or decategorizing) are formidable. There is first the existing legislation with its regulations interpreted according to a particular agency's objectives. To this must be added the congressional committees which guard the legislation, the build-up

aspects or elements help to describe its process: (1) comprehensiveness of services, which means that the service system is able to bring to bear upon individual problems the full range of services necessary to alleviate those problems and prevent their recurrence; (2) program consolidation, primarily an administrative concern to allocate societal resources in the most efficient manner; (3) inter-agency working relationships or linkages across agency lines, considered more limited but essential for achieving access to needed services provided by other agencies; and (4) general-purpose government relationships. The latter are of a different order but are included because they could become very important, operating as they do above line agencies. See Sid Gardner, "Service Integration in HEW: an Initial Report" (unpublished monograph, 1971). However one views services integration, it is not a goal in itself.

of agency personnel with their assorted attitudes, as well as the development (over years) of the constituent groups. While administrative simplification would help, even here there is little conformity among rulings and little flexibility in waiving state-wide requirements which could facilitate integration at the delivery level.

DIRECTION FOR SERVICES INTEGRATION

How can this integration best be accomplished while keeping the categorical programs in place? Social welfare professionals have focused understandably on developing models of integrated service systems at the point of delivery (which is where it happens and where it matters). Whether they have paid enough attention to other aspects which strongly shape the nature of the delivery system is debatable. Still unknown is what decentralization of services means in terms of economies of scale, what is involved in making facilities accessible, what is involved in breaking down jurisdictional lines among disciplines. As if that alone were not enough, there is a lack of clarity as to what the trade-offs are between resident participation (at which levels and with what functions), the strengthening of the planning capabilities of elected state and local officials, and the relative balance of authority between the federal, state, and local government. Since co-equal line agencies cannot integrate, who shall be in charge?

At a minimum, it appears reasonable to anticipate that changes in the direction of integration will take the form of facilitating program fund transfers, establishment of common eligibility requirements, and the development of a common funding stream. Simplification of plans, waiver of requirements, and single funding formulas are seen as strong incentives. While many of these changes do not directly deal with services integration, they do so indirectly through facilitating and enabling activities, through "gap-filling money" for services integration projects, and through money to build planning capabilities. It is hoped that, as a result, state plans will rationalize their program intentions and commit these intentions to paper. At present, these plans represent little more than ritualistic requisites for the receipt of funds.

Since any change has impact upon another, there is the question of the capacity of the federal level to review and reject the plans. Who ought to have what level of power over these plans? What appeals processes should be observed in instances of conflict? Who can opt-out and come directly to the Department of Health, Education, and Welfare? While these are just a few of the issues that surface around planning decisions, they are of significance in shaping the direction of the delivery systems.

In general, it is agreed that consumers of services ought to be involved in the planning process, that cities of a certain size should have the right to opt-out of the state planning process, that state and local government roles in services should be strengthened, and that the federal role should be that of technical assistance in designing and implementing systems to deal with local needs.

However, there are no easy answers. The desire is to avoid prescriptive modes and see what happens. Even while there is an emphasis on planning, not much is known as to how one shapes the planning processes into a discipline for choosing among competing alternatives. Even more important is the lack of knowledge as to how one uses the planning process to change operations. Resource allocation is, after all, highly political.

The private sector. The private sector is now counted upon to broaden the perspective of the service agencies beyond those of the poor. Through combined delivery mechanisms, private agencies would provide services on a fee basis, and the poor could benefit from a program which would be less stigmatized because it did not serve them exclusively. Coalition planning is considered to be a joint undertaking by the public and private sector, geared toward producing a plan for the allocation and delivery of resources. The expectation, then, is for increased funding for the purchase of voluntary services and extensive reliance on private and voluntary agencies. The issue, obviously, is the amount of money that will be available, for what services, and with what system of accountability.

Funding. In spite of the fact that the money available has never been equal to the exaggerated demands made for the services, the time is now past for acceptance of the notion that expanding service programs will significantly improve them. In fact, the Nixon Administration is determined to close the open end on social services, taking it for granted that the effort will be successful; the question is when and at what level.

If the proposed welfare reform legislation passes, supportive services for "employables" could be funded up to 100 percent. The Department of Labor would contract for services either through the public agency, or through utilizing purchase authority for other arrangements. For those categorized as "unemployable," funding would be substantially the same as now, possibly with a higher federal share, but with a ceiling on expenditures. The federal funding proposed for foster care and adoptions in 1970's service legislation is unchanged.

Again it is those services in support of manpower which will get the federal dollar. This brings us full circle to the dilemma as to the proper social role of the social services.

Clearly, a family-oriented, community-based, universal system of services is not in sight. Those who have a need for existing services may have to organize to make the need known and their demands effective. In the process may come new coalitions and shifts in professional emphasis. Already there is a change in codes of ethics from primary concern with the professional patient-client relationship to that of social responsibility and advocacy. A new breed of professional in medicine, law, architecture, and engineering has emerged. Perhaps in the refinement of techniques of advocacy and in the development of new concepts of social responsibility lies the hope for the social welfare field.

The Model Cities Program

I. AN ASSESSMENT

ROLAND L. WARREN

I̲T̲ ̲I̲S̲ ̲D̲I̲F̲F̲I̲C̲U̲L̲T̲ to summarize the goals which the Model Cities program was supposed to accomplish; not because the goals were not stated, but because there were so many of them. Further, the goals can be considered from many different points of view. For example, in many people's minds, Model Cities was "something for the blacks," a way of easing the social protest situation in the ghettos. For others, it was a step toward a more effective type of participation in decision-making on the part of a population largely shut out from sources of power. For some it was a foot in the door toward block grants and revenue sharing. For others, it was a program to "strengthen the Mayor's office" by giving him some leverage over such programs as education and urban renewal and housing, and also by helping him to build up competency in social planning.

The 1966 legislation speaks of "improving the quality of urban life" and then goes on to prescribe a combination of goals and conditions of acceptability which contain over twenty identifiable "program standards." The first one is for comprehensiveness. The legislation is clear in the intent to help cities

to plan, develop, and carry out locally prepared and scheduled comprehensive city demonstration programs containing new and imaginative proposals to rebuild or revitalize large slum and blighted areas; to expand housing, job, and income opportunities; to reduce dependence on welfare payments; to improve educational facilities and programs; to combat disease and ill health; to reduce the incidence of crime and delinquency; to enhance recreational and cultural opportunities; to establish better access between homes and jobs; and generally to improve living conditions for the people who live in such areas, and to accomplish these objectives through the most effective and economical concentration and coordination of Federal, State, and local public and private efforts to improve the quality of urban life.[1]

That certainly indicates an interest in comprehensiveness. Note also the opening phraseology concerning "new and imaginative proposals." These words express a widely held conviction that the conventional types of agency services were simply not good enough to do the job, and that a substantial degree of innovation would be necessary.

Another important goal or program standard relates to concentration—the idea that sufficient resources must be applied to the Model Cities neighborhood (which in turn should be no larger than one tenth of the city) so as to make a noticeable impact. One standard calls for "carrying out the program on a consolidated and coordinated basis." Another calls for "widespread citizen participation in the program." So we have what I call the four *C*'s: comprehensiveness, concentration, coordination, and citizen participation. Among the many remaining program standards are provisions for the maximum feasible use of costs-benefits analysis and program budgeting, for the "maximum possible use of new and improved technology and design, including cost reduction techniques," and for the projects to be initiated "within a reasonably short period of time."

It is probably true that not all of the program objectives can be attained fully at the same time. Beyond a certain point, at least, some are opposed to others, and choices must be made. Marris and Rein have analyzed the manner in which goal conflicts plagued earlier programs such as the Ford Foundation Grey Area programs and those of the President's Committee on Juvenile Delinquency and Youth Crime. They predicted correctly that the same would apply to the Economic Opportunities program.[2]

It seems both fair and realistic, therefore, to assess the Model Cities program liberally, acknowledging that any great enact-

[1] Demonstration Cities and Metropolitan Development Act of 1966.
[2] Peter Marris and Martin Rein, *Dilemmas of Social Reform: Poverty and Community Action in the United States* (New York: Atherton Press, 1967).

ment of even a combination of these goals would be highly worthwhile. Nevertheless, there is implicit in this mixture of goals and requirements a strategy for social change in the inner cities. It seems both fair and important to examine this underlying strategy and then to evaluate it in the light of what happened.

THE ASSUMPTIONS

The principal assumption was that existing agencies could be stimulated to engage in substantial changes in their performance, changes so substantial as to make a major impact on living conditions in the model neighborhoods. These changes would include greater efficiency in service delivery, through new technological methods and adequate coordination. As part of the same process, the service agencies would become more responsive to the needs and wishes of a disadvantaged clientele, mainly through the inclusion of an important input into program formulation from the residents of the neighborhood.

At the same time, the whole broad range of services would be geared more effectively toward removing the social problems at their roots, through a study of their causes and a modification of programs so as to address these causes in a concerted manner. For this reason, the cities were asked to identify the problems, to diagnose them, and to devise programs which would help remove them.

There was an important assumption concerning citizen participation—an implicit assumption that the local residents would be "responsible" in the sense of working with agencies rather than threatening them or challenging their existence; and that although there might be differences in viewpoint, these could be worked out amicably, because after all, "we are all working for the same thing."

Likewise, there were assumptions about the dynamics of this complex operation. It would receive its motive power from various sources. Although agency resistance to change is widely acknowledged, there is a consciousness on the part of many agencies that change is necessary, a consciousness rooted in professional ethics supporting effective and humane efforts to help people. In addition, there was the inducement of federal funds—a boon to the cities to provide services, and in many cases a boon to these very agencies in helping solve their budgetary problems. In order to get these funds, they would have to meet the federal requirements for adequate planning and sufficiently innovative and potentially effective programs. The participation of local residents would constitute an additional stimulus.

These assumptions seem reasonable. But a careful reading of Marris and Rein throws grave doubt on their feasibility. They show that in the programs they studied, the dilemmas of social reform stemmed not solely from faults in administration, but more importantly from deep-rooted constraints operating against the possibility of making the whole combination of strategies work. But it was assumed that lessons had been learned from these earlier programs and from the antipoverty program, which had been underway for only two years when Model Cities came along. Model Cities would be different. It would operate directly under City Hall, thus gaining the support of the mayor. It would not provide for unlimited community action, nor make excessive promises about the effectiveness of community action. It would have a much more comprehensive scope, much greater flexibility; would follow a much slower and more rational planning process; would have greater leverage over other federally supported programs operating in the city, and so on.

THE EXPERIENCE

The following observations are based on an intensive study of interorganizational behavior in nine cities,[3] over a period of several years. Although we have attempted to keep reasonably well informed on what has taken place elsewhere, the assessments are based primarily on the experience in these nine cities.

[3] The author's work is supported by a Public Health Service research career program award (number K3-MH-21,869) from the National Institute of Mental Health. The research project on the nine cities—Oakland (Calif.), Denver, San Antonio, Detroit, Columbus (Ohio), Atlanta (Ga.), Newark (N.J.), Boston, and Manchester (N.H.)—was supported by a grant from the National Institute of Mental Health.

The four *C's* are at the heart of the program. The Model Cities programs have been in operation for over a year now, based on an earlier planning period which lasted about a year also. Although the outcome of the program, originally conceived for five years, is still in doubt, there is already a firm basis of experience accumulated in the years since 1966.

1. *Comprehensiveness.* An examination of the specific programs, and the individual projects which make them up, in the nine cities indicates that the goal of comprehensiveness was rather persuasively accomplished.

Projects were developed in a wide range of sectors, such as health care, education, housing, manpower training, transportation, and so on. But it soon became apparent, especially to the new Administration, that this very comprehensiveness militated against the objective of concentration of sufficient efforts to be effective, and taxed the limited ability of the cities to coordinate these diverse projects.[4]

2. *Concentration.* This objective fared somewhat differently. The idea was that by limiting the size of the model neighborhood and pouring in a high concentration of resources and projects, a critical mass would be built up and, to change the metaphor, some sort of take-off point would be reached. While billions of dollars were anticipated for the supplemental programs over the years—that is, the money with which the cities could design their own programs to meet their needs—the stimulus of the program was expected to trigger a vast expansion of funding through the regular grant-in-aid channels, so that the total effort would be many times larger.

This ambitious and somewhat heady goal was not realized. Grant-in-aid programs did not expand as anticipated. Various efforts were made to integrate other grant-in-aid programs into Model Cities. But despite certain superficial though promising developments toward coordination and toward earmarking funds which would not otherwise have been available, the great multiplier effect of Model Cities funds was not forthcoming.

4 William Lilley, III, "Urban Report/Model Cities Program Faces Uncertain Future Despite Romney Overhaul," *Center for Political Research National Journal,* II (1970), 1467–80.

Another important factor, surprisingly, has been largely disregarded. It is the factor of mass. Here were 150 cities engaging in the most vigorous efforts, embroiled in great internal controversy, especially between local residents on the one hand and the agencies and City Hall on the other. Here was a full year's planning effort and the development of a five-year plan. And yet the total budget for Model Cities was $575 million for the fiscal year of 1970 and the same amount for fiscal 1971.

Consider this a moment. A massive impact on living conditions in the dilapidated sections of 150 cities was to be made with an expenditure equal to about one third of New York City's annual budget for public welfare! If the extremely limited amount of funds available had been kept a secret, one might have explained this anomaly as a massive betrayal of the trust of the American people. But the budgeted sums were known. Yet, through some strange process of self-deception, administrators in Washington and at the regional level, local city and agency officials, and local residents apparently believed that the niggardly sums allotted to each city would produce a sufficient concentration to start an upward cycle.

3. *Coordination.* Underlying this objective is the assumption that the billions of dollars now being spent in one urban program or another are largely without effect because they represent a fragmented approach. With each agency going its own way, the total effort has little effect, but with sufficient coordination it might add up to a much greater impact on the problems of the poor.

The actual components included in the over-all Model Cities programs of the nine cities constitute an array of highly disparate projects in a variety of different areas. To use the vernacular, these are "laundry lists" of projects rather than coordinated programs in any sense which is discernible either from the lists or from the lengthy project justifications and over-all planning rationale.

This outcome is hardly surprising, because the planning process itself, at least in the nine cities, resembled a series of interagency contests and negotiations accompanied by struggles between residents and City Hall for ultimate control of the program. Even where these struggles were kept under control, the planning process consisted of discrete planning efforts by different task forces with little relation to each other either within the task forces or among them.[5]

Our study did not indicate that the interaction among such agencies as we were studying in these cities was increased by the Model Cities program or that any appreciable coordination between pairs of organizations or larger combinations had taken place. Still, coordination is a most complex concept, and has numerous ramifications. The prerogative of the Model Cities agency to have the sign-off on federally funded projects within the model neighborhood gave these agencies a certain amount of leverage in bringing otherwise disparate programs into line with each other. This leverage was surprisingly seldom employed, however.

4. *Citizen participation.* In due time, the study will report in great detail on resident participation in these programs. Meantime, let me deny any personal romanticism about citizen participation as a cure-all. We have observed cases where citizens were given much greater measures of power than they were able to use; where they themselves conceded that their chief problem was not lack of power but rather bickering and ineffectiveness. Nevertheless, the citizen participation component of the Model Cities program has in one sense been dramatically successful. From one point of view, it has met in large measure each of its objectives, and must be considered an overwhelming success.

What objectives has it met so successfully? There, of course, is the rub. Mine is admittedly a cynical point of view.

Suppose, just suppose, you wanted to have citizen participation with objectives something like these:

1. To help reduce tension in the ghettos by giving residents a feeling that they were gaining power in community-level decision-making

2. To assure the existing agencies that citizen participation would not require them to change in any basic way, or threaten any of their major programs

5 Roland L. Warren, "Model Cities First Round: Politics, Planning, and Participation," *Journal of the American Institute of Planners*, XXXV, No. 4 (1969). Also included in Warren, *Truth, Love, and Social Change—and Other Essays on Community Change* (Chicago: Rand McNally & Co., 1971).

3. To give citizens the illusion that they were participating in major decisions but be assured that their participation would be relatively meaningless, and would not affect program development in any drastic way

4. To be able to convince many third parties—the federal agencies, the "man-in-the-street," the press, the legislature—that "widespread citizen participation" had really been given a fair trial

5. To be able to account for any program failure on the basis that it was caused by the ineptitude of low-income citizen participation.

I am not suggesting that the Model Cities program was conceived and administered with such malicious intent. Quite the contrary. I have high respect for the actual intent of the legislation and for the dedication with which the program was administered, to say nothing of the personal integrity of the officials involved. I am simply saying, hypothetically, that if one had such questionable intentions, the Model Cities program would have been well suited to realize them. Suppose, then, you did have these intentions. Here are some of the things that you could do:

1. Choose an arbitrary section of the city which had little relation to the natural neighborhoods and ethnic groups.

2. Arrange for lively competition and conflict among citizens "participating" in different federally funded programs, none of which was adequately funded.

3. Frustrate the citizens by insisting on deadlines for applications and for plans which are utterly unrealistic in terms of the process prescribed.

4. Enervate the citizens by rushing them as indicated and then delaying action for months on the proposals which they so frantically developed under pressure of your deadlines.

Months later, after the citizens were so frustrated with the delays that interest had tapered off, you could then release the money but point out that they would now have a new deadline for implementing the proposal and for submitting plans for the next year's effort.

If you could manage to have a change of mayors during the

period, the whole thing would be much easier. Better yet, if you could achieve a change in the National Administration through a federal election in which the other party wins, your chances of success would be still greater.

But just to be sure, have an important Administration official come out with a book which constitutes an assertion that it was largely the citizen action program which doomed the Economic Opportunities program. Get him to parody that program by some such title as *Maximum Feasible Misunderstanding*.[6] If this does not work, set up a presidential task force to evaluate the program to see if it should be continued at all. Appoint as its chairman a political scientist who has written:

The lower-class individual lives in the slum and sees little or no reason to complain. He does not care how dirty and dilapidated his housing is either inside or out, nor does he mind the inadequacy of such public facilities as schools, parks, and libraries: indeed, where such things exist he destroys them by acts of vandalism if he can. Features that make the slum repellent to others actually please him.[7]

Tell the citizens that the program must be innovative, and also keep reminding them that the law requires that such programs must be "scheduled to be initiated within a reasonably short period of time."

But enough. Underneath this cynicism is a point of great importance. Model Cities was hardly a fair trial of citizen participation. We really will never know how good or bad resident participation might have been under even moderate environmental and program conditions and constraints. The cards were stacked against it.

Disillusionment with citizen participation is not warranted by the Model Cities experience. Resident participation did not fail. It never had a chance to fail. It never had a chance at all. It operated under a truly impossible set of conditions. Those who

6 Daniel P. Moynihan, *Maximum Feasible Misunderstanding* (New York: Free Press, 1969).

7 Edward C. Banfield, *The Unheavenly City: the Nature and Future of Our Urban Crisis* (Boston: Little, Brown and Co., 1970), p. 62. Banfield states that the lower class, as so characterized, comprises only a small proportion of slum populations,

consider resident participation to be outmoded, unrealistic, a calamity, do so more as an indicator of changing ideological styles and climates than from a valid basis for assessment.

As one reviews the degree of attainment of the various Model Cities objectives or program standards, one should keep in mind some of the numerous practical difficulties which developed in administration of the programs.

1. The cooperation from other federal agencies in the form of coordinated effort and earmarking and carrying through of special funds for the Model Cities never developed to the hoped-for proportions.

2. The careful structure and process set up to review and monitor the planning and implementation of the programs across the country had the effect of interfering with continuity of local developments, causing endless delays and frustrations, discouraging innovation, making hasty planning decisions almost inevitable, and in general placing almost impossible constraints on the local planning process.

3. Planning in numerous cities was delayed by the extended contest between residents and City Hall for their respective measures of control over the program. Since city council approval was necessary, the programs were subject to the influence of organized pressure groups, including the existing agencies and city departments. Those new departures which in some way were seen as encroaching on the domains of agencies or interest groups tended to be sloughed off in response to the more powerful, established group interests, whether of labor unions, the police, the teachers, the medical establishment, or whatever.

While it is interesting to speculate what Model Cities might have been like if it had been optimally administered, and if some of these difficulties could have been foreseen and prepared for in advance, the importance of certain other aspects of the experience should not be overlooked.

Institutional change. Although institutional change is not mentioned in the basic Model Cities legislation, there has been considerable use of the term by the Model Cities administration, but with the usual, perhaps unconscious, ambiguity. The term is often used to reflect the assumption that major impact on ghetto problems cannot be made without changing the whole pattern of institutions which affect ghetto life and produce ghetto problems. This pattern includes structured unemployment, systematic racism, flawed systems of land ownership and housing exploitation, shoddy public services, including the school system, and so on through a list of basic institutional characteristics. Until these are changed, according to this view, we are dealing only with superficialities, putting band-aids on cancers, as the saying goes.

There is a much more restricted meaning of the term, however. It can denote simply the recognition that certain social agencies and certain patterns of service delivery are deficient, lack coordination, are too remote from the felt needs and wishes of the clients, and hence need change.

In my observation, this second, limited meaning has predominated over the first, not only in the actions of agencies and individuals who might be considered to be operating purely from self-interest or bureaucratic politics, but also with administrators, concerned professionals, and active residents. In the name of the first conception of institutional change, they have dealt almost exclusively only with the second conception.

This fact is apparent when one examines the actual project components which arose out of the Model Cities planning experience in the nine cities, and the way the cities used their supplemental funds—funds not confined to any specific grant-in-aid program—which could be used to meet their own special needs. A preliminary review indicates that very few of these projects could possibly be considered as dealing with institutional change in the first, broader meaning of the term, as contrasted with the further elaboration of social services and the attempt at improving service delivery.

Problem diagnosis. In a related matter, it early became apparent to the project staff that in the nine cities one of the principal aspects of the planning strategy was being not merely neglected, but ignored. This was the process of problem diagnosis. The cities were supposed to identify the problems of their model neighborhoods, to diagnose them, and on the basis of this diagnosis, to build their comprehensive programs to improve the conditions of living. They all skipped directly from problem identification to program planning without any attempt, good or bad, to relate their programs to a diagnosis of the causes of the problems and the manner in which programs would prevent these problems. As a result, the programs were almost completely remedial. They chiefly provided services to people victimized by the problems rather than even claiming to attack the problems themselves. They all seem to have defined "problems" immediately in terms of a lack of sufficient agency services, with the predictable result that the program proposed was for more agency services. One might add that the very modest innovations involved in these services had largely to do with service delivery patterns rather than with any new strategy of intervention into the problems themselves.

THE IMPLICATIONS

These somewhat disappointing aspects of the Model Cities experience are all closely related. They all are related to the basic strategy underlying the program, and to the basic assumption on which that strategy was based. I believe now that the basic strategy was faulty because the basic assumption was fallacious. I did not bring this belief to the study, but quite the contrary, it forced itself upon me and the other members of the staff as we tried to understand why things were happening as they did.

The assumptions. The Model Cities strategy is based on two assumptions. One is the assumption of individual deficiency as the root of social problems; the other is the assumption that a more effective coordination of remedial social services will remove the problems, or at least reduce them to an acceptable minimum.

As indicated, the objective of institutional change can be interpreted to mean that the principal difficulty lies within the institutional structure: in structured unemployment which manpower programs cannot relieve in a declining economy; in systematic deficiencies in the school system which tend to be shoved into the background when we begin to define the issue in terms of a dropout problem; in economic exploitation; in systematic racist discrimination, as in the construction industry. Yet, even those agency officials who use the term "institutional change" in this more basic sense most often propose remedial services and coordinative efforts as the solution when it comes to the actual test in experience. Even the low-income residents themselves accept the solutions which the professionals tell them represent this year's cutting edge of progress—neighborhood service centers, storefront delivery units, crisis intervention.

Regarding the second assumption, the potential effectiveness of greater coordination of remedial social services, the outcome seems similarly unconvincing. Some modest accomplishments have been made in virtually all of the cities studied. I cannot even conceive how these changes might reasonably be expected to make a significant impact on the incidence of the major social problems which these cities listed in their original Model Cities planning applications: extensive substandard housing, extensive unemployment, extensive juvenile delinquency, crime, drug addiction, alcoholism, family breakdown. At best, they are palliatives.

I feel a sense of outrage that we fool ourselves into believing we are going to make a substantial impact on these problems through the projects which have come out of Model Cities. In this context, the great emphasis now on coordination, on systems analysis, on advanced techniques of program budgeting, on data banks, on the social and technical means of bringing about greater coordination of agency services—this whole effort may have some modestly worthwhile results, I am convinced. But I really believe that its side effects are more disadvantageous than its benefits, to use economic terms, or, in sociological terms, that its manifest function is minimal while its latent function is great and dysfunctional. In ordinary English, it does more harm than good.

It distracts our attention from the aspects of the institutional structure which produce poverty and the social problems of poverty. It facilitates the self-deception that some technology will help us be effective by making more efficient a strategy which is patently inadequate and in large part misdirected. It is this sort of emphasis which immunizes our professional strategies from the hard test of reality. It helps to explain how we can take seriously the expectation that $575 million a year will improve conditions of living in the slums of 150 cities—through greater coordination, of course. It helps us to talk seriously about the need to force able-bodied welfare recipients to work at a time when engineers and highly trained employees in many fields are being laid off because of national economic policies. And it helps a great many relatively well-to-do professionals to make a living from engaging in activities which, whatever their justification on other grounds, are not going to do anything at all to attack the underlying problems of poverty.

The strategy. The strategy is expected to produce basic changes —even if only in service delivery systems—through a collaborative process which makes it mandatory to work with and through existing agencies. Such a strategy can be expected to produce little change which the agencies find incompatible with their own interests. This comment is hardly new. We have known this for years. The agencies concerned themselves with Model Cities principally for two related purposes: to prevent any threat to their own domains and their own viability, and, where possible, to benefit from the program by increasing their budgets or enlarging their domains. That is the nature of all organizations. To expect them to do otherwise is like expecting human beings voluntarily to stop breathing.

We went through this a century ago with the charities organization movement, then with the council movement, then with the poverty program, now with Model Cities. How long will we continue to deceive ourselves that a collaborative strategy with some sort of bait like federal funds will bring local agencies together to attack the roots of poverty? There was little excuse for choosing this ineffective, bankrupt strategy. Many people felt it might still be worth a try, provided we had learned the lessons of the Office of Economic Opportunity experience. I say, never again this deception. And I say it with anger. We already know that it does not work and we already know why it does not work—not all of the why, but enough to know that it is a blind alley and a deception.

Never again should we ask the slum residents of 150 American cities to come to endless rounds of frustrating meetings, to be lectured on what a splendid opportunity they have to improve their neighborhoods if they will only participate responsibly in decision-making; never again should we expect them to jump through the same old participation hoops, with the help of the same old expert professionals at their elbows telling them why this or that innovation is impractical; never again should we promise them the improvement of living conditions in 150 cities for $575 million a year. It is an insult to their intelligence and integrity as human beings, and to our own.

I do not want to discount the gains that have been made through Model Cities. There are some. But if we had been serious about it, we would have needed a budget at least four times as large. That would have been the minimum for the program to have a serious possibility of making some appreciable impact.

Nor do I want to discount the value of improving largely remedial social services. Of course we need help for young people who have been damaged, body and soul, by physical and spiritual victimization. Of course we need an array of social services to help people in various forms of misery. But these things do not get at the root of our social problems and neither does the Model Cities program.

I have really come to question the ability of the conventional social agencies to bring about institutional change in any fundamental sense, even though we acknowledge to each other in abstract terms that services alone will never do the job. We constitute, ourselves, part of the socially structured resistance to significant change, though we usually do not realize this or do not wish to acknowledge it.

The gains. In my estimation, there are three gains.

1. The Model Cities program has brought about some modest improvement in social services—extremely modest.

2. It is giving some city administrations experience in social planning across a wide area of concern, and the cities are beginning to learn about this difficult task. The process is one of strengthening City Hall, strengthening its clout, strengthening its commitment, and strengthening its ability to deal with the city's problems. As the saying now goes, "Model Cities is not a program, it is a process." Of course, if that is the case, then we really have deceived the thousands of neighborhood residents as well as the professionals who worked their heads off on Model Cities because they believed it *was* a program, because they believed they were going to see some tangible results in the quality of their neighborhoods, not just in City Hall's planning competence. So one way of looking at this slogan is that it is a great "cop-out," saying in effect: we never promised tangible results; we just thought of the program as a sort of advanced in-service training program for city officials. I look at it this way. But I also look at it the other way. This slogan represents an attempt to be honest with people who have been willfully or unwillfully deceived into thinking it would be more than it could possibly be.

3. Model Cities has enacted what at best is a modest but meaningful experiment in participation of slum area residents in local policy-making. While this may be little more than a pageant in many cities, even pageants have their symbolic value. At least it is becoming more difficult for agency officials to plan programs of physical change or social services in almost total disregard of the opinions of those who will be affected by them. "They are beginning to learn how to participate," say some of the enthusiasts. But the disquieting question is whether they are not learning to participate in a charade.

THE ALTERNATIVES

It is easy to criticize, difficult to offer constructive alternatives. There are no panaceas. Resident participation is no panacea, although we have not heard the last of it by any means. Strengthening City Hall is no panacea. Coordination *cum* systems analysis is no panacea. Neither are new towns, the program that seems destined to be the next overemphasized, overadvertised, alleged cure for the diverse problems of urban living and urban population growth. Revenue sharing offers some fiscal help, but offers little evidence that more effective programs to solve the problems of poverty and discrimination will be developed. On the contrary, it seems to offer fresh guarantees that the agencies will continue to develop programs of the band-aid type.

Three developments appear to have great potential importance. First is the gradual recognition among more and more people that a large part of the population is poor because it lacks money, not because it lacks social services. The answer is to supply it with money, not with social services. This development makes for strange political bedfellows, both in support and in resistance. It constitutes an important alternative to the notion that coordination of services is going to take us very far. And it will cost a good deal more than $575 million a year. Let us not fool ourselves about that.

The second development is less important but equally welcome. It is the gradual growth of a knowledgeable resistance to what might be called the "naïve cult of coordination." Over the past century we have tried to work toward eliminating duplication of services, toward coordinating the efforts of agencies. The quest has never been completely successful, but as it approaches success, it inadvertently accumulates formidable disadvantages along with its alleged advantages. It tends to create a monopoly situation, to limit free competition, and to reduce the options to the client. Meantime, we do not even have the alleged duplication of services, in the sense of wasteful superabundance. There is no reason, after a century of this, to believe that a monopoly situation induces nonprofit agencies to give the consumer a better break any more than it induces profit organizations to do so.

Many people believe that the situation would be better if clients had the opportunity to select from a variety of agencies the ones which they like the best, and if this preference reflected itself in the agencies' income or lack of income through financial credits of one type or another. This is a highly complex question. The broader use of the economic "market" is more appropriate for some type of services than for others. We really do not know enough about this yet, so arguments wax heated and rhetorical.

Nevertheless, I see some hope in a shift in emphasis from a position where we limit competition wherever we can, to one where we promote competition wherever feasible. It is certainly no panacea, but I believe it will become more important in the next decade.

The third development is still more important. It is the gradual growth of a host of new and experimental settings and structures for social service delivery, many of them definitely antiestablishment in the sense of trying to break with conventional patterns of agency structure and function. There are the free clinics, the free schools, the cooperatives, the ethnically oriented centers.

A group of young people at the National Student Association is developing a national directory of these and other countercultural or alternative institutions or facilities. It will soon be available with listings under fourteen major institutional headings with numerous subheadings—a sort of national "yellow-page" directory including many of these types of services, to be called the Source Catalogue. It would seem to be a "must" for anyone interested in innovation in the social welfare field.

I do not mean to imply that all these services are or will be "better." I believe that some of them already are, and others will be, but not all by a long shot. Nevertheless, with my disenchantment concerning agency innovation in the nine cities of our study, I think that anyone interested in innovation must look for its motive force outside the system of the established agencies. In this connection, I believe we should take a long, hard look at the simple assumption that one should always work with and through established agencies. More recently, this doctrine has been made official by the Model Cities Administration. The basis is that if lasting institutional change, even in the narrower sense, is to be brought about, it must involve these basic established agencies rather than set up fly-by-night attempts to bypass them or substitute for them.

There is much logic behind this position. It is politically realistic and is welcomed by the agencies—a large and powerful constituency. But in the long run, I believe, it is myopic. It does not risk enough, it does not venture enough, to get the effective innovation it allegedly aspires to but will not achieve. In effect, on the one hand we talk about experimenting with new structures, new methods; but when they come along, we cut them down to the conventional professional size and place them securely under the control of the very agencies whose operations they must challenge if they are to bring significant change. Rather than discouraging the emergence of new structures, with new constituencies and new methods, we should encourage them by allocating a part of federally funded program budgets explicitly for new organizations, including client organizations, which seek to develop radical as well as less radical alternatives to present agency structures and programs.

But do we really *want* innovation? Again, let us be honest with ourselves and with the people we claim to serve.

I have a high regard for the people in the Model Cities Administration, most of whom are very serious about bringing about change in the inner cities. Much the same is true of other agencies on the federal and regional level, and on the local level as well. Some gains have been made, and other gains could undoubtedly be made through administrative improvements in the program and through more limited and realistic goal-setting. But this is a very limited route. We do not need another program like Model Cities to learn that.

When we talk about building competence in City Hall and building competence in citizen participation, part of this competence should consist of a realistic awareness of the limitations of the collaborative planning route. We must develop other alternatives, and we must have the courage to follow them.

II. A MEXICAN AMERICAN VIEW

JUAN J. PATLAN

BEING A CHICANO, being Mexican American, being brown and a minority, has certain advantages.

For one thing, Chicanos recognize quite clearly the contrast between what should be and what actually is in our society. On a practical level this means that we do not make frustrating attempts to retread traditional delivery systems in health and welfare services. Our vision is of new and perhaps radical ways of doing things. In view of the massive poverty of our group, we are extremely anxious to short-cut the present way of getting things done. We are firm believers in the axiom that the shortest distance between two points is a straight line. Everywhere, Mexican Americans are making strenuous efforts to redefine the social problems that harass our group. We reject any further surveys and studies that focus on Chicanos as *the* social problem while branding us as social misfits. We think that our predicaments are just one part of a larger problem caused by society's inadequate institutions.

In the writings of social scientists, we find much evidence to support our intuitions. Dr. Warren has presented an example of writings by the new sociologists that document the same basic theme: "the social solutions of the 1930s are no longer relevant." Our social problems occur in the midst of complex and interwoven institutions. They call for comprehensive solutions that are based on sophisticated knowledge about vested interests and institutions. Just as importantly, these solutions must be based on values that stress human liberation and responsibility.

What we actually experience are social problems that are resolved because of pragmatic political reasons. The results are fraud, tokenism, and disillusionment among our citizens. Let me apply Dr. Warren's general comments to the actual experience in San Antonio, Texas. Here is what happened and what is happening in that city's Model Cities program.

To paraphrase Warren:

Suppose, just suppose, you wanted to conduct psychological warfare on the minds of a large, restless group of Mexican Americans who live, for the most part, in a section of San Antonio called the West Side. The area is crowded and poverty-stricken. For generations these people have provided the sweat and muscle for the Anglo community. They are, in the main, San Antonio's maids and handymen.

There are definite signs that they no longer will accept this low-status position in the community. How would you go about keeping things the ways things are? How would you keep these Chicanos poor but happy? You would try the following strategies:

1. Limit them, contain them, with a massive birth-control program.

2. Amuse them by building two mini-parks. Call one of them Smith Park to remind them of their debt to the Anglo establishment.

3. Divide them by relocating them, splitting up the warmth and loyalty and dependency on one another that come about because of stable neighborhoods albeit poor ones.

4. Place Mexican Americans in leadership roles, but be sure that they remain loyal to the establishment.

5. Embitter and further isolate them by making all kinds of promises. Take surveys, hold town hall meetings that go on for hours and accomplish nothing that has relevance to problems of poverty and ill-housing.

6. Identify and isolate the troublemakers by having plain-clothes policemen at meetings and "Human Resources" personnel noting names and car licenses. Place some of them on the Model Cities Board and subcommittees, giving them publicity and a sense of power.

7. Divert them by creating highly visible programs that have nothing to do with root causes. Institute nutrition programs that teach the right things to eat even though the area's residents cannot afford the proper amounts of food. Provide puppet shows and recreational vans, all properly marked with Model Cities propaganda. Put signs all over the West Side announcing that such and such will be a Model Cities project.

8. Have the Mayor announce: "The Bandera Freeway is a must." This is a freeway that is scheduled to go right through th middle of the Model Cities area. This further confuses and diverts people by making them defend the integrity of their area.

9. Finally, consolidate and maintain power by passing a $60 million bond issue, thus uniting city departments, real estate interests, and the construction interests. Meanwhile, the residents

of the Model Cities neighborhoods remain poor, ill-housed, underemployed, and unhealthy.

Let me cite examples of the four *C*'s which Dr. Warren discussed.

CITIZEN PARTICIPATION

There is no effective citizen participation in San Antonio Model Cities. For almost three years, residents of the Model Cities area have been sitting on component review committees and the overall Citizens Participation Policy Commission, sincerely believing that they are making policy, providing substantive input into what develops out of Model Cities. The evidence in three instances indicates something else.

The Citizens Board:

1. Four times said *no* to a massive birth control program, only to have the City Council approve it.

2. Approved a pilot housing rehabilitation program for fifty houses, only to have the City Council say *no*.

3. Approved a housing counseling program by a community organization, only to have it disapproved by the City Council.

COMPREHENSIVENESS

Let us analyze the housing situation as an example.

Fifteen thousand homes, according to the statement of the problem for Model Cities, need extensive rehabilitation, and hundreds are being added every year. Substantial construction of new, scattered, individual homes should be undertaken through Model Cities, and the feasibility of building some other types should be explored. To date, *no* homes have been rehabilitated, less than one hundred new, scattered, individual homes have been built, and only a few hundred units of multifamily housing have been constructed.

This is hardly, after three years, a comprehensive approach to housing, one of the most physically glaring problems of the Model Cities area. No rehabilitation project has been undertaken through Model Cities because the only pilot project was submitted by the Mexican American Unity Council, which was on the "outs" with City Hall. Very little scattered-site home building has been done because mass production of that kind of home is not possible in a densely populated urban center. The only type of construction considered and actively pursued was multifamily housing, which is taboo in the Mexican American barrios of San Antonio. Several thousand units were designed and planned, and the home builders could see the green stuff coming in. The ire of the citizens, particularly of the officials of a heavily predominant Mexican American school district, was so great that a battle over this issue raged for months. Only a few projects were built. And all that the citizens were saying was that we would go along with this type of home if we were shown a total housing plan which offered a comprehensive and balanced approach to the entire problem.

COORDINATION

As for coordination, the last time I looked there was none. Independent of Model Cities funding, the Mexican American Unity Council planned to launch a small housing rehabilitation project in one of the most thoroughly depressed barrios of the West Side, the Casiano Park area. There was no place where we could check what was already planned for that section. To make sure that we would not be building in an area scheduled for another activity we ended up going to:

1. F.H.A.: for site inspection and tentative approval

2. Urban Renewal: for creek expansion and ascertainment of rehabilitation building standards

3. Parks and Recreation Department: to make sure that a nearby park was not scheduled to be expanded into our project area

4. The School District: to make sure that a nearby school was also not going to be expanded into our project area

5. The San Antonio River Authority: because the homes were in an area near a creek which in 1921 reached flood stage

6. The U.S. Corps of Engineers: to verify our suspicion that the 1921 holdings were no longer relevant

7. The Transportation Department: to check if a nearby major thoroughfare would be redirected over the homes.

CONCENTRATION

Concentration was imagined when San Antonio heard that it would be allocated $9.5 million a year for five years to spend in the Model Cities area only. Figures given to me by the Model Cities staff show the following.

	Total Grant	*Total Spent*
First action year	$9,590,000	$3,350,403
Second action year	9,590,000	1,233,886

Model Cities was intended to be an innovative program. Well, it has not been. It has proceeded to pump funds into established city programs and departments, like the San Antonio River Authority, urban renewal, school districts, and so forth, that have no intention of changing their attitudes and entire *modus operandi*. What has happened is that their budgets have been fattened so that they could continue operating on the basis of their present perception of the problem, that of increasing presently formulated services.

No innovativeness has been shown on the part of those who staff Model Cities, not because they may lack know-how, but because they are not permitted to do other than what they are told. They are not permitted to think for themselves.

There is no innovativeness because completely new organizations, constituted of political friends, have been formed overnight to handle such important and technically tough programs as economic development.

ALTERNATIVES

There should be an area designated as an impacted area, but there should not be a Model Cities agency. It is too much to expect a new agency headed by a man with little or no status effectively to coordinate the efforts of agencies headed by persons who have been for many years entrenched in their positions of power. There are just too many vested interests to protect.

As Dr. Warren points out, there are no panaceas, and although

it is true that a large part of the population are poor because
they lack money, not because they lack social services, I refuse to
agree that *the* answer is to supply them with more money.
Money in hand is a good start, because it provides immediate
relief, but it needs to be accompanied by a radical change in the
premise on which present institutions attack the problems.
There needs to be a radical change in the manner in which
Chicano children from non-English-speaking homes are taught.
There needs to be a radical change in hiring procedures, and by
that I do not necessarily mean just doing away with discrimination based on sex, creed, or color. There needs to be a radical
change so that earnings and capital are accumulated and retained
in the barrios. There needs to be a radical change in the delivery
of health services. There needs to be a radical change in how
homes are built.

But who, pray tell, is going to do all of these things? Certainly
not the established institutions. What is needed, then, is what I
call a community development corporation, free-floating agents
with a technical competence and, more important, with firsthand
knowledge of the day-to-day problems of the barrios and with
direct accountability to those people whom they are set up to
serve. They must be free of restrictive guidelines and multi-
special-condition grants.

Where are those community development corporations, those
free-floating agents? As Dr. Warren points out, they are emerging
in most urban centers, a result of pressure groups that applied
confrontation tactics in days gone by. And there is one in San
Antonio, called the Mexican American Unity Council.

MEXICAN AMERICAN UNITY COUNCIL

The Unity Council is an organization operating in the West
Side of San Antonio. Its chief strengths are intimate understanding and knowledge of the low-income Mexican American community and the ability to match the priorities and the resources
of that community with the vast array of private and federal
programs. It fills the gap between bureaucratic limitations, the
limited budgets, red tape, and low-income peer and family life

styles as specifically expressed by Mexican Americans. More positively, it maintains a flexible, interdisciplinary approach to the problems that arise from the varied and changing needs of our clientele.

The Mental Health Center in San Antonio wanted to extend its services into West San Antonio. The National Institute of Mental Health (NIMH) made a grant to the Mental Health Center, which wished to subcontract with the Unity Council.

It was a staffing grant, providing for a director, psychiatrist, social worker, registered nurse, narcotics specialist, youth coordinator, and ten field workers. All but the psychiatrist, nurse, and social worker are paraprofessionals, many of them not even high school graduates. The only requirements were that they be of good moral character, be able to read and write, speak both Spanish and English, and know the barrio, the people who live there, their customs and traditions. No tests were given. Salaries are somewhat higher than a person with comparable training and experience could elsewhere earn. NIMH, a couple of months ago, evaluated the program, and it passed with flying colors. The correspondence that transpired between the Mental Health Center administrator and the Unity Council in the beginning overflowed with cautiousness and skepticism.

It is said that lending institutions commonly prefer that a man have some money of his own to invest in the business which he wishes to enter. The Unity Council acquired the first Mexican-American-owned McDonald's Hamburger franchise in the entire country just recently. But since McDonald's corporate practice is to deal with an individual manager, we had to find someone smart enough and hard-working enough to manage the business. That was no problem, or so we thought: Mexican Americans manage most of the big businesses in San Antonio, but do not own them. The problem was that our chosen manager did not have enough money for his share of the investment and he could not borrow it from any bank. The Unity Council convinced McDonald's, the Small Business Administration, and others that we would lend our manager his share of the equity. At first everyone balked, but we finally convinced them. So, not only did we put a man in business, but we brought about a little institutional change with three institutions: McDonald's, the bank, and the Small Business Administration.

Four young elementary school students, Mexican Americans, reached the point where, because of a lack of successful experience in the classroom, they were unable to deal with the institution and the institution was unable to deal with them. Preparations were made to send them to reform school. The Unity Council intervened, and the school agreed to give us responsibility for the youngsters and for their tutoring. The principal was so impressed by the results that two months later she wanted to turn over more students to us.

Essentially, the Mexican American Unity Council operates as a community-based organization that will:

1. Provide new opportunities to develop and retain the talents of barrio residents

2. Bring in and retain capital in the barrios

3. Halt the process of obsolescence and increase the tax base of the barrios by improving dwellings and establishing new businesses

4. Lead to the integration of the low-income neighborhood into the social, political, and economic systems of the larger community.

The Mexican American Unity Council is a new experiment and experience for the Chicano community in San Antonio and Bexar County. It is not a mass-membership organization, nor was it created to give any one organization a "base." Rather, the Council is a device by which neighborhood organizations working on the many fronts of Mexican American concerns can explore their common ground, develop mutual support, and share common services and technical assistance.

We believe that our organization is akin to other Chicano groups throughout the country because we share the same goals:

1. A radical decentralization of power with active participation of Chicanos in the decision-making processes of our basic institutions

2. The elimination of racism and the building of a pluralism of cultural and ethnic diversity in our society

3. A reorganization of the human services and professions, opening them to new styles, people, and practice and making them accountable to those they serve

4. The humanization of technology and bureaucracy to serve the needs of Chicanos as they themselves define their needs rather than the interest of any bureaucratic establishment, whether its measure of worth be profit or efficiency.

Community Control of Health and Welfare Programs

GARY A. LLOYD
and JOHN MICHAEL DALEY, JR.

COMMUNITY CONTROL of public schools and educational facilities has been a hotly debated issue in some sections of the country during recent years. There has been less discussion in the popular press or professional journals about community control of health and welfare services. Because the public welfare system seems overpowering and monolithic, and the health services system appears specialized and remote, community groups have not yet placed these institutions under siege. We anticipate that the question of community control will become a central concern for the health and welfare systems during the 1970s.

It is impossible to predict, from the experience of educators and lay people jousting for control of schools in delimited areas of a few large cities, the direction and future thrust toward community control of health and welfare services. Assuming that the thrust will come, believing that health and welfare personnel are unready for debate or action, and recognizing that few case studies exist, we raise many questions and offer few answers. We acknowledge that such exercises are frustrating, but we believe that there is rather urgent need for examination of the issue of community control, and for separation of rhetoric from organizational, professional, and political realities.

In order to observe our own admonitions, we need to make our bias clear. We believe that community control of health and welfare service systems is desirable. But, we must acknowledge that, as yet, we have no clear image of the forms that control might take, and we believe that the odds against community control are high.

The ideal of community participation and citizen participation [1] has a long history in Western thought and in this nation. A rallying point both for defenders of the status quo and for agitators for change, citizen participation has tended to be defined in safely vague terms. Rhetoric about citizen participation has supported our historical myths about a classless society while at the same time providing a rationale for the continuing practice of *noblesse oblige.*

It does not denigrate a noble concept to point out how infrequently word has been matched with deed. To be sure, the town hall meetings were prototypes for today's efforts to increase citizen participation in community affairs. Social settlements for a time attempted to create new institutions within which the abstract concept "participation" might be moved to a more operational—or, as the settlement residents liked to stress, "practical" —level. The seminal but short-lived Cincinnati Social Unit Experiment foreshadowed much of the mid-twentieth-century credo of participation which was forged in the civil rights movement and the skirmish on poverty, and elevated by the Economic Opportunity Act into "maximum feasible participation" of the poor. All of these experiments failed to give voice to the "previously unheard," and were opposed by those whom Eduard Lindeman once remarked were "at heart frightened by the democratic process when it moves into actuality and practice." [2]

Community control is a form of the more widely discussed citizen participation. As citizen participation has evolved over the past few years, its most frequently heard definition has progressed from a rather innocuous introduction of the poor or powerless into the formalities of participation by assigning representatives to advisory groups and discussion forums, through a more political phase involving minority voting rights, to the current demand for the most politicized form of citizen participa-

1 We use these terms interchangeably.
2 Eduard C. Lindeman, "New Patterns of Community Organization," in *Proceedings of the National Conference of Social Work, 1937,* (Chicago: University of Chicago Press, 1937), p. 322.

tion, community control. Today, all of these definitions are still used, with the earlier versions often becoming the source of considerable cynicism on the part of those expected to participate.[3]

Community control cannot become reality without citizen participation, but citizen participation does not necessarily imply that participants have power actually to control or even to influence decision-making and resource allocation. Oversimply, citizen participation *may* entail advice and consent; community control *requires* both.[4] In sum, we differentiate citizen participation from community control on the basis of the degree of power exercised by local groups.

Community control is the decision-making power exercised by a group of people who live in a defined geographical area (usually a neighborhood) over the policies of, and resource allocation to, services. Exercised through community corporations, neighborhood school boards, or local policy-making boards, community control depends upon power to create and guide programs and policies, upon access to information in the larger social system, and upon some degree of autonomy. Given the interrelationships and linkages of social and political structures of our cities, full autonomy and control are implausible goals. But if community control is to be more than another slogan, the group "controlling" must have more than a "right to participate" and must be more than a rubber stamp for professional proposals and directives. The group must have more than "veto" power. Community control must rest upon what Ralph Nader has called "initiatory democracy"[5] under which official irresponsibility can be met by initiating actions of redress. Community control can be said to be "working" only to the degree that both reaction to events and initiation of action are within the capacity of the group.

[3] Sherry Arnstein, "A Ladder of Citizen Participation," *Journal of the American Institute of Planners*, XXXV (1969), 216.

[4] For a discussion of decentralization, which is often confused with community control, see Nathan Glazer, "For White and Black, Community Control is the Issue," New York *Times Magazine*, April 27, 1969, p. 36; Alan A. Altshuler, *Community Control* (New York: Western Publishing Co., 1970), p. 64.

[5] Quoted by Julius Duscha in "Stop! In the Public Interest!" New York *Times Magazine*, March 21, 1971, p. 16.

START

ISSUES

Community control has been dismissed by many people as unworkable and undesirable. A variety of reasons has been offered to support such points of view. Altshuler has reviewed many of them.[6] Leaving aside the either-or resistance to, or acceptance of, the idea itself, there are several issues raised by the concept of community control which require discussion.

Resource distribution. The central issue of community control will almost inevitably become one of resource distribution. To what degree community control as a process can succeed, even in a delimited form, is a difficult question. We concur with assertions that control is no substitute for resources and services. Control is a means but not an end in itself. It is quite obvious that, because of the symbolic connotation of community control, some socially, politically, and economically disfranchised groups attribute to other groups a higher degree of control over their own destiny than exists in fact. To the black or Chicano unemployed father in a ghetto, it may appear that the white suburbanite has great control over his destiny when in fact, the suburbanite's potential for self-determination is limited by economic, social, and political factors far beyond the scope of individual influence. But, keeping these constraints in mind, there is little doubt that some groups are "more equal" than others, in terms of access to resources and control of processes important to their lives.

Movement toward community control must be inspired by a sense of being "left out." The goal must be creation of a network of power relationships wherein those who are now have-nots secure the right to participate effectively, to contest for control of relevant aspects of community life, and to contribute to determination of social priorities. Miller and Rein term such change a transformation of power, not a transfer of power.[7]

Professionals, bureaucracies, and community control. A false

---

[6] Altshuler, *op. cit.*, Chaps. I and II.
[7] S. M. Miller and Martin Rein, "Participation, Poverty, and Administration," *Public Administration Review*, XXIX (1969), 24.

assumption of a finite amount of power and resources has caused
the community control movement to be particularly threatening
to many relatively well-off groups, including professionals. Control exercised by local groups implies to some people a loss of
institutional or professional autonomy.

Undoubtedly, community control would force some redefini-
tion of professional roles. While professional functions might be
modified, we doubt that they would be entirely supplanted. The
perceived threat to role and to autonomy is so strong, however,
that powerful defensive mechanisms are brought into play, sometimes even by those who espouse the ideal of participation or
control. Professionals and bureaucracies in the health and welfare fields have had considerable experience in fending off threats
to their territory from politicians, special interest groups, and
each other. Such experience can be used to block attempts at
community control of health and welfare programs. The arts of
dividing and conquering, of co-optation, and of manipulation of
emotional and fiscal rewards are not unknown to bureaucracies
and professionals. This is not to demean the real efforts of many
health and welfare workers across the country to expand participation of, and control by, consumers. However, organizations,
including professionally oriented organizations, are designed to
survive. Despite individual good will, their structures can be used
to minimize—if not quell—the drive first toward meaningful
participation in decision-making, and then toward community
control.

With respect to the ability of the poor to wrest and keep control of their communities, it must be pointed out that the bu-
reaucratized professional and municipal agencies are potent ad-
versaries. If a local group survives the politics and strains within
its own ranks, it must contend with the relatively greater power
and endurance of official agencies. Community control, to repeat,
involves redistributing something, that "something" usually being power. Milton Kotler summarizes the response of agencies to
a threat to their power:

There is nothing more terrifying to a bureaucrat than the prospect
of losing control over the lives of his clients. To lose these small
opportunities for tyranny means the loss of the personal power that

our paternalistic system gives bureaucrats as a fringe benefit and calls moral obligation. Having no political liberty themselves, administrators cannot understand the claim of local liberty—let alone appreciate it. Their little control over a few lives brings them to their own political oppression in a life of privilege without liberty.[8]

Faced with opponents who can mobilize considerable strength, local groups in quest of control have limited resources with which to play the game of community control. Commitment of the few—the existence of a "little band of prophets"—is essential. Community control must ultimately involve some kind of mass support, but it is initiated by commitment of a few persons, and not by a large membership. The initial partisans, and (later) at least some of the wider participant base, must have expertise in the political system, and a highly developed political sense. Advocates of community control must be "true believers" lest their commitment be shallow, but they must also be sensitive to the forces arrayed against them. Community control may ultimately come not through outright confrontation, although that is a viable means, but through negotiation and compromise. The political sense that leads to compromise must also be accompanied by willingness to take the calculated risk. These three attributes (commitment, political sense, willingness to risk) may be difficult to find in even the best of circumstances. When massive external forces are arrayed against the group, the fragility of coalition politics, of defense tactics, and of individual ardor may prove to be fatal.

Pluralism and community control. Any discussion of community control must touch upon a philosophically puzzling and perhaps unanswerable question: how much heterogeneity can a theoretically open society tolerate? Very slowly we are beginning to give up our belief in the melting pot. Are we now making an equally fallacious assumption that numbers of "centers of identity" or of control in an urban nation are infinite? Does community control as an ideology assume that there are no common bonds that can unite people into a sense of common cause? Has our "common cause" been an illusory image projected by those

[8] Milton Kotler, *Neighborhood Government* (Indianapolis: Bobbs-Merrill, 1969), p. 77.

who have benefited most from existing arrangements? These questions cannot be answered in an either-or fashion. Community control of urban subsystems or institutions would provide basic building blocks for a coalition style of participation and politics, but would also broaden possibilities for "war of all against all." In a pluralistic society, we must avoid the dual myths of absolute heterogeneity and absolute homogeneity.

Efficiency and effectiveness. Closely related to these questions are others having to do with the potential fragmentation of authority and accountability which community control would entail. The most common defense against community control (and even milder forms of citizen participation, for that matter) has been that inefficiency would result. This argument has been heard particularly from health and welfare personnel. Such a point of view obviously assumes that what we now have to offer is designed and provided efficiently. We would be hard put to defend such a point of view. But unless one does assume that we are producing and delivering services efficiently, one is left to conclude that a local group, neighborhood, or community controlling its own services might do just as well (which might be saying very little), or much better than their "caretakers." We know of no qualitative definition of "efficiency" which can be applied to service delivery in health and welfare. It seems to us that the efficiency argument against community control is weak and may becloud the more important issue of effectiveness of services.[9] We wonder if a graver concern of the professionals is that community-controlled services would be less predictable. Predictability of response and not efficiency of service delivery seems to be the crucial issue.

Community control and the public interest. Community control would also challenge predictability of definitions of the public good. Given community control, how can the good of the individual or group be balanced with the public good? Health and welfare personnel have traditionally assumed that they

---

[9] "Efficiency" here refers to the ratio of input to output. "Effectiveness" refers to the production of desired results, without specific reference to input-output ratio. The central question must be: does the system achieve the desired goals?

spoke for both their geographical and their functional communities. Indeed, one of the ancient platitudes of social work (thankfully heard very little these days) was that social work was the conscience of the community. That little rubric expressed more than a rather awesome professional ethnocentricity. Contained within it was the notion that the professional technician had a monopoly upon judgments about what should or could be done, and what should not or could not be done; what "the community" wanted, and what "the community" did not want. That "the community" often reflected the views of only some of the larger community interest groups obscured the fact that in the geographical areas we call cities there were many communities. The "public good" never touched the good of many communities nor reflected the interests and needs of minorities. Today, groups seeking more control over their lives attack this concept of a public good, and state unequivocally that the welfare of other segments of the social system is of little concern to them. What may seem a parochial outlook on the part of emerging leadership is a necessary point of view if local group integrity and unity are to be preserved.

CONSTRAINTS UPON CONTROL

Thus far, it is difficult to see where significant social changes have occurred because of citizen participation which increasingly is more narrowly defined by professionals as consumer participation, and by some neighborhood-based groups as control. To be sure, participation by the poor in decision-making through Community Action programs helped create, in some places, at least, a substantial and sophisticated corps of men and women adept in the arts of urban politics.[10] Through participation in forums and organizations, many people are probably more aware of the forces which affect their lives than they were before. Despite all our talk about participation, however, we still have not found—and cannot find?—a social invention which gives every man a fairly equal chance to participate and to be heard,

[10] Jon Van Til and Sally Bould Van Til, "Citizen Participation in Social Policy: the End of the Cycle?" *Social Problems*, XVII (1970), 319.

to say not only "whether" something will be done, but also "how." The seemingly endless numbers of doctoral dissertations, learned articles, and confrontations of the past half-decade symbolize our frustration with the ideological and theoretical gap between the kinds of citizen participation which are possible and those which seem even barely probable.

Professionals in all fields seem to have less difficulty accepting participation than they do control. Citizen participation—allowing people to have some influence, but not necessarily power, in decision-making—was, like most motive ideas in American social reform, a creation of middle-class professionals. Indeed, one might find some evidence that professionals have used programmed "citizen participation" as a means of co-opting spontaneous citizen groups threatening to attack social welfare agencies and programs.[11] Thursz's comment about consumer involvement can be applied to community control: consumer involvement "is an idea that runs counter to the traditional view of *noblesse oblige* and the modern thrust of professionalism."[12] Demands for community control usually do not come from professionals but from people who want to take responsibility for their own destiny. Participation has come to imply a sharing of labor between professionals and nonprofessionals, with the former in a dominant position. The opposite is true with community control: the professionals would be to some degree subject to their clientele, and in most instances would have to compete for, rather than assume without question, a leadership role.

Community control, both in preachment and limited practice, has evolved as a social response to perceived neglect or exploitation. It is demanded by individuals and groups who have had little opportunity heretofore to influence directly significant institutions which bear upon them, and who have grown cynical about continued promises of participation. For poor, frustrated, and politically alienated people, community control is a potent

11 Piven offers one example in which an official citizen participation structure was established to counteract spontaneous citizen participation which seemed to threaten urban renewal programs. Frances Piven, "Participation of Residents in Neighborhood Community Action Programs," *Social Work*, XI, No. 1 (1966), 73–80.

12 Daniel Thursz, *Consumer Involvement in Rehabilitation* (Washington, D.C.: U.S. Department of Health, Education and Welfare, 1969), p. 1.

idea and symbol. Surrounded by poverty, ready evidence of inequitable distribution of resources, and seeming indifference of church, school, health, and welfare institutions, the minority poor in particular recognize fully that access to the resources of "the communities of solution" for their problems is restricted. That being so, the only alternative, at least for the most militant, is to create their own "community of solution" through community control.[13]

As both idea and ideal, community control is a fragile creation. No one can debate its merits or demerits dispassionately. The prospect of operationalizing the concept threatens a wide range of vested interests, while at the same time it attracts partisans who may overestimate control as a solution for powerlessness. Clearly, community control challenges political hegemonies, the elusive power elites of our urban places, fundamental assumptions about consumer-professional relationships, and perhaps the role-status structure of the very society itself.

Proponents of community control must tread warily between the realities of co-optation and the fantasies of total autonomy. They must develop an independent power base, while recognizing that diplomatic relations must be maintained with institutions which they wish to influence or supersede. Established institutions cannot be depended upon to provide resources to be used to destroy themselves, but neither can advocates of control indulge themselves in the fictions of resources without imposed restrictions. Community control must come from some group of local people, and must be an emotional response to the conditions about which professionals prefer to be "rational" and "objective." Community control must also extend, as Glazer has implied, beyond the point of rage or conflict to the provision of service.[14]

Because the degree of control (particularly of resources) varies with the issues, it should be possible to establish a community profile of control reflecting for one point in time, the degree to which that community controls resources in various areas of

[13] The concept of "community of solution" is borrowed from National Commission on Community Health Services, *Health is a Community Affair* (Cambridge, Mass.: Harvard University Press, 1966), p. 129.

[14] Glazer, *op. cit.*, p. 52.

community life.[15] Arnstein's "ladder of participation," with rungs beginning with manipulation (nonparticipation) and ending with community control, provides one formulation of degrees of control. A group in search of control may be found on different rungs of the ladder for different issues, and may move up or down the ladder on a single issue. Community control, like social reform, is dynamic. It will succeed and fail, become elipsed, and be resurrected.

Reactions to community control—and to citizen participation, for that matter—are apt to be more ideological than analytic. In practice, neither can be supported for very long on purely objective or theoretical grounds. The comments of Spiegel and Mittenthal about citizen participation can be applied easily to a discussion of community control. They observe that citizen participation in planning is a "phenomenon of infinite complex and subtle dimension." The evidence available to us, they go on, is "contradictory, inconclusive, particularistic, and over qualified by the dictates of time, place, and circumstance." [16] Whether rationalized as a means of increasing the citizen's or consumer's stake in a whole society or a particular agency, or as a means of instilling democratic values, or as a way to provide entry employment to the poor, citizen participation and community control defy both definition and empirical exploration.

The rationales for both citizen participation and community control are similar. Dubey, for example, rationalizes community participation on the grounds of correcting program inadequacy or irrelevance, creating a power base or improving service delivery, and enhancing participatory democracy.[17] Burke lists as purposes of citizen participation, education therapy, behavioral change, staff supplementation, co-optation, and sharing of community power.[18]

15 See Altshuler, *op. cit.,* p. 44.
16 Hans B. C. Spiegel and Stephen D. Mittenthal, "The Many Faces of Citizen Participation: a Bibliographic Overview," in Hans B. C. Spiegel, ed., *Citizen Participation in Urban Development* (Washington, D.C.: NTL Institute, 1968), pp. 3–4.
17 Sumati N. Dubey, "Community Action Programs and Citizen Participation: Issues and Confusions," *Social Work,* XV, No. 1 (1970), 77–79.
18 Edmund M. Burke, "Citizen Participation Strategies," *Journal of the American Institute of Planners,* XXXIV (1968), 287–94.

Dubey's point of view bears a distinct resemblance to that held by partisans of community control. Burke expresses a more traditional perspective, implying the ways in which the strategies of citizen participation can be used by professionals to maintain control of decision-making and allocative processes.

From the reports of community control experiments, it appears that we have attained neither the ideal of democracy held forth by partisans of participation nor the chaos of anarchy predicted by the critics of control. We have learned that, as a social invention, participation or control is messy, inconvenient for the professionals involved, time-consuming, and inefficient. Neither participation nor control insures the application of expertise, or wise judgments.

Community control has, in the past, been justified on the grounds that participatory democracy must be fostered if our society is to resolve its "social question." This argument has been applied to citizen participation by professionals, and to some degree has been heard in the battles for community control of schools. Although it still figures in debates, we suspect that participatory democracy as a rationale will be less used in the future. Instead, we believe that groups striving to control a school, or a service system, will appeal less abstractly to individual or community vested interests. Faced with unresponsiveness of municipal agencies, schools and social welfare and health services, differing definitions of need, and lack of influence upon allocation, supporters of community control must turn increasingly to development of political power based upon a finely honed sense of discrimination and injustice, and upon ethnic pride. To succeed in wresting and keeping control of local communities, groups will need to form themselves on a model similar to the ward organizations of old, and become adept in the arts of patronage, coalition formation, and handling the trade-off. Even with these skills, survival will be a moot point for many local organizations.

AUTHENTICITY, PARTICIPATION, AND CONTROL

Citizen participation, particularly in the form of community control, entails social costs. The most obvious of these is the potential for increased, and perhaps debilitating, social conflict as more groups maneuver for influence. The sense of displacement felt by professionals and others of the "have" group may not elicit much sympathy in some quarters, but must be reckoned as a potentially devastating social cost. More subtle are the social costs to the entire society of "inauthentic" participation. We are compelled to offer a caveat about those costs to professional workers in the health and welfare fields.

In a provocative article Etzioni discusses at some length the consequences of an unresponsive social structure:

We see . . . that a whole category of structures, which appear as if they were responsive, may actually be highly alienating, with their participatory façades adding some alienating effects of their own to the underlying, unresponsive, structures.

He goes on to refer to social conditions as

authentic, when the appearance and the underlying structure are both responsive to basic human needs; as *alienating,* when both the appearances and the structures are unresponsive; and as *inauthentic,* when the underlying structure is unresponsive but an institutional or symbolic front of responsiveness is maintained.[19]

Without attempting to force Etzioni's point of view into the framework of a different issue, it seems to us that the likelihood of community control of health and welfare service being "authentic" is rather low, while the potential for the erection of "participatory façades," pseudo participation, and pseudo control is rather high.

Invitations for people to participate may have a hollow ring if the means for their participation are limited. Participation and control can be easily proffered, but may be difficult for professionals to live with. If "authentic" participation is not the manifest goal of professional workers, participation should not be talked about, even if good public relations seems to demand it. Pseudo participation is well known in the cities of America. Further instances of it can only contribute to the growing number of disbelieving, cynical people who already have dis-

19 Amitai Etzioni, "Basic Human Needs, Alienation, and Inauthenticity," *American Sociological Review,* XXXIII (1968), 880–881.

cerned the discrepancy between soothing mottoes of participatory democracy and the harsher realities of organizational maintenance and survival.

We have not intended to suggest specific structures for community control. Kotler, Weismantel, and Jencks,[20] among others, have elsewhere proposed what well might prove workable structures. We believe that the issue of community control has broad implications for our society:

The democratic process, including citizen involvement, does not assure wisdom. The end result may indeed be inferior to the professional's carefully studied proposal. The gains to be made cannot be measured in short terms. At stake is nothing less than the type of society we wish to develop.[21]

[20] Kotler, *op. cit.;* Christopher Jencks, "Is the Public School Obsolete?" *Public Interest,* No. 2 (1966), pp. 18–27; William Weismantel, "A Credit Card System for Model Cities," *Journal of the American Institute of Planners,* XXXV (1969), 49–51.

[21] Thursz, *op. cit.,* p. 14.

Clients' Participation in Institutional Change

ARTHUR J. KATZ

INSTITUTIONAL CHANGE is an "unspoken" objective of Head Start because it does not appear directly in any of the literature or policy statements published by the federal agency. Yet, a multitude of activity has been identified as institutional change efforts and has been documented and assessed as successful over the short period of Head Start's history.

The current emphasis emanating from the federal agency to the regional offices and local programs seems to point in the direction that the Head Start program should return to its basic charge of direct delivery of service focused almost exclusively on the child and his immediate family.

It has also been suggested that the institutional change objective is no longer considered a legitimate goal for Head Start.

One can only speculate as to why such a change in orientation has taken place. The most obvious assumption is connected with the political factor. The current Administration seems to be demanding a stringent withdrawal by any federal programs from areas of potential political controversy. The second assumption is related to a genuine desire on the part of the federal agency to strengthen and institutionalize a high standard of child development service which could become a prototype for a vast complex of future child care programs. In an effort to protect the integrity of such high standards and to assure its institutionalization, it seems reasonable to dedicate all resources toward that end and remain free from the dangers of political conflict.

It is difficult to argue against this rationale if one's primary focus is direct-service delivery. However, if social welfare is also seen as an agent for institutional change, it is difficult to accept the notion of service delivery alone as an adequate one.

Project Head Start must not be limited to the child development function. It has important roots in institutional change and has indeed demonstrated a successful contribution toward such efforts. It can potentially make increasingly significant contributions. Head Start need not compromise its aspirations for a high standard of service in child development programs. Rather, a strong institutional change focus accompanying the service program can assure the success of the child development objective which otherwise may be severely limited and even curtailed.

CONCEPTION OF INSTITUTIONAL CHANGE

The concept of institutional change is often used synonymously with that of social change. When one thinks of social change it is difficult to conceive of efforts to affect an entire society. One thinks rather of particular components which as organized systems fall under the rubric of "social institutions."

In defining social change Irwin T. Sanders gives us a point of departure for a definition of institutional change: "Any change which becomes incorporated in the system to such an extent that it modifies the structure of the system (the arrangements among its components) or the operation of the system (communication, allocation of power, social mobility, and the like)." [1]

Lloyd Ohlin and Martin Rein deal with the concept of socializing institutions, which they define as, "those organized structures of persons, facilities, and resources which have as their end the preparation of persons to play various types of social and cultural roles." [2] Such socializing institutions, which include welfare, education, and health among others, are likely to be managed by decision-makers who are far removed from the individual directly involved. Often the individual is not knowledge-

[1] Irwin T. Sanders, "Approaches to Social Change for Social Work," in *1960 Proceedings, 8th Annual Program Meeting* (New York: Council on Social Work Education, 1960), pp. 3–33.
[2] Lloyd E. Ohlin and Martin Rein, "Social Planning for Institutional Change," in *The Social Welfare Forum, 1964* (New York: Columbia University Press, 1964), p. 86.

able about appropriate channels needed to be employed in order
to influence decisions which are made for operation of these institutions. Knowledge of these complex systems and methods of
negotiating them are particularly absent in our economically
deprived population.

One major task for professionals in social welfare is, therefore, planning for institutional change which can make these
systems more sensitive and responsive to the consumers of services, particularly in economically deprived areas. Ohlin and
Rein identify four types of institutional acts which have the
effect of creating personal and social problems for individuals
and suggest that such acts might be initial points of engagement
in institutional change efforts: the process of labeling; access to
institutional resources; distribution of rewards and promotions;
and postinstitutional linkage with opportunity.[3]

The more specific points at which these important institutions
can be changed in order to help them operate maximally on
behalf of poor people are many, and they range from modifying
organization structure to changing policies, such as simplifying
admissions criteria.

A variety of strategies exists for accomplishing change:

> There can be as many strategies for change as there are ways in
> which institutions change. As yet our knowledge about the processes
> of institutional change do not enable us to design such efforts with
> as much confidence concerning the outcome as we are able to do in
> working with individual and family problems.[4]

Rein suggests three major strategies for institutional change:
parallelism, redistribution, and social choice and incremental-
ism.[5]

PROJECT HEAD START

The Head Start program, originally administered through the
community action title of the Economic Opportunity Act of
1964, is currently part of the Office of Child Development of

---

[3] *Ibid.*, p. 91.   [4] *Ibid.*, p. 95.
[5] Martin Rein, *Social Policy: Issues of Choice and Change* (New York: Random
House, 1970).

the Department of Health, Education, and Welfare. Despite occasional attacks upon the program by a variety of groups for differing reasons, it has survived, albeit in weakened condition.

Although the program has been severely underfunded from its inception, the same comment is true about most federal programs related to the antipoverty effort. Nevertheless, Head Start over the years has achieved support on a broad front so that it begins to take on a "movement" character. Enlisting in the Head Start effort is a wide spectrum of professionals, paraprofessionals, and middle-class lay citizens. It has also engendered the enthusiasm of large numbers of its low-income consumers. Despite the regular attempts to discredit the program values of the child development component Head Start has been relatively free from political controversy. This is a blessing to those interested in pursuing the child development objectives. The program will continue to arouse little political conflict if it maintains a focus exclusive on the objectives of personal development of preschool children and increased social services to families, relatively benign and noncontroversial areas.

Head Start, however, is an outstanding example of a national social welfare program with unusual potential for contributing to community institutional change efforts. Indeed, it has already given evidence of this. Other national social welfare programs which have successfully demonstrated this process can be found within the so-called "self-help" groups, specifically, the Association for the Help of Retarded Children (AHRC) and United Cerebral Palsy.

AHRC, for instance, has been successful in effecting changes within the nation's educational system on countless local fronts as well as on state-level systems for the benefit of retarded youngsters. Its influence has been felt on all levels in relation to vocational services, in the economic institutions, and in research and training in higher education. Other national agencies focused on specific demographic or problem characteristics can make similar claims to successful institutional change efforts on behalf of their clientele. Their methods, however, have been those of the traditional approach to policy change; namely, the use of lobbying techniques on local levels with boards of education and on state and federal legislatures. These methods have been utilized primarily by middle-class agents to whom the process of influence through power-source identity is familiar and available.

Head Start is a national level agency created by federal administrative and legislative policy. As such it suffers from the same problem in institutional change efforts that attends all government programs; namely, the difficulty in utilizing direct political channels.

Much of the motivation in organizations such as AHRC originates from parents (the essential force in self-help groups). Mental retardation cuts across all socioeconomic lines. Middle-class parents are politically sophisticated, organizationally wise, and familiar with sources of financial support. Head Start has no such middle-class parent base. Head Start's institutional change strategies of necessity need to be selectively different. Parents of poor kids are generally not politically sophisticated or organizationally wise, nor do they have access to funds for engaging technical assistance.

Despite such limitations, Head Start's influence on community institutions suggests extremely high potential for change and, in fact, already has evidenced impact worthy of note.

Head Start's original charge in relation to the institutional change objective is concerned with the original intent of locating the program under the community action title of the Economic Opportunity Act. Was this decision merely an expedient one, or was there a purpose?

The community action programs were designed to be the nucleus of the Economic Opportunity Act's system. It seemed reasonable and expedient in 1964 to locate all service activities within the community action structure. Yet all community action program activities, including Head Start, were mandated to conform with policies designed to achieve a major objective of the Economic Opportunity Act as follows: "Bettering the conditions under which people live, learn and work." [6] Project Head

6 Economic Opportunity Act of 1964, Title II.

Start in its relationship to the OEO effort could be expressed as "helping individuals and their families in their struggle against poverty." [7] The concept of "bettering conditions" implies a clear rationale for an institutional change strategy for all community action activities, moving beyond the concept of dealing with individual cases of poverty and beyond the notion of individual child development.

The original conception of Head Start included the institutional change notion. As in other social policy developments, a wide gap exists between intent, policy formulation, and organizational implementation.

Head Start has a relationship to the educational institution in a special way. Its special mission within that institution is related to economic development of its consumer group, an objective not formally accepted by education generally. President Nixon's Task Force in Urban Education indicated that the dimensions of the new federal role in education be set forth as "fostering institutional change for the improvement of economic, social, health and educational conditions of impoverished groups . . . and becoming an advocate on behalf of impoverished groups." [8] Obviously, neither the federal educational establishment nor local community education systems have as yet accepted these new directions. Title I's impact raises serious questions.

Social welfare is constantly forced to identify with a point of view suggesting a dichotomy and inherent conflict in program objectives between service delivery and institutional change. It is constantly suggested that a choice must be made since no social welfare agency can effectively manage both. Unfortunately, we seem to have limited success in managing either. Specht, among others, points out the feasibility for social welfare workers to utilize a flexible approach so that they can function as service deliverers as well as institutional change agents.[9] The dichotomy seems to be a spurious one.

[7] *Ibid.*   [8] *Congressional Record,* January, 1970.
[9] Harry Specht, "Social Policy Formulation: the Role of the Social Caseworker," in *Social Work Practice, 1967* (New York: Columbia University Press, 1967), pp. 72–94.

There is an equally spurious distinction being made between the objectives of individual, personal development and institutional change. If we can agree that the four types of institutional acts which Ohlin and Rein identify as creating personal and social problems are valid, it is simple to make the connection between institutional change, service delivery, and individual human development. There exists no "necessary dichotomy" except as one is fostered by those who seek to maintain social welfare efforts in an exclusive preoccupation. Given that we need to develop a greater knowledge base for both understanding and doing in the larger system, there must be a greater emphasis upon institutional change functions within organized social welfare activities. Nevertheless, the critical notion to be maintained is that the two functions, service delivery and institutional change, are symbiotic parts of an integral approach to an effective community social welfare system.

Can a social welfare program like Head Start engage in, and successfully accomplish objectives in, both areas? It can and it must if it is to accomplish its broadest objective of improvement of the human condition of poor people. Head Start is doomed to failure on all counts if it measures its success solely on the instrumental objective of immediate personal development for young children, or delivery of certain services to individuals and families. Long-term effectiveness of any efforts toward personal development are limited if they do not become institutionalized into the broader community systems.

We are not discussing methods of change, strategies of change, or rates of change in relation to time. Radical, immediate changes may well be needed in some community institutions. On the other hand, it may not be desirable for Head Start or any other program to adopt a revolutionary rather than an incremental approach to change. The time-honored principle in social work, put into contemporary language, still prevails, namely, "different strokes for different folks."

Institutional change efforts within the social welfare framework seem to have been most successful when related to a service program area for which community support has been developed and where trust and recognition for competency have been established.

The development of a high-quality service program is therefore almost a prerequisite for enlisting the interest and involvement of grass-roots support (usually an important component in institutional change strategy with low-income people). The use of grass-roots support is not the only strategy employed in institutional change. The elite strategy is another. Here the responsibility for planning and implementing a change process is given to highly specialized professionals, a group of sophisticated, interested lay people or a combination of both. Recent developments have made us cautious of elitist strategy. Too often the elite cadre is subject to political, economic, and social pressures and can be "bought off" in a variety of ways. When elitist groups have a personal, emotional, or ideological commitment, such as in the case of the middle-class AHRC parent, such "buying off" may not take place.

Despite the limitations associated with effective utilization of the grass-roots strategy, we have come to recognize the special potential inherent in this strategy for successful institutional change. Grass-roots processes demand high levels of organization and are usually provided leadership at some point by elite forces. How ready the elite force (professional or otherwise) is to give up power is a critical issue.

Head Start has within its structure the possibility for combining both these strategies. Head Start has a committed consumer group. It also has a committed professional and paraprofessional group. This professional group, at this point, has a high service delivery orientation. The child development staff component is by definition oriented to classroom experiences. The social service component within Head Start has been until recently poorly defined. Social work with its tradition of social reform and community development could have made a more meaningful contribution to the institutional change objective than it has. For the most part, social work has been represented in Head Start primarily by individuals without training, experience, or professional tradition. The single most misunderstood function within the Head Start profession complex is that of "social worker."

The parent involvement component has in the past offered the most effective possible arena for institutional change purposes. In most Head Start centers parent involvement runs the gamut from coffee *klatsches* and sewing groups to adult education with limited focus on institutional change or social action efforts.

Any program interested in institutional change clearly defines and limits its scope. Many successful attempts have focused on particular areas of interest where the agency seeking change has demonstrated knowledge, competency, and authority in addition to the important factor of a power base. The nature of knowledge needed to analyze, understand, and intervene for the purpose of complex system change makes it impossible for any but the most highly sophisticated agency to engage in a multiplicity of efforts simultaneously.

Head Start can best address institutional change efforts to arenas appropriate to its knowledge, competency, experience, authority, and power. The community institutions most clearly identified as target goals in relation to these criteria are public education, health, and welfare.

All three of these institutions are directly related to the lives of Head Start children and their families. There is a corresponding component within the Head Start program which actively relates to each of these larger community institutions as service providers to Head Start families.

A critical objective of the Office of Economic Opportunity (OEO) was to affect such existing community resources so that they functioned more effectively on behalf of the poor. These are also the institutional systems with which Head Start personnel deal on a regular basis and about which they are most knowledgeable. It is the dysfunctional quality of some of these institutions which prevents their effective utilization and impairs their maintenance or rehabilitative functions.

One social work objective for institutional change is to make those institutions charged with service delivery more account-able and responsible to those they serve so that they operate at maximum effectiveness on behalf of service consumers. The best definers of effective service and evaluators of service quality are consumers. Our free-market economic system has accepted the proposition of the primacy of the consumer. There is little ra-tionale to deny the same prerogative to the consumer of non-profit services.

Should the Head Start program continue to maintain a focus on institutional change as a major objective? Should this objec-tive be strengthened? Head Start has a history which admirably fits it to play this role. The ideals of most social welfare programs are committed to the democratic principle of self-determination for consumers. Yet many programs are conducted in a less than democratic fashion. Head Start, like other OEO programs, has a similar set of ideals. The community action context focused more attention on involvement and participation of the service user. Despite the labeling of this development as a major "mis-understanding," [10] participation attempts by these various pro-grams were sound in purpose although at times ill-conceived in operation. Despite a vast number of operational misfortunes, history may well record that the OEO period of grass-roots orga-nization was integrally connected with major developments, we are currently observing, representing a rebirth of a populist movement involving efforts of large masses of people concerned with social justice for minorities, income redistribution, and war resistance.

Head Start has built-in policies to assure the involvement of service consumers in policy determination. The policy advisory committees on the local center level and advisory councils on the city-wide or county level offer opportunity for participation by consumers. Head Start is a pioneer in this development. To be sure, in many places this development is "tokenism," yet there are many Head Start center operations where parents have a significant and critical impact.

[10] See Daniel P. Moynihan, *Maximum Feasible Misunderstanding* (New York: Free Press, 1969).

The concept of parent involvement which Head Start has also built into its program is not a new one since group work agencies have utilized it for many years. Nevertheless, it represents a structured opportunity for access to large numbers of poor people with a vital stake as service consumers. They are vulnerable to the dysfunctions of community institutions.

The parent involvement program can also play a major role in personal growth of parents: The ability to feel good enough about self to struggle (in a group) with formidable institutional forces represents growth for many.

Although the parent involvement program in Head Start is not currently considered as an institutional change force, it could easily become one. This component also can help parents learn organizational skills, methods of political expression, and approaches to understanding complex systems. Such knowledge can be effectively utilized outside the Head Start program when children enter the public schools. Experiences of parents in Head Start are easily integrated into other arenas. In many parts of the country former Head Start parents have contributed effectively to change efforts within the public school system.

THE KIRSCHNER REPORT

The final issue is that of Head Start's experience with institutional change efforts. This question was posed by the Office of Research and Evaluation of Project Head Start and studied in depth by the Kirschner Associates. Their report, released in May of 1970, begins with the assumption that Head Start "is also vitally concerned with influencing the environment in ways deemed beneficial to children of low income families. This is inferred from many of the Head Start goals which can not be accomplished solely as a result of the association of a child or his family with Head Start." [11]

The objectives of the research project were:

1. To determine if there have been changes in local educational and health institutions relevant to the objectives of Project Head Start

11 Kirschner Associates, Inc., *A National Survey of the Impacts of Head Start Centers on Community Institutions* (Washington, D.C.: Project Head Start, Office of Child Development, U.S. Department of Health, Education, and Welfare, 1970), p. 1.

2. To determine if local Head Start centers were influential in bringing about relevant changes in community institutions
3. To analyze how Head Start was involved in the institutional change process
4. To describe the different impacts on community institutions of various Head Start characteristics and approaches.[12]

The second objective was to study the more general issue of achieving institutional change through an intervention strategy known as "educational innovation." The basic findings of the study identified four change areas as a result of Head Start intervention in local educational and health institutions:

1. Increased involvement of the poor with institutions, particularly at decision-making levels and in decision-making capacities
2. Increased institutional employment of local persons in paraprofessional occupations
3. Greater educational emphasis on the particular needs of the poor and of minorities.
4. Modification of health institutions and practices to serve the poor better and more sensitively.[13]

Institutional changes consistent with Head Start goals were identified in all 58 communities studied. A total of 1,496 changes was noted. Within each community the number of such changes ranged from 14 to 40. In over half of the communities surveyed more than 25 such changes were identified. "Thus, while it can not be stated at this stage of the analysis that Head Start *caused* these prevalent institutional changes, it can be seen that changes of a type desired by Head Start have generally occurred in substantial numbers." [14]

Of the 1,496 changes in the 58 communities, 1,055 were within the educational and 441 within the health institutions. All communities reported both health and education changes.

The study also investigated comparison communities (those without Head Start centers) and found almost no relevant institutional changes.

The study concludes: "The data thus indicate not only that community changes consistent with Head Start goals have occurred on a widespread basis but that these changes are prevalent in both educational and health fields, two of the areas

12 *Ibid.,* pp. 1–3.   13 *Ibid.,* pp. 4–5.   14 *Ibid.* p. 5.

of predominate Head Start concern." [15] The report cites many interesting case examples of institutional change which specify the nature of the processes involved.

The study also adds to our knowledge of how the process of institutional change takes place. Seven stages in the process are conceptualized as: the background; the ideal proposal; the support for adoption; authorization; resource fund provision; execution; and support during change. In 94 percent of the changes identified, Head Start was involved in one or more of the stages. In a majority of changes, Head Start was involved at three or more stages.

The full significance of changes in the education and health institutions can only be appreciated if one recognizes the traditionally removed stance of both of these institutions from consumer contact and consumer control. "In the brief period of less than half a decade, concurrent with the life of Head Start, these institutions have changed remarkably." [16] Although the report recognizes that these two institutions are nowhere near fully responsive to the needs of poor people, given the short period of time and a relatively small investment of resources, Head Start has been closely identified with a series of fundamental changes in two of the most crucial institutions in our society. "Head Start has been a successful strategy in that it has widely achieved its goals of modifying local institutions so they are more responsive to the needs and desires of the poor." [17]

To summarize briefly, social welfare has an equally deep commitment to institutional change and to service delivery. These two fundamental objectives can never be seen as dichotomous but rather as part of an integral approach. The Head Start program, with an OEO community action tradition, has an ideological commitment to institutional change as well as to child development services. Head Start has developed a structure capable of carrying out institutional change objectives and in its short experience has manifested that it can successfully affect community institutions toward change on behalf of poor people.

[15] *Ibid.,* p. 5.   [16] *Ibid.,* p. 5.   [17] *Ibid.,* p. 19.

Appendix A: Program

THEME: HUMAN ASPIRATIONS AND NATIONAL PRIORITIES

SUNDAY, MAY 16

ORIENTATION FOR NEWCOMERS AND EXPOSITION TOUR
Presiding and speaker: Alexander J. Allen, Jr., National Urban League, New York
Speaker: Sara Lee Berkman, NCSW, New York

U.S. COMMITTEE GENERAL SESSION
Presiding: Charles I. Schottland, Brandeis University, Waltham, Mass.; President, ICSW
Speakers: Norman V. Lourie, Pennsylvania Department of Public Welfare, Harrisburg
Bernard E. Nash, National Association of Retired Teachers–American Association of Retired Persons, Washington
Sponsor: U.S. Committee of ICSW

OPENING GENERAL SESSION: THE PEOPLE, YES!
Invocation: Gen. John F. McMahon, Volunteers of America, New York
Introduction: Mitchell I. Ginsberg, Columbia University, New York
Welcome from City of Dallas: George Allen, Dallas City Council
Speaker: Margaret E. Berry, National Federation of Settlements and Neighborhood Centers, New York; President, NCSW

CONFERENCE RECEPTION

MONDAY, MAY 17

GENERAL SESSION: THE SOUTHWEST—A SAGA OF
HUMAN ASPIRATION
Presiding: Rabbi David Jacobson, Temple Beth-El, San Antonio, Texas
Speaker: Jorge Lara-Braud, Hispanic-American Institute, Austin, Texas

A DECADE OF SOCIAL ACTION—AN APPRAISAL OF THE 1960s
Presiding: Ron Linton, Washington
Speaker: Rev. Andrew J. Young, Atlanta, Ga.

WELFARE REFORM
Presiding: Donald S. Howard, University of California, Los Angeles
Speaker: John C. Montgomery, HEW Washington
Discussant: Mrs. Johnnie Tillmon, National Welfare Rights Organization, Los Angeles

PURCHASE OF SOCIAL SERVICES: WILL IT MAKE
THE DIFFERENCE IN DELIVERY OF SERVICES?
Presiding: Elaine Rothenberg, Virginia Commonwealth University,
Richmond, Va.
Speakers: Mary Lou Linton, Clinicare Corp., Milwaukee
John Erickson, Milwaukee
Rev. Benjamin Gjenvick, Milwaukee

COMMUNITY MENTAL HEALTH—THE DREAM,
THE DEVELOPMENT, AND ITS DELIVERY
Presiding: Fred DelliQuadri, University of Wisconsin, Milwaukee
Speakers: Bertram Brown, HEW, Chevy Chase, Md.
Robert Dovenmuehle, Dallas County Mental Health and Retardation
Center, Dallas.

AGING: THE GOLDEN YEARS—A TARNISHED MYTH
Presiding: Cecil Sheps, M.D., University of North Carolina, Chapel Hill
Speaker: Jack Ossofsky, National Council on the Aging, Washington

CHILD ADVOCACY
Presiding: Robert Quinn, National Institute of Mental Health, Chevy
Chase, Md.
Speaker: Paul Renger, De Paul Community Health Clinic, New Orleans

NEW CONCEPTS OF LEISURE TODAY (Lindeman Memorial Lecture)
Presiding: Lilian Sharpley, Voluntary Agencies, Hartsdale, N.Y.
Speaker: Max Kaplan, University of South Florida, Tampa

SUBURBIA CONFRONTS CHANGE
Presiding: Mrs. Corinne H. Wolfe, HEW, Washington
Panelists: Gerald Greenwald, Arlington Commission on Human Resources, Arlington, Va.
Stanley Mayer, Department of Human Resources, Arlington Co.,
Arlington, Va.
Mrs. Geraldine Hart, Family and Child Welfare, Arlington, Va.
John Robinson, Community Action Program, Arlington, Co., Arlington, Va.

DELIVERY OF SERVICES AS A VEHICLE FOR
PREVENTION IN CHILDREN
Presiding: Delwin Anderson, Veterans Administration, Washington
Speaker: Herbert I. Levit, Woodville State Hospital, Carnegie, Pa.
Discussant: Al Abrego, Guadalupe Community Center, San Antonio,
Texas

THE ROLE AS ADVOCATE
Presiding and panelist: Roosevelt Johnson, Jr., Dallas Urban League
Barbara Lusk, Community Council of Greater Dallas
Carolyn Blackburn, State Department of Welfare, Dallas
John Igo, State Department of Welfare, Dallas
Rudy Folsom, Dallas

THE DOUBLE BIND IN PUBLIC WELFARE:
HELP THAT STIGMATIZES
Presiding: Martin B. Loeb, University of Wisconsin, Madison
Speaker: Jeanne Mueller, University of Wisconsin, Madison
Discussant: Edward T. Weaver, Illinois Department of Children and Family Services, Springfield

THE MODEL CITIES PROGRAM: ASSUMPTIONS,
EXPERIENCE, IMPLICATIONS
Presiding: Edward H. Palmer, SPA/REDCO, Inc., Chicago
Speaker: Roland L. Warren, Brandeis University, Waltham, Mass.
Discussant: Juan J. Patlan, Mexican American Unity Council, San Antonio, Texas

SOCIAL MOVEMENTS: CRITERIA FOR SUCCESS OR FAILURE
Presiding: Mrs. Peggy Curtin, University Hospital, Columbus, Ohio
Speaker: William Whitaker, South Side Settlement House, Columbus, Ohio

WHO WILL FUND SOCIAL CHANGE?
Speaker: David Hunter, Stern Fund, New York
Reactor: C. F. McNeil, National Assembly for Social Policy and Development, New York

A NEW TOOL FOR SOCIAL CHANGE
Presiding: Adele Braude, New York
Speakers: Ralph Rogers, Public Television Foundation for North Texas, Dallas
Jim Lehrer, KERA-TV, Dallas

NEW PERSPECTIVES IN CROSS-CULTURAL COOPERATION IN
INTERNATIONAL AND NATIONAL SOCIAL WELFARE
Presiding: Ellen Winston, National Council for Homemaker-Home Health Aide Services, Raleigh, N.C.
Speakers: Mary Catherine Jennings, HEW, Washington
Genevieve W. Carter, University of Southern California, Los Angeles
William Miner, U.S. Department of State, Washington
Charles Prigmore, University of Alabama, Birmingham
Sponsor: U.S. Committee of ICSW

AUTHORS' FORUM: GROUPS
Presiding: John McDowell, National Council of the Churches of Christ in the U.S.A., New York
Speakers: William A. Apaka, Jr., Queen Liliuokalani Children's Center, Honolulu (paper coauthored by Gillman T. M. Chu, Tomly Komatsubara, Stephen K. Morse, David S. Nakamoto, Georgian K. Padeken, Joseph W. A. Richard, Betty Ann B. Rocha, and Gene K. Uno)
Maeda Galinsky, University of North Carolina, Chapel Hill
Janice H. Schopler, University of North Carolina, Chapel Hill
Paul Abels, Case Western Reserve University, Cleveland
Elliot V. Levin, North Shore Child Guidance Center, Manhasset, N.Y.

A RADICAL VIEW OF SOCIAL PROBLEMS AND SOLUTIONS
Presiding: Daniel Thursz, University of Maryland, Baltimore
Speaker: Eugene Guerrero, *Great Speckled Bird*, Atlanta, Ga.
Discussant: Alvin L. Schorr, New York University

THE WIN PROGRAM: AN APPRAISAL
Presiding: Fred Romero, Department of Labor, Washington
Speakers: William Ford, Michigan Employment Security Commission,
Detroit
Sheldon Steinberg, University Research Corp., Washington
Eunice O. Schatz, University Research Corp., Washington.

THE FUTURE OF SOCIAL SERVICES
Presiding: Mrs. Dorothy Bird Daly, Catholic University of America,
Washington
Speaker: Shirley Buttrick, HEW, Washington
Respondents: Don W. Russell, Virginia Department of Vocational
Rehabilitation, Richmond
Trina Rivera de Rios, Lehman College, New York
Discussant reactor: Martin B. Loeb, University of Wisconsin, Madison

PRIVATE FOUNDATIONS AND SOCIAL WELFARE—
A BETTER PARTNERSHIP
Presiding: C. F. McNeil, National Assembly for Social Policy and
Development, New York
Speaker: Samuel J. Silberman, Lois and Samuel Silberman Fund, New
York
Reactor: Edward Protz, Moody Foundation, Galveston, Texas

COMMUNITY MENTAL HEALTH: DILEMMAS AND
NEW DIRECTIONS AT LOCAL LEVEL
Presiding: Mrs. V. Besselle Attwell, Julia C. Hester House, Houston,
Texas
Speakers: Stanley J. Matek, Mental Health Planning, Milwaukee Co.,
Milwaukee
George G. Meyer, M.D., University of Texas Medical School, San
Antonio

AGENCY ADMINISTRATIVE EFFECTIVENESS IN
SOCIAL WORK PROGRAMS
Presiding: Edward Weaver, Illinois Department of Children and
Family Service, Springfield
Speakers: Phillip Fellin, University of Michigan, Ann Arbor
Arthur K. Berliner, National Institute of Mental Health Clinical
Research Center, Fort Worth, Texas
Reactor: Clark W. Blackburn, Family Service Association of America,
New York

ACTION RESEARCH: THE INTERPLAY OF THEORY,
RESEARCH, AND AGENCY PROGRAM DEVELOPMENT
> *Presiding:* E. F. Christman, Jr., Family Service Center of Houston and Harris County, Houston, Texas
> *Speakers:* Elam Nunnaly, University of Wisconsin, Milwaukee
> Sherod Miller, Augsburg College, Minneapolis
> Bruce Campbell, University of Minnesota
> Earl J. Beatt, Family and Children's Service, Minneapolis

MIDDLE MANAGEMENT—THE REAL INFLUENCE IN
ADMINISTRATION OF PROGRAMS
> *Presiding and discussant:* Bernard Neugeboren, Rutgers—the State University, New Brunswick, N.J.
> *Speakers:* Richard J. Bond, Department of Family and Children Services, Springfield, Ill.
> Nathan Markus, University of Toronto, Canada

RURAL LEGAL SERVICES—TEXAS LEADS THE WAY
> *Presiding:* Jack Otis, University of Texas, Austin
> *Speaker:* James De Anda, Corpus Christi, Texas
> *Reactor:* Jack Eisenberg, Austin, Texas

DEVELOPMENT OF DRUG ABUSE PROGRAMS FOR
UNDERPRIVILEGED BLACK AREAS
> *Presiding:* H. Jack Geiger, M.D., Tufts Medical College, Boston
> *Speaker:* Ashton Brisolara, Committee on Alcoholism and Drug Abuse for Greater New Orleans
> *Discussants:* Herbert Newman, New Orleans
> Curtis Johnson, New Orleans
> Martin Thibodeaux, New Orleans

REDEFINING THE ROLE AND FUNCTION OF
HOSPITAL SOCIAL WORK
> *Presiding:* Mrs. Marjorie Berlatsky, Jacobi Hospital, New York
> *Speaker:* Emanuel Hallowitz, University of Chicago

THE ROLE OF THE FAMILY IN THE
REHABILITATION PROCESS
> *Presiding:* Andrew Dobelstein, University of North Carolina, Chapel Hill
> *Speaker:* Leslie J. Shellhase, University of Alabama, University

ABORTION AND PREMATURITY
> *Presiding:* John Longres, Portland State University, Portland, Oreg.
> *Speaker:* S. Wayne Klein, M.D., Nassau County Medical Center, East Meadow, N.Y.

PUBLIC HEALTH, PUBLIC WELFARE, AND THE QUESTION
OF COMMUNITY CONTROL
> *Presiding:* Rosa C. Marin, University of Puerto Rico, Rio Piedras
> *Speakers:* Gary A. Lloyd, Tulane University, New Orleans

John Michael Daley, Jr., Tulane University, New Orleans
Discussant: Willard Olsen, HEW, Dallas

SPECIFIC URBAN ILLS: HOW MAY LEISURE BECOME
AN INTEGRAL PART OF EASING SUCH ILLS?
  Presiding: Norma J. Sims, YWCA, Hartsdale, N.Y.
  Speaker and moderator: Dorothea C. Spellman, University of Denver

HEAD START—AN INSTITUTIONAL CHANGE AGENT
  Presiding: Charles Farris, Barry College, Miami Shores, Fla.
  Speaker: Arthur Katz, University of Kansas, Lawrence
  Discussant: Fred Souflee, HEW, Washington

THE WHITE HOUSE CONFERENCE ON AGING: PLANS FOR
IMPLEMENTATION OF POLICY RECOMMENDATIONS
  Presiding: Mrs. Marian H. Miller, HEW, Washington
  Speakers: Willis W. Atwell, HEW, Washington
  Mrs. Donna Johnson, Governor's Committee on Aging, Austin, Texas
  Angela Dickey, Paris, Texas
  James Sherry, Governor's Committee on Aging, Austin, Texas

LET'S BE POLITICALLY PRACTICAL ABOUT
DELIVERING HUMAN WELFARE SERVICES
  Presiding: Raymond Gordon, Health and Welfare Association of
  Allegheny County, Pittsburgh
  Speaker: Leon L. Haley, University of Pittsburgh

EVALUATION OF MULTIPURPOSE NEIGHBORHOOD CENTER
  Presiding: Sherman Merle, Catholic University of America, Washington
  Speaker: Robert Wilson, University of Delaware, Newark, Del.
  Discussant: John Hiland, Jr., State Department of Heatlh and Social
  Services, Wilmington, Del.

FAMILY ADVOCACY
  Presiding: John E. Dearman, San Francisco Family Service Society,
  San Francisco
  Speakers: Mrs. Frances Brisbane, Family Service Association of America,
  Dallas
  Mrs. Ruth G. Joyner, Family Service of Memphis, Memphis, Tenn.
  John E. Dearman, San Francisco Family Service Society
  Discussant: Herman Curiel, Harris County Mental Health and Mental
  Retardation Center, Houston, Texas

ENLISTING COMMUNITY SUPPORT FOR CORRECTIONS
  Presiding: James T. Speight, Southeast Neighborhood House, Washington
  Speakers: Harry Walsh, D.C. Department of Corrections, Washington
  Allen M. Avery, D.C. Department of Corrections, Washington

THE AMERICAN INDIAN MOVEMENT: ISSUES,
PERSPECTIVES, AND DEVELOPMENTS
   Presiding: Robert Overacker, Indian Health Service, Tucson, Ariz.
   Panelists: Gordon Denipah, Tucson, Ariz.
   Anthony Purley, American Indian Culture Center, Los Angeles
   Paul Ortega, Intertribal Council of California, Sacramento, Calif.
   Mrs. Leah K. Manning, Intertribal Council of Nevada, Reno
   John Mackey, Council on Social Work Education, Vermillion, S. Dak.
   Ernest Stevens, Bureau of Indian Affairs, Washington

A MIDWAY PROGRESS REPORT ON SOCIAL WELFARE
AND REHABILITATION MANPOWER
   Presiding: Mrs. Jean Szaloczi Fine, HEW, Washington
   Speakers: Raymond A. Katzell, New York University
   Eugene Litwak, University of Michigan, Ann Arbor
   Robert Teare, University of Georgia, Athens

WHO WILL FUND SOCIAL CHANGE?
   Speakers: William Fitzpatrick, Legal Aid Society of Albuquerque,
   Albuquerque, N. Mex.
   Bernard Wohl, South Side Settlement House, Columbus, Ohio

EXPANDING HOUSING THROUGH A HOUSING
DEVELOPMENT CORPORATION
   Presiding: John H. Ballard, Welfare Council of Metropolitan Chicago
   Speaker: Edward H. Palmer, SPA/REDCO, Inc., Chicago

PLANNING THE NATION'S ECONOMY (Lindeman Memorial Lecture)
   Presiding: Henry B. Ollendorff, Council of International Programs for
   Youth Leaders and Social Workers, Cleveland
   Speakers: Michael Harrington, New York
   Harold Demsetz, University of Chicago

WORLD POPULATION DEVELOPMENTS:
IMPLICATIONS FOR SOCIAL WELFARE
   Presiding: Mrs. Katherine B. Oettinger, Canterbury, Va.
   Speakers: Philip M. Hauser, University of Chicago
   Halvor Gille, United Nations, New York
Sponsor: U.S. Committee of ICSW

AUTHORS' FORUM: EDUCATION
   Presiding: Darwin Palmiere, University of Michigan, Ann Arbor
   Speakers: J. R. Pearman, Florida State University, Tallahassee
   Morton S. Perlmutter, University of Wisconsin, Madison
   Imogene S. Young, University of Illinois, Chicago

CHICANO APPRAISAL AND CRITIQUE OF
SOCIAL WELFARE SYSTEMS
   Speakers and planners: Alejandro Garcia, National Association of
   Social Workers, New York

Manuel Soto, HEW, Dallas
Juan J. Acosta, HEW, Dallas

MANPOWER PROGRAMS AND MINORITY GROUPS
Speakers: Mrs. Sirel Forster, East Central Area Welfare Planning Council, Los Angeles
Juan Ramos, National Institute of Mental Health, Chevy Chase, Md.
Reactors: Frances Arrendondo, Dallas Community College
Berta Hernandez, Houston, Texas
Rene Martinez, Dallas Community Relations Commission

CAN YOUTH WORK WITHIN THE SYSTEM?
Presiding: Jeanne Mueller, University of Wisconsin, Madison
Speakers: Michael Garazini, White House Conference on Youth, St. Louis
Mrs. John D. Crain, Wisconsin League of Women Voters, Beloit
Mary J. Denton, Wisconsin Department of Health and Social Services, Madison

FAMILY APPROACH TO TREATMENT OF ALCOHOLISM
Presiding: Mrs. Grace W. Bell, National Institute of Mental Health, Chevy Chase, Md.
Speaker: Merrilee Atkins, Family Service of the Cincinnati Area
Reactor: Mrs. Grace W. Bell, National Institute of Mental Health, Chevy Chase, Md.

NEW WAYS TO DELIVER SOCIAL SERVICE TO RURAL AREAS
Presiding: Orlando Romero, Denver Department of Public Welfare
Speakers: Kenneth R. Russell, Colorado State Hospital, Pueblo
Christian E. Hinz, Colorado State Hospital, Pueblo
Orlando Martinez, Alamosa, Colo.
Edward Montoya, Colorado State Hospital, Pueblo

FACTORS IN HETEROSEXUAL DEVELOPMENT OF
ADOLESCENT BLIND MALES
Presiding: Euzelia C. Smart, North Carolina Memorial Hospital, Chapel Hill
Speakers: Marcialito Cam, Department of Public Welfare, Philadelphia
Merle Broberg, Bryn Mawr College, Bryn Mawr, Pa.

CONSUMER CONTROL AND PUBLIC ACCOUNTABILITY:
THE CASE OF NEIGHBORHOOD HEALTH CENTERS
Presiding: Fred Sutherland, Tulane University, New Orleans
Speaker: Peter Kong New, Tufts University School of Medicine, Boston

DEVELOPMENT OF DRUG ABUSE PROGRAMS FOR
UNDERPRIVILEGED MINORITY GROUPS IN THE SOUTHWEST
Presiding: Kathryn Fritz, National Institute of Mental Health, Dallas
Speaker: Eduardo Villarreal, Clinical Research Center, San Antonio, Texas

THE RESEARCH FIELD PLACEMENT IN SOCIAL WORK
Speaker: Melvin N. Brenner, University of Wisconsin, Madison

USE OF LEISURE IN SENIOR COMMUNITY SERVICE AIDES
PROJECTS OF AARP AND NRTA
Presiding and speaking: Edwin C. Doulin, American Association of
Retired Persons—National Retired Teachers Association, Washington
Discussants: Mary Lou Engram, Cleveland
Robert Yzaguirre, Good Neighbor Settlement House, Brownsville,
Texas

THE PRESENT ROLE OF STATE AGENCIES ON AGING
Presiding: H. S. Geldon, HEW, Dallas
Speakers: Charles E. Wells, HEW, Washington
Mrs. Carter Clopton, Governor's Committee on Aging, Austin, Texas

CHILD NEGLECT IN RURAL APPALACHIA
Presiding: Abraham S. Levine, HEW, Washington
Speaker: Christine DeSaix, University of Georgia, Athens
Discussant: Jirina Polivka, Catholic University of America, Washington

REAPPRAISAL OF HEALTH AND WELFARE SERVICES—
A CASE STUDY
Presiding: Morton Coleman, University of Pittsburgh
Speaker: Raymond Gordon, Health and Welfare Association of Al-
legheny County, Pittsburgh

CONSTRUCTING A COMMUNITY SERVICE DELIVERY SYSTEM
Presiding: Maurine Currin, Texas Department of Public Welfare,
Austin
Speaker: Ruth Pauley, HEW, Washington

EMERGING ORGANIZATIONAL PATTERNS TO
COMBAT RACISMS
Presiding: Karim Childs, Parkway Community House, Chicago
Speaker: H. Frederick Brown, University of Illinois, Chicago
Panelists: Jerome Stevenson, Community Fund, Chicago
Benjamin Finley, Afro-Amer Family and Community Services, Chicago

THE "NEW" SOCIAL WORK STUDENT
Presiding: Eddie C. Thompkins, Jr., Welfare Council of Metropolitan
Chicago
Speaker: Lynne Riehman, Bronx State Hospital, New York
Panelists: Arnita Boswell, University of Chicago
DeWana Gray, University of Chicago

AUTHORS' FORUM: FAMILY
Presiding: Charline J. Birkins, Colorado Department of Social Services,
Denver
Speakers: Alice H. Collins, Field Study of the Neighborhood Family
Day Care System, Portland, Oreg.

Col. Jack A. Davis, USAF Medical Center, Lackland Air Force Base, Texas
Charles Garvin, University of Michigan, Ann Arbor
Richard B. Joelson, North Shore Guidance Center, Manhassett, N.Y.

GENERAL SESSION: THE ROLE OF STATE GOVERNMENT IN PUBLIC WELFARE
Presiding: Nelson C. Jackson, National Association of Social Workers, New York
Speaker: Hon. John J. Gilligan, Governor, State of Ohio, Columbus
Presentation of NCSW Awards and 50-Year Plaques

TUESDAY, MAY 18

GENERAL SESSION: SOCIAL REVOLUTION IN THE SOUTHWEST
Presiding: Santos Reyes, Jr., University of Texas, Austin

ROLE OF PUBLIC AND PRIVATE AGENCIES IN LEADERSHIP FOR PROGRAMS FOR THE ELDERLY
Presiding: D. Ned Linegar, National Retired Teachers Association–American Association of Retired Persons, Dallas
Speaker: Elias Cohen, University of Pennsylvania, Philadelphia
Discussants: Clarence Lambright, HEW, Dallas
Herbert Shore, M.D., Dallas Home for Jewish Aged
Cosponsors: American Association of Retired Persons; National Retired Teachers Association; American Home Economics Association; American Public Welfare Association (Group Meeting 1); Family Service Association of America (Group Meeting 1); the Salvation Army (Group Meeting 1)

THE ADVOCATE ROLE OF CHILD PROTECTIVE SERVICES
Presiding: Maurine Currin, Texas Department of Public Welfare, Austin
Speaker: John T. McTigue, Nassau County Department of Social Services, Mineola, N.Y.
Discussant: Phillip Dolinger, Hennepin County Welfare Department, Minneapolis
Cosponsors: American Humane Association, Children's Division; American Legion, National Commission on Children and Youth; American Public Welfare Association (Group Meeting 2); Child Welfare League of America (Group Meeting 1); National Council on Crime and Delinquency

MUSHROOMING SERVICES FOR CHILDREN—HOW TO DELIVER QUALITY
Presiding: Ellen Winston, National Council for Homemaker-Home Health Aide Services, Raleigh, N.C.
Speakers: Mrs. Deborah B. Leighton, Great Hartford Community Planning, West Hartford, Conn.
Norman W. Paget, Children's Home of Cincinnati
Sylvia Mitchell, State Department of Public Welfare, Dallas

Cosponsors: Child Welfare League of America (Group Meeting 2); Florence Crittenton Association of America (Group Meeting 1); National Council for Homemaker-Home Health Aide Services (Group Meeting 1)

A NEW FOCUS ON MOTIVATION: BILINGUAL
EDUCATION FOR CHILDREN
> *Presiding:* Mrs. Eunice Garcia, Child and Family Service, Austin, Texas
> *Speakers:* Victor Curz-Aedo, Texas Education Agency, Austin
> Mrs. Frances Vargas, Creedmoor Elementary Bilingual School, Travis Co., Texas

Cosponsors: Child Welfare League of America (Group Meeting 3); Florence Crittenton Association of America (Group Meeting 2); National Council for Homemaker-Home Health Aide Services (Group Meeting 2)

AGENCY MERGERS—A BURNING QUESTION
> *Presiding:* John McDowell, National Council of the Churches of Christ in the U.S.A., New York
> *Speaker:* Charles Zibbell, Council of Jewish Federations and Welfare Funds, New York
> *Discussants:* Rev. James H. Garland, Catholic Charities, Dayton, Ohio
> Dorothy Mundt, Lutheran Council of the U.S.A., New York

Cosponsors: Council of Jewish Federations and Welfare Funds; National Conference of Catholic Charities; Committee on Social Welfare, National Council of Churches of Christ in the U.S.A.

CHANGES IN SOCIAL WORK EDUCATION:
IMPLICATIONS FOR PRACTICE
> *Presiding:* C. F. McNeil, National Assembly for Social Policy and Development, New York
> *Speaker:* Arnulf M. Pins, Council on Social Work Education, New York

Sponsor: Council on Social Work Education

ORGANIZING FOR UNIVERSAL DAY CARE SERVICES
> *Presiding:* Theodore Taylor, Day Care and Child Development Center of America, Washington
> *Panelists:* Alfred J. Kahn, Columbia University, New York
> Mrs. Thelma Peters, Massachusetts Head Start Parents, Dorchester
> Kenton Williams, HEW, Kansas City, Mo.

Sponsor: Day Care and Child Development Council of America

EDUCATION FOR CHANGE—A NEW PATTERN FOR
STAFF DEVELOPMENT
> *Presiding:* Jack Otis, Dean, University of Texas, Austin
> *Speaker:* Pauline Cohen, Family Service Association of America, New York
> *Discussants:* Mrs. Lucille Levitan, United Charities of Chicago
> Henry Ovadia, Jewish Family Service, Cincinnati

Sponsor: Family Service Association of America (Group Meeting 2)

DAUGHTERS-PARENTS INTERACTION GROUPS AS
SOLUTIONS TO PREGNANCY CRISIS
  Presiding: Nic Knoph, Florence Crittenton Association of America,
  Knoxville, Tenn.
  Panelists: Mrs. Camille W. Smith, Florence Crittenton Services, Houston,
  Texas
  Mrs. Marie Jacobson, Florence Crittenton Services, Houston, Texas
  Mrs. Marguerite Papademetriou, Florence Crittenton Services, Houston,
  Texas
  Discussants: Mrs. Norma Robinson, Florence Crittenton Services, Hous-
  ton, Texas
  Sidney Fuqua, Florence Crittenton Services, Houston, Texas
  Rev. Larry D. Spencer, Florence Crittenton Services, Houston, Texas
Cosponsors: Florence Crittenton Association of America (Group Meeting
3); Child Welfare League of America (Group Meeting 4); National Council
of Illegitimacy (Group Meeting 1)

EMERGING ROLE OF STATE ORGANIZATIONS IN
HEALTH AND WELFARE
  Presiding: Warren B. Goodwin, Texas United Community Services,
  Austin
  Speaker: Richard S. Bachman, Community Services of Pennsylvania,
  Harrisburg
Sponsor: National Association for Statewide Health and Welfare

BLACK RELIGION: SEEDBED FOR SOCIAL ACTION
  Presiding: Larry D. Hybertson, Brandeis University, Waltham, Mass.
  Speakers: Timothy Smith, Johns Hopkins University, Baltimore
  Michael Haynes, Massachusetts State Board of Parole, Boston
Sponsor: National Association of Christians in Social Welfare

NASW—THE PROFESSION IN ACTION
National Social Worker of the Year Award presented by Dr. Allan D. Wade,
President, National Association of Social Workers, to Mrs. Edna Wagner,
Director, Medical Social Services, M .D. Anderson Hospital and Tumor
Institute, University of Texas, Houston
  Presiding: A. Gerald Spaulding, Suicide Prevention of Dallas
  Speakers: Chauncey A. Alexander, National Association of Social
  Workers, New York
  Mitchell I. Ginsberg, Columbia University, New York
Sponsor: National Association of Social Workers

WICS: VOLUNTEERS IN COALITION
  Presiding: Mrs. Maxwell H. Stokes, National Council of Catholic
  Women, Washington
Cosponsors: National Council of Jewish Women; WICS Coalition

OUR OLDER POPULATION: A NATIONAL RESOURCE
AND/OR A SOCIETAL PROBLEM
  Presiding: Hobart C. Jackson, Stephen Smith Home for the Aged,
  Philadelphia

Speaker: Charles E. Odell, U.S. Department of Labor, Washington
Cosponsors: National Council on the Aging; American Foundation for the Blind

ALCOHOLISM IN THE PUBLIC DOMAIN
Presiding: Mrs. Bernice Shepard, Community Council of Greater New York
Speaker: John R. Butler, New York State Department of Mental Hygiene, Albany
Sponsor: National Council on Alcoholism

PREVENTION OF UNWED PREGNANCY
Presiding: Mrs. Marcus Ginsburg, Fort Worth, Texas
Speaker: Robert Beavers, M.D., University of Texas, Dallas
Reactors: Kenneth Pepper, Pastor Counseling and Education Center, Dallas
Sid Fitzwater, United High School Council, Fort Worth, Texas
Mrs. Robert J. Stout, Fort Worth Council of Parents and Teachers, Fort Worth, Texas
Cosponsors: National Council on Illegitimacy (Group Meeting 2); Child Welfare League of America (Group Meeting 5); Family Service Association of America (Group Meeting 3); Florence Crittenton Association of America (Group Meeting 4); the Salvation Army (Group Meeting 2); the Volunteers of America

ETHNIC CONSCIOUSNESS, RESPONSIBILITY, AND
THE SOCIAL SERVICES
Presiding: Antonio A. Medina, United Presbyterian Health, Education, and Welfare Association, Espanola, N. Mex.
Speaker: Tomas Atencio, La Academia de la Nueva Raza, Dixon, N. Mex.
Sponsor: United Presbyterian Health, Education, and Welfare Association, Southwest Region

VOLUNTEERS IN COURTS AND CORRECTION:
THE EMERGING PARTNERSHIP OF
PROFESSIONALS AND VOLUNTEERS
Presiding: Mrs. Elliott Jacobson, Association of Volunteer Bureaus of America, Kansas City, Mo.
Speakers: Keith J. Leenhouts, Volunteers in Probation, Royal Oak, Mich.
James Jorgensen, University of Denver
Sponsor: United Way of America–Association of Volunteer Bureaus

UNICEF: A TWO-WAY RELATIONSHIP
Presiding: Hon. Sarah T. Hughs, Dallas
Speakers: Olcutt Saunders, U.S. Committee for UNICEF
Michael N. Scelsi, New York
Sponsor: U.S. Committee for UNICEF

TRANSPORTATION FOR THE ELDERLY AND HANDICAPPED
   Presiding: Lora G. Buckingham, National Retired Teachers Association–
   American Association of Retired Persons, Washington
   Speakers: Richard Andryshak, U.S. Department of Transportation,
   Washington
   Rhoda Gellman, National Easter Seal Society for Crippled Children
   and Adults, Chicago
Cosponsors: American Association of Retired Persons (Group Meeting 1);
National Retired Teachers Association (Group Meeting 1); American
Public Welfare Association; National Easter Seal Society for Crippled
Children and Adults (Group Meeting 1); the Salvation Army (Group
Meeting 1); United Way of America (Group Meeting 1)

NEEDS AND ASPIRATIONS OF PUERTO RICANS
   Presiding: Julian Rivera, Association of Puerto Rican Social Service
   Workers
   Speakers: Margarita Olivieri, Association of Puerto Rican Social Service
   Workers, New York
   Lijia Vasquez de Rodriguez, University of Puerto Rico, Rio Piedras
   Julio Morales, Jr., City University of New York
Cosponsors: Association of Puerto Rican Social Service Workers; Colegio
de Trabajadores Sociales de Puerto Rico

NEW TRENDS IN ADOPTION: A CHALLENGE TO THE AGENCY
   Presiding: Mrs. Elizabeth Philbrick, Colorado Department of Social
   Services, Denver
   Speakers: Ruth E. Reynolds, Denver Department of Welfare
   John P. Califf, Lutheran Service Society of Colorado, Denver
   Discussant: Mrs. Ethel G. Rollins, Denver
Cosponsors: Child Welfare League of America (Group Meeting 1); Florence
Crittenton Association of America (Group Meeting 1)

A NATIONAL CHILDREN'S LOBBY—OMBUDSMEN FOR
CHILDREN'S SERVICES
   Presiding: Fernando G. Torgerson, University of Texas, Arlington
   Speaker: Fred DelliQuadri, University of Wisconsin, Milwaukee
Cosponsors: Child Welfare League of America (Group Meeting 2); Florence
Crittenton Association of America (Group Meeting 2); National Council for
Homemaker-Home Health Services (Group Meeting 1)

CHANGING ATTITUDES TOWARD TRANSRACIAL ADOPTION
   Presiding: Sproesser Wynn, Fort Worth, Texas
   Speaker: Peter Forsythe, State Department of Social Services, Lansing,
   Mich.
Cosponsors: Child Welfare League of America (Group Meeting 3); Florence
Crittenton Association of America (Group Meeting 3)

ETHNIC MINORITIES IN SOCIAL WORK EDUCATION:
ISSUES, TRENDS, AND DEVELOPMENTS
   Presiding: John F. Longres, Portland State University, Portland, Oreg.

Speaker: Carl A. Scott, Council on Social Work Education, New York
Cosponsor: Council on Social Work Education

PLANNING, STRATEGY, AND ACTION MEETING
Presiding: Theodore Taylor, Day Care and Child Development Center of America, Washington
Speakers: Alfred J. Kahn, Columbia University, New York
Mrs. Thelma Peters, Massachusetts Head Start Parents, Dorchester
Kenton Williams, HEW, Kansas City, Mo.
Sponsor: Day Care and Child Development Council of America

WHAT MAKES SOCIAL WORKERS GROW?

CAN AGENCIES RISK IT?
Presiding: Earl J. Beatt, Family and Children's Service, Minneapolis
Speaker: Louise Koch, Family and Children's Service, Minneapolis
Sponsor: Family Service Association of America (Group Meeting 1)

A NEWSMAN LOOKS AT STATE HEALTH AND

WELFARE ORGANIZATIONS
Presiding: Rabbi David Jacobson, Temple Beth-El, San Antonio, Texas
Speaker: Bert Holmes, Dallas *Times Herald*
Sponsor: National Association for Statewide Health and Welfare

RACISM IN SOCIAL WORK PRACTICE
Presiding, discussant, and reactor: Albert T. T. Cook, Jr., Houston, Texas
Speakers. Mrs. Robert W. Claytor, YWCA of the U.S.A., New York
Mrs. Elizabeth Jackson, YWCA of the U.S.A., New York
Sponsor: National Association of Social Workers (Group Meeting 1)

CERTIFYING COMPETENCE IN SOCIAL WORK PRACTICE
Presiding: Mrs. Ruth I. Knee, National Institute of Mental Health, Chevy Chase, Md.
Speakers: Lewis W. Carr, Catholic University of America, Washington
Lillian D. Terris, Professional Examination Service, New York
Sponsor: National Association of Social Workers (Group Meeting 2)

DEVELOPING AN ACCREDITATION PLAN FOR

HOMEMAKER-HOME HEALTH AIDE SERVICES
Presiding: Ellen Winston, National Council for Homemaker-Home Health Aide Services, Raleigh, N.C.
Speaker: Peter G. Meek, National Health Council, New York
Discussants: Joe M. Jenkins, Child and Family Services, Chicago
Donald L. Schmid, Public Welfare Board of North Dakota, Bismarck
Cosponsors: National Council for Homemaker-Home Health Aide Services (Group Meeting 2); American Association of Retired Persons (Group Meeting 2); American Home Economics Association; Child Welfare League of America (Group Meeting 4); Family Service Association of America (Group Meeting 2); National Easter Seal Society for Crippled Children and Adults (Group Meeting 2); National Retired Teachers Association (Group Meeting 2)

DIVERSION OF JUVENILES FROM THE CRIMINAL
JUSTICE SYSTEM
>   *Presiding:* Carl Flaxman, Dallas
>   *Speakers:* Fred Howlett, National Council on Crime and Delinquency,
>   Austin, Texas
>   John M. Freas, Wake Forest University, Winston-Salem, N.C.
>   Russ Delatour, Community Council of Greater Dallas, Dallas

Cosponsors: National Council on Crime and Delinquency; Child Welfare
League of America (Group Meeting 5); Family Service Association of America (Group Meeting 3); the Volunteers of America (Group Meeting 1)

A LOOK AT SERVICES EXTENDED BY PUBLIC AGENCIES:
LEGAL MEDICAL, AND SOCIAL
>   *Presiding:* Lt. Col. Belle Leach, Volunteers of America, New York
>   *Speaker:* Charles P. Gershenson, HEW, Washington

Cosponsors: National Council on Illegitimacy; Child Welfare League of
America (Group Meeting 6); Family Service Association of America (Group
Meeting 4); Florence Crittenton Association of America (Group Meeting 4);
the Salvation Army (Group Meeting 2); the Volunteers of America (Group
Meeting 2)

MY BARRIO IS MY HOME: SELF-DETERMINATION AT THE
NEIGHBORHOOD LEVEL—BARRIO-GHETTO-NEIGHBORHOOD
>   *Presiding:* John S. Chavez, Dallas
>   *Speaker:* Antonio Tinajero, National Hispanic Resources Center, San
>   Antonio, Texas
>   *Discussants:* Clarence Laws, Office for Civil Rights, Dallas
>   John Belindo, National Indian Leadership Training Program, Albu-
>   querque, N. Mex.
>   Andrew Gallegas, National Federation of Settlements and Neighbor-
>   hood Centers

Sponsor: National Federation of Settlements and Neighborhood Centers

INFORMATION AND REFERRAL ROUND TABLE: A ROUNDUP
OF FEDERAL INFORMATION AND REFERRAL PROGRAMS—
IMPLICATIONS FOR THE LOCAL SCENE
>   *Presiding:* Mrs. Corazon Esteva Doyle, Phoenix Community Council,
>   Phoenix, Ariz.
>   *Speaker:* Alfred J. Kahn, Columbia University, New York
>   *Discussant:* Manuel F. Fimbres, Social Planning Council of Santa Clara
>   Co., Santa Clara, Calif.
>   *Speaker:* Lt. Col. Frank Montalvo, Department of the Army, Wash-
>   ington

Sponsor: United Way of America (Group Meeting 2)

EDUCATING BACCALAUREATE SOCIAL WORKERS FOR
PRACTICE: A REPORT OF THE VETERANS ADMINISTRATION–
SYRACUSE UNIVERSITY CURRICULUM PROJECT
>   *Presiding:* Delwin M. Anderson, Veterans Administration, Washington
>   *Speakers:* Thomas Briggs, Syracuse University, Syracuse, N.Y.

Lester J. Glick, Syracuse University, Syracuse, N.Y.
Sponsor: Veterans Administration

VIOLENCE AND THE AGING
Presiding: D. Ned Linegar, National Retired Teachers Association–
American Association of Retired Persons, Dallas
Speakers: Daniel Schorr, Austin College, Sherman, Texas
Mrs. Ola Moore, North Texas State University Center for Studies on
Aging, Denton, Texas
Charles Hunter, Bishop College, Dallas
Lt. A. M. Eberhardt, Police Department, Dallas
Cosponsors: American Association of Retired Persons (Group Meeting 1);
National Retired Teachers Association (Group Meeting 1); National Council
on Crime and Delinquency (Group Meeting 1); the Salvation Army (Group
Meeting 1)

FOSTER PARENTS ASSOCIATION: WHAT ARE THEY AND
WHAT ARE THEY GOING TO BE?
Presiding: Mrs. Betty Althaus, De Pelchin Faith Home, Houston, Texas
Speaker: Beatrice Garrett, HEW, Washington
Panelists: Mr. and Mrs. Joe Barry, Children's Bureau, Dallas
Mr. and Mrs. James Oliver, Lena Pope Children's Home, Fort Worth,
Texas
Mr. and Mrs. Larry Young, Lena Pope Children's Home, Fort Worth,
Texas
Sponsor: Child Welfare League of America (Group Meeting 1)

THE ROLE OF THE AGENCY BOARD AS ADVOCATE
FOR CHILDREN
Presiding: Mrs. Ralph Hanna, Austin, Texas
Speakers: Mrs. Irwin Lieb, Austin, Texas
Mrs. Harold C. Yates, Waco, Texas
Jerome Meyer, Houston, Texas
Cosponsors: Child Welfare League of America (Group Meeting 2); Florence
Crittenton Association of America (Group Meeting 1); National Council
for Homemaker-Home Health Aide Service (Group Meeting 1)

PREPARATION FOR INTERNAL AND EXTERNAL ADVOCACY
Presiding: Mary Margaret Carr, Child Service and Family Counseling
Center, Atlanta, Ga.
Speakers: Jack Howley, Child Service and Family Counseling Center,
Atlanta, Ga.
Tim Ramey, Family Counseling Service, Seattle
Mrs. Frances Brisbane, Family Service Association of America, Dallas
Cosponsors: Family Service Association of America (Group Meeting 1);
Travelers Aid Association of America

NEW USES OF MATERNITY HOME RESOURCES
Presiding: Seth Low Weeks, Florence Crittenton Association of America,
Chattanooga, Tenn.
Speakers: Mrs. Lydia Kelly, Los Angeles Florence Crittenton Services

Mrs. Regene Schroeder, Florence Crittenton Services of Arizona, Phoenix
Cosponsors: Florence Crittenton Association of America (Group Meeting 2); National Council on Illegitimacy (Group Meeting 1)

FEDERAL REVENUE SHARING—COMMUNITY DEVELOPMENT
    Presiding: Warren B. Goodwin, Texas United Community Services, Austin
    Speaker: Floyd H. Hyde, U.S. Department of Housing and Urban Development, Washington
Sponsor: National Association for Statewide Health and Welfare

BEACON HILL TO ROXBURY: ADMINISTRATIVE TENSIONS
RESULTING FROM AGENCY COMMITMENTS TO
SOCIAL ACTION
    Presiding: Alan R. Gruber, Boston Children's Services, Boston
    Speakers: Larry D. Hybertson, Brandeis University, Waltham, Mass.
    Keith Rawlins, Public Welfare Department, Commonwealth of Massachusetts, Quincy
    Discussant: Charles Bates, Boston Children's Services, Boston
Sponsor: National Association of Christians in Social Welfare

EVALUATING AGENCIES
    Presiding: Lorenzo H. Traylor, Equal Employment Opportunity Commission, Los Angeles
    Speaker: Rev. Bernard J. Coughlin, St. Louis University, St. Louis
Sponsor: National Association of Social Workers

PROGRAM AND ISSUES AT THE ICJCS
    Presiding: Earnest Siegel, Julius Schepps Community Center, Dallas
    Speaker: Arnulf M. Pins, Council on Social Work Education, New York
Sponsor: National Conference of Jewish Communal Service

APPROACHES TO COORDINATED TRAINING AND DELIVERY
OF HOMEMAKER-HOME HEALTH AIDE SERVICES
    Presiding: Inez Haynes, University of Texas, Austin
    Speakers: Brahna Trager, San Geronimo, Calif.
    Richard L. D. Morse, Kansas State University, Manhattan
Cosponsors: National Council for Homemaker-Home Health Aide Services (Group Meeting 2); American Association of Retired Persons (Group Meeting 2); American Home Economics Association; Child Welfare League of America (Group Meeting 3); Family Service Association of America (Group Meeting 2); National Easter Seal Society for Crippled Children and Adults; National Retired Teachers Association (Group Meeting 2)

DIVERSION OF JUVENILES FROM THE CRIMINAL
JUSTICE SYSTEM
    Presiding: Carl Flaxman, Dallas
    Panelists: Fred Howlett, National Council on Crime and Delinquency, Austin, Texas

John M. Freas, Wake Forest University, Winston-Salem, N.C.
Russ Delatour, Community Council of Greater Dallas, Dallas
Cosponsors: National Council on Crime and Delinquency (Group Meeting 2); Child Welfare League of America (Group Meeting 4); Family Service Association of America (Group Meeting 3); the Volunteers of America (Group Meeting 1)

A LOOK AT SERVICES EXTENDED BY PUBLIC AGENCIES:
LEGAL, MEDICAL, AND SOCIAL
Presiding: Lt. Col. Belle Leach, Volunteers of America, New York
Speaker: Charles P. Gershenson, HEW, Washington
Cosponsors: National Council on Illegitimacy (Group Meeting 2); Child Welfare League of America (Group Meeting 5); Family Service Association of America (Group Meeting 4); Florence Crittenton Association of America (Group Meeting 3); the Salvation Army (Group Meeting 2); the Volunteers of America (Group Meeting 2)

VETERANS ADMINISTRATION DEVELOPMENTS
RELEVANT TO SOCIAL WORK
Presiding: Delwin M. Anderson, Veterans Administration, Washington
Panelists: Claire R. Lustman, Veterans Administration, Washington
John R. Reida, Veterans Administration, Washington
Sponsor: Veterans Administration

SOCIAL ISSUES FORUM
Presiding: Ruth I. Knee, National Institute of Mental Health, Chevy Chase, Md.

WEDNESDAY, MAY 19

GENERAL SESSION: HEALTH CARE—NO TIME FOR
A MODEL T SYSTEM
Presiding: Sue W. Spencer, University of Tennessee, Nashville
Speaker: Leonard Woodcock, International Union, United Automobile Workers of America, Detroit

NEW PLAYERS IN THE POLITICAL GAME
Presiding: Duane W. Beck, Community Council of the Atlanta Area, Atlanta, Ga.
Speakers: Mrs. June Cofer, Clark College, Atlanta, Ga.
Robert Waymer, Atlanta University, Atlanta, Ga.

THE AMERICAN ECONOMY IN 1971 AND ITS IMPACT ON
SOCIAL WELFARE PROGRAMS (Lindeman Memorial Lecture)
Presiding: Ewan Clague, Washington
Speaker: Charles C. Holt, Sr., Urban Institute, Washington

CLINICAL AND TEACHING APPLICATION OF
MULTIMEDIUM TECHNOLOGIES IN
SOCIAL SERVICE PROGRAMS
Presiding: James McBride, Aboussie Electronic Systems, Dallas

Speakers: Irving A. Kraft, M.D., Baylor College of Medicine, Houston
Robert Del Vecchio, Sandos Pharmaceutical Company-Wonder, Inc.,
Hanover, N.J.
Wayne Holtzman, University of Texas, Austin

POLITICKING FOR SOCIAL WORKERS
Presiding: Halloway C. Sells, Seven Hills Neighborhood House, Inc.,
Cincinnati
Speakers: John Hansan, State Department of Public Welfare, Colum-
bus, Ohio
Hon. Howard N. Lee, Chapel Hill, N.C.
John Alaniz, San Antonio, Texas

PROPOSED NATIONAL HEALTH PROGRAMS
Presiding: Mottram Torre, M.D., De Paul Community Mental Health
Clinic, New Orleans
Panelists: James H. Sammons, M.D., Baytown, Texas
Robert E. Toomey, Greenville, S.C.

NEW PATTERNS OF RECREATIONAL SERVICES
Presiding: Alexander J. Allen, Jr., National Urban League, New York
Speakers: R. Edward Lee, Community Church of New York
Ollie A. Randall, New York State Recreational Council for the Elderly,
New York
Louis B. Houston, Department of Parks and Recreation, City of Dallas

SOCIAL PLANNING IN NEW TOWNS
Presiding: Virginia Tannar, HEW, Washington
Speaker: James I. Shelton, New Dimensions in Training, Philadelphia

MANPOWER FOR SOCIAL SERVICES AND
INCOME MAINTENANCE
Presiding: Frank C. Caracciolo, HEW, Washington
Speakers: Mrs. Dorothy Bird Daly, Catholic University of America,
Washington
Joseph B. Bracy, HEW, Washington
Discussant: Rodolpho B. Sanchez, San Diego State College, San Diego,
Calif.

SYSTEMATIC APPROACH TO THE ANALYSIS AND
DEVELOPMENT OF SOCIAL POLICIES
Presiding: Charles P. Gershenson, HEW, Washington
Speaker: David G. Gil, Brandeis University, Waltham, Mass.

THE PRESIDENTIAL COMMISSION: INSTRUMENT OF
CHANGE OR CONTROL
Presiding: Chauncey A. Alexander, National Association of Social
Workers, New York
Speaker: Thomas Wolanin, Harvard University, Cambridge, Mass.

AMERICA, FALLING APART?
Speaker: Jack Conway, Common Cause, Washington

TOWARD INTERNATIONAL SOCIAL WELFARE—RECENT
TRENDS IN PROVIDING SOCIAL SECURITY AND
SOCIAL SERVICES
Presiding: Jay L. Roney, HEW, Baltimore
Speakers: Paul Fisher, HEW, Washington
Dorothy Lally, HEW, Washington
Sponsor: U.S. Committee of ICSW

AUTHORS' FORUM: CORRECTIONS
Presiding: Andrew G. Freeman, Philadelphia Urban League, Phila-
delphia
Speakers: Harris Chaiklin, University of Maryland, Baltimore
Ronald A. Feldman, Washington University, St. Louis
Sheldon D. Rose, University of Wisconsin, Madison
Cordell H. Thomas, Temple University, Philadelphia

AFTER THE PERUVIAN EARTHQUAKE, WHAT?
Discussion leader: Olcutt Sanders, UNICEF, New York
Sponsor: U.S. Committee for UNICEF

THE WORKER WITHIN THE SYSTEM: THE SOCIAL
WORKER'S DILEMMA
Presiding: Hobart A. Burch, United Church of Christ, New York
Speaker: Roy H. Schlachter, Cleveland Metropolitan General Hospital,
Cleveland Heights, Ohio
Panelists: Mrs. Rachel Ghiselin, Houston, Texas
Mrs. Kilby Lee Jayne, Houston, Texas
Mrs. Jewel E. Kelley, Houston, Texas
Reactors: Mrs. Josephine Brown, Dallas
Mrs. Ophelia Garay, San Antonio, Texas

GUARANTEED ANNUAL POVERTY: A CLIENT'S VIEW OF
INCOME-MAINTENANCE PROGRAMS FOR OLDER ADULTS
Presiding: Mrs. Frances Lomas Feldman, University of Southern Cali-
fornia, Los Angeles
Speaker: Molly Piontkowski, Committee for the Rights of the Disabled,
Los Angeles
Panelist: Norma E. Robertson, Lomita, Calif.

NATIONAL MANPOWER LEGISLATION
Presiding: Jules Berman, University of Maryland, Baltimore
Speakers: Malcolm R. Lovell, Jr., U.S. Department of Labor, Wash-
ington
Raleigh C. Hobson, Department of Employment and Social Services,
Baltimore

POVERTY STANDARDS
Presiding: Genevieve W. Carter, University of Southern California,
Los Angeles
Speakers: David Beverly, University of South Carolina, Columbia
Mollie Orshansky, HEW, Washington

THE 4-C's CAN MAKE IMPACT ON DEVELOPING
COMPREHENSIVE SERVICES FOR CHILDREN
  Presiding: Thomas B. Sullivan, HEW, Dallas
  Speakers: Preston Bruce, HEW, Washington
  S. M. Murphy, HEW, Dallas
  Roger Bost, Arkansas State 4-C Policy Board, Little Rock
  Raymond Hill, Child Care Council of Greater Houston, Houston,
  Texas

MIGRATION CONDITIONS—1971
  Presiding: Lionel J. Castillo, Diocese of Galveston–Houston, Houston,
  Texas
  Speakers: Harry S. Lipscomb, Baylor College of Medicine, Houston,
  Texas
  William Chandler, United Farm Workers of America, Houston, Texas

EMERGING ROLE OF CRIMINAL JUSTICE EDUCATION
  Presiding: Frank Dyson, Police Department, City of Dallas
  Speaker: John J. Hughes, Catholic University of America, Washington
  William Hewitt, University of Wisconsin, Milwaukee

MANAGEMENT PROGRAM—A TRIPLE PARTNERSHIP IN
SOCIAL WORK EDUCATION
  Presiding: Howard B. Gundy, University of Alabama, University
  Panelists: Edward T. Weaver, Illinois Department of Children and
  Family Services, Springfield
  Donald E. Brieland, University of Illinois, Urbana
  Bruce Gross, University of Illinois, Urbana

THE POLITICAL ECONOMY OF THE AMERICAN
HEALTH SYSTEM
  Presiding: Milton I. Roemer, M.D., University of California, Los
  Angeles
  Speaker: Robert R. Alford, Columbia University, New York

RECREATION SERVICES FOR PEOPLE WITH SPECIAL NEEDS
  Presiding: Etha Forman, Community Council of Greater Dallas
  Speaker: Earnest Siegel, Julius Schepps Community Center, Dallas
  Panelists: Rene Martinez, Dallas Community Relations Commission
  Robert W. Beames, U.S. Bureau of Indian Affairs, Dallas
  V. Besselle Atwell, Julia C. Hester House, Houston, Texas

COMMUNITY SERVICE ROLES FOR OLDER PERSONS:
PAID AND VOLUNTEER
  Presiding: Frank Nicholson, Atlanta, Ga.
  Speakers: Wally Gursch, Social and Rehabilitation Service, Dallas
  Edwin C. Doulin, National Association of Retired Teachers–American
  Association of Retired Persons, Washington
  John B. Keller, HEW, Washington

DETERMINING THE NEED, DELIVERING THE SERVICE,
AND WEIGHING THE RESULTS
Presiding: Leon Haley, University of Pittsburgh
Speaker: T. Willard Fair, Greater Miami Urban League

SOCIAL WELFARE RESEARCH CENTERS—
IMPLICATIONS FOR THE FUTURE
Presiding: Jack Otis, University of Texas, Austin
Speaker: Abraham S. Levine, HEW, Washington

DAY CARE AS ONE ALTERNATIVE TO FOSTER CARE IN
PROTECTIVE SERVICES
Presiding: Mildred Arnold, HEW, Washington
Speaker: James B. Harvey, Texas State Department of Public Welfare,
Austin

UTILIZATION OF MANPOWER—UTAH DEMONSTRATION
Presiding: Frank C. Caracciolo, HEW, Washington
Speaker: Evan E. Jones, Jr., Utah Department of Health and Social
Services, Salt Lake City
Discussants: Ernique Salinos, State Department of Public Welfare, San
Antonio, Texas
Sidney Fine, W. E. Upjohn Institute for Employment Research,
Washington

FROM NEW PROFESSIONALS THROUGH OLDER PROFESSIONAL
Presiding: Morton Coleman, University of Pittsburgh
Speaker: Barbara K. Shore, University of Pittsburgh
Discussant: Beuford Farris, University of Texas, Austin

DELIVERY OF SOCIAL AND REHABILITATION SERVICES—
WHERE WE ARE AND WHERE WE ARE GOING
Presiding: Joseph H. Reid, Child Welfare League of America, New
York
Speaker: Edward Newman, HEW, Washington, D.C.

AMERICA, FALLING APART?
Presiding: Mrs. Billy Brown, Neighborhood House, Columbus, Ohio
Speaker: Richard Keyes, California Association for African Studies,
Fresno
Respondents: Mrs. Lydia Aguirre, El Paso, Texas
Mrs. Amelia Castillo, El Paso, Texas
Manuel de la Rosa, El Paso, Texas
Otto Landron, Houston, Texas
Juan J. Patlan, Mexican American Unity Council, San Antonio, Texas

YOUNG AMERICANS AS AGENTS OF CHANGE IN
DEVELOPING COUNTRIES OR AMERICAN GHETTOS
Presiding: Jeffrey Binda, Office of Economic Opportunity, Washington
Speakers: Stephen Cummings, HEW, Washington

Chris Thorne, HEW, Washington
Discussant: Grace Lloyd, Dallas
Panelist: Hector Sanchez, National Catholic School of Social Work
Sponsor: U.S. Committee of ICSW

ANNUAL MEETING OF NCSW MEMBERS
GENERAL SESSION: IS THERE A SOCIAL POLICY?
FACT OR FANCY?
Presiding: Margaret E. Berry, National Federation of Settlements and Neighborhood Centers, New York; President, NCSW
Speaker: Hon. Sol M. Linowitz, National Urban Coalition, Washington

THURSDAY, MAY 20

AMERICA: MELTING POT? CULTURAL PLURALISM?
Presiding: Dorothy Demby, American Foundation for the Blind, New York
Moderator: Dorothy I. Height, YWCA of the U.S.A., New York
Speaker: Rabbi Levi A. Olan, Temple Emanu-El, Dallas
Reactors: Rev. Zan W. Holmes, Jr., Texas State Legislature, Dallas
L. A. Velarde, Jr., U.S. Catholic Conference, El Paso, Texas
Sponsor: Combined Associate Groups

GAMES AGENCIES PLAY: INTRODUCTORY LECTURE/
DEMONSTRATION FOR WORKSHOPS 1, 2, 3, AND 4
Speakers: Jack Rothman, University of Michigan, Ann Arbor
Armand A. Lauffer, University of Michigan, Ann Arbor

THE COMMUNITY PLANNING GAME (Workshop 1)
Director: Armand A. Lauffer, University of Michigan, Ann Arbor

THE LOBBYING GAME (Workshop 2)
Director: David Williams, Brandeis University, Waltham, Mass.

THE WELFARE RIGHTS GAME (Workshop 3)
Directors: Jarl Nischan, Michigan Division of Youth Services, Lansing
Celeste Sturdevant, University of Michigan, Ann Arbor

WELFARE MONOPOLY (Workshop 4)
Director: Ann Kraemer, New Detroit Speakers' Bureau, Detroit

SENIOR POWER—WHAT IT'S ALL ABOUT
Presiding: Elias Cohen, University of Pennsylvania, Philadelphia
Speakers: Fran Faris, Community Council of Greater Dallas
David Jeffreys, National Center for Voluntary Action, Washington
Frank I. Millar, Southern Methodist University, Dallas
Cosponsors: American Association of Retired Persons (Group Meeting 1); National Retired Teachers Association (Group Meeting 1); National Council for Homemaker-Home Health Aide Services; the Salvation Army (Group Meeting 1)

TERMINATION OF PARENTAL RIGHTS—
BALANCING THE EQUITIES
  Presiding: Jeanette Harris, HEW, San Francisco
  Speaker: Vincent De Francis, American Humane Association, Denver
  Discussant: Ray Myrick, HEW, Denver
Cosponsors: American Humane Association, Children's Division; American Legion, National Commission on Children and Youth; American Public Welfare Association (Group Meeting 1); Child Welfare League of America (Group Meeting 1); National Council on Crime and Delinquency

ADOLESCENCE, GROUP LIVING, AND THE CHILD CARE STAFF
  Presiding: Charles E. McBrayer, DePelchin Faith Home, Houston, Texas
  Speaker: Morris F. Mayer, Bellefaire, Cleveland
Cosponsors: Child Welfare League of America (Group Meeting 2); Florence Crittenton Association of America (Group Meeting 1)

STANDARD-SETTING IN GRADUATE AND UNDERGRADUATE
SOCIAL WORK EDUCATION: IMPLICATIONS FOR
THE PROFESSION
  Presiding: Mark P. Hale, University of Illinois, Urbana
  Speakers: Frank M. Loewenberg, Council on Social Work Education, New York
  Alfred Stamm, Council on Social Work Education, New York
Sponsor: Council on Social Work Education

DYNAMIC NEW PROGRAMS INVOLVING THE AGING
  Presiding: Richard M. Standifer, Child and Family Services, Austin, Texas
  Speakers: Mrs. Marilyn Sutherland, Child and Family Service, Austin, Texas
  Arthur Goldberg, Jewish Family and Children's Service, St. Louis
  Byron L. Pinsky, Jewish Family Service of Trenton, Trenton, N.J.
  Bernard Goldstein, Jewish Family Service, Dallas
Cosponsors: Family Service Association of America (Group Meeting 1); American Association of Retired Persons (Group Meeting 2); National Retired Teachers Association (Group Meeting 2)

VOLUNTARISM—DEAD OR ALIVE?
  Presiding: Mrs. Carolyn Busch, University of Texas, Arlington
  Speaker: Clark W. Blackburn, Family Service Association of America, New York
  Discussants: Tom Connelly, National Center for Voluntary Action, Washington
  C. F. McNeil, National Assembly for Social Policy and Development, New York
Cosponsors: National Assembly for Social Policy and Development; National Association for Statewide Health and Welfare (Group Meeting 1); United Way of America–Association of Volunteer Bureaus

RELATIONSHIPS WITH NATIONAL ORGANIZATIONS
  Presiding: Warren B. Goodwin, Texas United Community Services, Austin
  Speaker: Robert S. Burgess, Rhode Island Council of Community Services, Providence
Sponsor: National Association for Statewide Health and Welfare (Group Meeting 2)

PREVENTION: A DARING ATTEMPT
  Presiding: A. D. Buchmueller, National Congress of Parents and Teachers, Chicago
  Speaker: Merwin R. Crow, Orchard Place Residential Treatment Center for Children, Des Moines, Iowa
  Discussant: Donald Yohe, United Charities of Chicago
Sponsor: National Association of Christians in Social Welfare

FOUR EXPECTANT MOTHERS SPEAK OUT
  Presiding: Mrs. Ruby Lee Piester, Edna Gladney Home, Fort Worth, Texas
  Reactors: Martha Henderson, Hope Cottage Association, Dallas
  Rev. Dale W. Blackwell, Episcopal Pastoral Center, Fort Worth, Texas
  Austin Foster, Edna Gladney Home, Fort Worth, Texas
Cosponsors: National Council on Illegitimacy; Child Welfare League of America (Group Meeting 3); Family Service Association of America (Group Meeting 2); Florence Crittenton Association of America (Group Meeting 2); the Salvation Army (Group Meeting 2); the Volunteers of America

PATTERNS OF PARTNERSHIP OF GOVERNMENTAL AND
NONGOVERNMENTAL ORGANIZATIONS SERVING THE AGING
  Presiding: The Hon. Oswin Chrisman, Dallas
  Speaker: Cleonice Tavani; Office of Economic Opportunity, Washington
  Reactors: Freeman T. Pollard, Urban Coalition, Washington
  Marjorie Collins, National Council on the Aging, Washington
Cosponsors: National Council on the Aging; American Foundation for the Blind

ESTABLISHING PROGRAM PRIORITIES AND STRATEGIES
FOR SOCIAL AND POLITICAL ACTON
  Presiding: Walter L. Smart, National Federation of Settlements and Neighborhood Centers, New York
  Speakers: Lionel Castillo, Catholic Council on Community Relations, Houston, Texas
  Donald E. Hamilton, the Lighthouse, Philadelphia
Sponsor: National Federation of Settlements and Neighborhood Centers

THE CHICAGO MOVEMENT
  Presiding: Santos Reyes, Jr., University of Texas, Austin
  Panelists: Magdalena Santos, University of Texas, Arlington
  Joe Gonzales, Block Partnership, Fort Worth, Texas
  Frank Reyes, Borger, Texas

Mrs. Eloise Campos, Model Neighborhood Program, Austin, Texas
Sponsor: Trabajadores Sociales de La Raza

FACING SOCIAL CHANGE
Presiding: Lt. Col. John D. Needham, the Salvation Army, Richmond, Va.
Sponsor: The Salvation Army

MEAL SERVICES FOR OLDER PEOPLE
Presiding: Lora G. Buckingham, National Retired Teachers Association–American Association of Retired Persons, Washington
Speakers: Mrs. Jeannette Pelcovitz, HEW, Washington
Howard Wallach, National Retired Teachers Association–American Association of Retired Persons, Washington
John Hutchinson, Office of Economic Opportunity, Washington
Cosponsors: American Association of Retired Persons; National Retired Teachers Association; American Home Economics Association; National Council for Homemaker-Home Health Aide Services; the Salvation Army (Group Meeting 1)

SIMULATION GAMES: A HUMAN RELATIONS TRAINING UNIT
Presiding: Oscar Cohen, Anti-Defamation League of B'nai B'rith, New York
Sponsor: Anti-Defamation League of B'nai B'rith

POSTPLACEMENT SERVICE TO THE ADOPTED CHILD
IN LATER LIFE
Presiding: Mrs. Margaret Dean, Children's Bureau, Dallas
Speaker: Mrs. Marietta Spencer, Children's Home Society of Minnesota, St. Paul
Cosponsors: Child Welfare League of America (Group Meeting 1); Florence Crittenton Association of America (Group Meeting 1)

STANDARDS FOR UNMARRIED PARENTS—THE LATEST LOOK
Presiding: Mrs. Eleanor Campbell, Edna Gladney Home, Fort Worth, Texas
Speakers: Gloria Chevers, Child Welfare League of America, New York
Mrs. Charlotte S. Creighton, Northaven, Rochester, N.Y.
Cosponsors: Child Welfare League of America (Group Meeting 2); Florence Crittenton Association of America (Group Meeting 2)

A VOLUNTARY SOCIAL AGENCY CHARTS NEW
DIRECTIONS TO MEET NEEDS
Presiding: Jack Otis, University of Texas, Austin
Speakers: Robert H. Mulreany, Community Service Society of New York
James G. Emerson, Jr., Community Service Society of New York
Edward J. Mullen, Community Service Society of New York
Sponsor: Community Service Society of New York

TEACHING AS A CAREER IN SOCIAL WORK
> *Presiding:* Daniel E. Jennings, Our Lady of the Lake College, San Antonio, Texas
> *Speaker:* Leon H. Ginsberg, West Virginia University, Morgantown
> *Sponsor:* Council on Social Work Education (Group Meeting 1)

THE CARE OF BLACK CHILDREN IN LOUISIANA, 1869–1960
> *Presiding:* Eleanor M. Hynes, University of Houston, Texas
> *Speaker:* Robert Moran, Southern University, Baton Rouge, La.
> *Discussant:* Philip Lichtenberg, Bryn Mawr College, Bryn Mawr, Pa.
> *Cosponsors:* Council on Social Work Education (Group Meeting 2); Social Welfare History Group

PLAYS FOR A LIVING—A TOOL FOR COMMUNITY
EDUCATION INVOLVEMENT
> *Presiding:* Al L. Henry, United Fund of Houston and Harris County, Houston, Texas
> *Speaker:* Gerda Hansen Smith, Family Service Center of Houston and Harris County, Houston, Texas
> *Discussants:* Mrs. Harriet Roberts, Family Service Center of Houston and Harris County, Houston, Texas
> Mrs. Mary Benavidez, Family Service Center of Houston and Harris County, Houston, Texas
> *Cosponsors:* Family Service Association of America (Group Meeting 1); Plays for Living—A Division of Family Service Association of America

WORKSHOP ON PROBLEMS OF STATE ORGANIZATIONS
> *Presiding:* Burt Shulimson, Missouri Association for Social Welfare, Jefferson City
> *Discussants:* James W. Wimberly, Texas United Community Services, Austin
> A. Rowland Todd, Wisconsin Welfare Council, Madison
> Cecil S. Feldman, Community Services of Pennsylvania, Harrisburg
> *Sponsor:* National Association for Statewide Health and Welfare

ABORTION: MEDICAL, PSYCHOLOGICAL, SOCIAL, LEGAL,
AND THEOLOGICAL IMPLICATIONS
> *Presiding:* Mary Louise Allen, Florence Crittenton Association of America, Chicago
> *Speakers:* Mildred Beck, National Center for Family Planning, Rockville, Md.
> J. Olcott Phillips, Fort Worth, Texas
> Pelham P. Staples, M.D., John Peter Smith Hospital, Fort Worth, Texas
> Rev. Ruben E. Spannaus, Lutheran Welfare Association of Illinois, River Forest
> *Cosponsors:* National Council on Illegitimacy; Child Welfare League of America (Group Meeting 3); Family Service Association of America (Group

Meeting 2); Florence Crittenton Association of America (Group Meeting 3); the Salvation Army (Group Meeting 2); the Volunteers of America

BETTER LIVING WITHOUT CHEMISTRY
Presiding: Ruby L. Hubert, Neighborhood House Association, San Diego, Calif.
Speakers: John F. Austin, James Weldon Johnson Community Center, New York
Joel Carp, Mid-Westchester Young Men and Women's Hebrew Association of America, Scarsdale, N.Y.
Melvin Goldstein, Samuel Field Young Men and Young Women's Hebrew Association, Little Neck, N.Y.
Cosponsors: National Federation of Settlements and Neighborhood Centers; National Jewish Welfare Board

THE NATIONAL URBAN LEAGUE IN THE RURAL SOUTH
Presiding: Clarence D. Coleman, National Urban League, Atlanta, Ga.
Speakers: Alvin Brown, Atlanta University, Atlanta, Ga.
Charleyenne Bloodworth, Atlanta University, Atlanta, Ga.
Mrs. Willie M. Strickland, National Urban League, Atlanta, Ga.
Hon. William Branch, Atlanta, Ga
Panelists: James W. Brinkley, National Urban League, Atlanta, Ga.
Mrs. Sarah E. Curry, National Urban League, Atlanta, Ga.
Felton Alexander, National Urban League, Atlanta, Ga.
Discussant: Mrs. Genevieve Hill, Atlanta University, Atlanta, Ga.
Sponsor: National Urban League

CONSUMER EDUCATION FOR OLDER PEOPLE
Presiding: Lora G. Buckingham, National Retired Teachers Association–American Association of Retired Persons, Washington
Speakers: Barbara Fazenbaker, National Retired Teachers Association–American Association of Retired Persons, Washington
Samuel Carusi, Federal Trade Commission, Dallas
Lynn Hubbert, Texas Bank and Trust Company of Dallas
Harold Bryson, Department of Agriculture, Dallas
Cosponsors: American Association of Retired Persons; National Retired Teachers Association; American Home Economics Association: American Public Welfare Association: National Council for Homemaker-Home Health Aide Services; the Salvation Army (Group Meeting 1)

ANNUAL MEETING—NASHAW
Presiding: Cecil S. Feldman, Community Services of Pennsylvania, Harrisburg
Sponsor: National Association for Statewide Health and Welfare

ABORTION: MEDICAL, PSYCHOLOGICAL, SOCIAL, LEGAL, AND THEOLOGICAL IMPLICATIONS
Presiding: Mary Louise Allen, Florence Crittenton Association of America, Chicago

Speakers: Mildred Beck, National Center for Family Planning, Rockville, Md.

J. Olcott Phillips, Fort Worth, Texas

Pelham P. Staples, M.D., John Peter Smith Hospital, Fort Worth, Texas

Rev. Ruben E. Spannaus, Lutheran Welfare Association of Illinois, River Forest

Cosponsors: National Council on Illegitimacy; Child Welfare League of America; Family Service Association of America; Florence Crittenton Association of America; the Salvation Army (Group Meeting 2); the Volunteers of America

EVERYTHING YOU HAVE ALWAYS WANTED TO KNOW
ABOUT POLITICS AND SOCIAL WORK, BUT WERE AFRAID
TO ASK (Howard F. Gustafson Memorial Lecture)

Presiding: Margaret E. Berry, National Federation of Settlements and Neighborhood Centers, New York; President, NCSW

Speaker: Hon. Howard N. Lee, Chapel Hill, N.C.

Cosponsors: Indianapolis Howard F. Gustafson Memorial Committee; National Association of Social Workers; National Conference on Social Welfare

FRIDAY, MAY 21

BLAMING THE VICTIM

Presiding: Laura B. Morris, Department of Public Welfare, Commonwealth of Massachusetts, Boston

Speakers: William Ryan, Boston College, Boston

Eugene M. Cox, United Way of America, New York

Discussant: Patricia Johnson, HEW, Washington

SOCIAL SECURITY—NEW FRONTIERS

Presiding: Daniel O. Price, University of Texas, Austin

Speaker: Robert M. Ball, HEW, Baltimore

Discussant: Jerry Johnson, American Association of Retired Persons, Dallas

INCOME MAINTENANCE IN OPERATION

Presiding: Hortense E. Kilpatrick, University of Texas, Austin

Speakers: W. Joseph Heffernan, University of Wisconsin, Madison

Terence Kelly, Urban Institute, Washington

IMPACT OF FAMILY ASSISTANCE PROGRAM PROPOSAL ON
THE ADMINISTRATION OF PUBLIC SOCIAL SERVICES

Presiding: Harold Richman, University of Chicago

Speakers: Stephen P. Simonds, HEW, Washington

Richard P. Lindsay, Utah State Department of Social Services, Salt Lake City

DELINQUENCY: INNOVATIONS AND NEW APPROACHES
Presiding: Manuel Soto, HEW, Dallas
Speaker: Robert Gemignani, HEW, Washington

ROLE OF SOCIAL WORK IN REGIONAL MEDICAL PROGRAMS
AND COMPREHENSIVE HEALTH PLANNING
Presiding: Clyde E. Madden, University of Southern California School
of Medicine, Alhambra
Panelists: Veronica L. Conley, HEW, Bethesda, Md.
Mrs. Bernice Catherine Harper, HEW, Rockville, Md.
George O. Ebersole, California State Department of Public Health,
Sacramento

AUTOMATION IN THE HEALTH AND WELFARE FIELD
Presiding: Joseph J. Bevilacqua, Walter Reed General Hospital, Washington
Speakers: Myron Pulier, M.D., U.S. Army Health Clinic, Washington
Theron K. Fuller, HEW, Washington
Jack Silver, Walter Reed General Hospital, Washington
William B. McCurdy, Information Management, Processing, Analysis,
and Communication for Voluntary Social Agencies, New York
John Noble, HEW, Washington

SOME USES OF THE ARTS IN A SOCIAL WELFARE SYSTEM
Presiding and speaker: Ronald Federico, University of Maryland, College Park
Speaker: Richard Santos, WAI-TV, San Antonio

DELIVERING SOCIAL SERVICES THROUGH THE USE
OF TEAMS
Presiding: Sydney Beane, Jr., Cook Christian Training School, Tempe,
Ariz.
Speaker: Thomas Briggs, Syracuse University, Syracuse, N.Y.
Discussants: E. F. Christman, Jr., Family Service Center of Houston
and Harris County, Houston, Texas
Gabriel Russo, Monroe County Department of Social Services,
Rochester, N.Y.

INCOME MAINTENANCE AND HEALTH INSURANCE—WHAT
WILL HAPPEN TO SOCIAL SERVICES?
Presiding: Anne Wilkens, University of Texas, Austin
Speaker: Martin B. Loeb, University of Wisconsin, Madison

AUTHORS' FORUM: PLANNING
Presiding: Cecil S. Feldman, Director, Community Services of Pennsylvania, Harrisburg
Speakers: Lillian Feldman, New York
Phyllis R. Miller, University of Maryland, Baltimore
Robert A. Porter, West Virginia University, Morgantown
Kenneth D. Viegas, University of Oregon, Eugene

CLOSING GENERAL SESSION
A Tribute to Whitney M. Young, Jr., "Bridge Builder"; Executive Director, National Urban League; President, National Association of Social Workers; Past President, NCSW; deceased March 11, 1971.
> *Presiding:* Margaret E. Berry, National Federation of Settlements and Neighborhood Centers, New York; President, NCSW
> *Invocation:* Rev. David Cardenas, Sacred Heart-Guadalupe Parish, Dallas
> *Speaker:* Hon. Charles B. Rangel, New York

Introduction of NCSW President for 1971–72
Sponsors: National Urban League; National Conference on Social Welfare

NCSW FILM THEATER

Sponsored by the NCSW Audio-Visual Committee

Alcoholism: a Disease in Disguise
Appalachia: Rich Land, Poor People
Battle of East Saint Louis
Boys in Conflict
Care and Activation
A Case of Suicide
Color Us Black
Crisis in Medicine
Diary of a Harlem Family
Drugs: Facts Everyone Needs to Know
Drugs in the Tenderloin
Fifth of Despair
For All My Students
Fragile Egos
Guidance Office
I Just Don't Dig Him
The Living Dead
Many Good Years
Mexican Americans: an Historic Profile
Mexican Americans: Invisible Minority
Mississippi Summer Project
The Neglected
The Search
Social Problems and the Impact on the Life Cycle
The South: Health and Hunger
Them People
The Trip Back
Volunteer Story
Youth Turns On: Portrait of a Drug User

Appendix B: Business Organization of the Conference for 1971

NCSW OFFICERS

President: Margaret E. Berry, New York
First Vice President: Arthur Logan, M.D., New York
Third Vice President: Sue W. Spencer, Nashville, Tenn.
Secretary: Nelson C. Jackson, New York
Treasurer: Emerson C. Wollam, Columbus, Ohio
Past President: Wilbur J. Cohen, Ann Arbor, Mich.
President-elect: James R. Dumpson, New York
Executive Secretary: Joe R. Hoffer, Columbus, Ohio

NCSW NATIONAL BOARD
(includes officers listed above)

Term expires 1971: Donald D. Brewer, Athens, Ga.; Mrs. Wayne Coy, Washington; Franklin M. Foote, M.D., Hartford, Conn.; Andrew F. Juras, Salem, Oreg.; Mrs. Ruth I. Knee, Chevy Chase, Md.; Mrs. Henry Steeger, New York; Fred H. Steininger, Atlanta, Ga.

Term expires 1972: Alexander J. Allen, New York; Hon. Elmer L. Anderson, St. Paul, Minn.; Robert M. Ball, Washington; Charline J. Birkins, Denver; Robert S. Burgess, Providence, R.I.; Philip Hauser, Chicago; Darwin Palmiere, Ann Arbor, Mich.

Term expires 1973: Harold Baron, Evanston, Ill.; Andrew G. Freeman, Philadelphia; Mrs. Sue Easterling Kobak, Cambridge, Mass.; Patrick McCuan, Baltimore; Halloway C. Sells, Jr., Cincinnati; T. George Silcott, New York; John Trevino, Austin, Texas

Representative from Committee on Public Relations and Development: John H. McMahon, New York

Representative from National Association for Statewide Health and Welfare: Cecil S. Feldman, Harrisburg, Pa.

Chairman, U. S. Committee of ICSW: Kenneth W. Kindelsperger, Louisville, Ky.

Legal Consultant: Rudolph Janata, Columbus, Ohio

NCSW COMMITTEE ON NOMINATIONS

Chairman: Raleigh C. Hobson, Baltimore
Vice Chairman: Melvin A. Glasser, Detroit

Term expires 1971: Mildred Arnold, Washington; Melvin A. Glasser, Detroit; Arthur Hillman, Chicago; Raleigh C. Hobson, Baltimore; Mildred Sikkema, Honolulu; Sue W. Spencer, Nashville, Tenn.; Roy C. Votaw, Sacramento, Calif.
Term expires 1972: Mark Battle, Washington; Maurice P. Beck, Lansing, Mich.; Clark W. Blackburn, New York; William J. Brown, Hartford, Conn.; Malvin Morton, Chicago; Sebastian C. Owens, Denver; Mrs. David A. Whitman, Winchester, Mass.
Term expires 1973: Richard S. Bachman, Harrisburg, Pa.; Ernest C. Cooper, Cleveland; Suzanne D. Cope, Philadelphia; Ruth B. Freeman, Baltimore; Mrs. Howard F. Gustafson, Indianapolis; Geneva Mathiason, Woodside, N.Y.; Daniel E. O'Keefe, Houston, Texas

NCSW COMMITTEE ON PUBLIC RELATIONS AND DEVELOPMENT

Chairman: John H. McMahon, New York
Vice Chairman: Mrs. Alice Adler, New York
Term expires 1971: Helen Christopherson, New York; Mrs. Virginia R. Doscher, Washington; Herbert S. Fowler, Washington; Mrs. Frances A. Koestler, Brooklyn, N.Y.; Paul Mendenhall, New York; Philip E. Ryan, Washington
Term expires 1972: Adele Braude, New York; Mrs. Elma Phillipson Cole, New York; Frank Driscoll, New York; Mrs. Elly Robbins, New York; Layhmond Robinson, New York; William C. Tracy, New York
Term expires 1973: Donald F. Bates, New York; Edward Gant, New York; James Ortiz, New York; William E. Perry, Jr., New York; the Very Rev. Msgr Thomas J. Reese, Wilmington, Del.; Ira Sherman, Flushing, N.Y.; Theodore R. Thackrey, New York
Consultant: Harold N. Weiner, New York

NCSW TELLERS COMMITTEE

Chairman: Merriss Cornell, Columbus, Ohio

NCSW EDITORIAL COMMITTEE

Chairman: Arthur Katz, Lawrence, Kans.
Members: Delwin M. Anderson, Washington; Virginia Tannar, Washington; Harold R. White, Morgantown, W. Va.; Anne Wilkens, Austin, Texas

NCSW CENTENNIAL COMMITTEE

Chairman: C. Virgil Martin, Chicago

AD HOC COMMITTEE ON THE FUTURE OF NCSW

Chairman: Robert S. Burgess, Providence, R.I.

Members: Margaret E. Berry, New York; Cecil S. Feldman, Harrisburg, Pa.; Mitchell I. Ginsberg, New York; Patrick McCuan, Baltimore; Darwin Palmiere, Ann Arbor, Mich.; T. George Silcott, New York; Mrs. Henry Steeger, New York

NCSW SEARCH COMMITTEE

Chairman: Wayne Vasey, Ann Arbor, Mich.

U. S. COMMITTEE OF ICSW

Chairman: Kenneth W. Kindelsperger, Louisville, Ky.
Vice Chairman: Norman V. Lourie, Harrisburg, Pa.
Secretary: Martha Branscombe, Arlington, Va.
Treasurer: Nelson C. Jackson, New York
Representatives of National Organizations: American Council of Voluntary Agencies for Foreign Service, Eugene Shenefield, New York; American Public Welfare Association, Raleigh C. Hobson, Baltimore; Council of International Programs for Youth Leaders and Social Workers, Henry B. Ollendorff, Cleveland; Council on Social Work Education, Katherine A. Kendall, New York; National Assembly for Social Policy and Development, Mrs. Alexander B. Ripley, Los Angeles; National Association of Social Workers, Donald E. Brieland, Urbana, Ill.; U.S. Department of Health, Education, and Welfare, Dorothy Lally, Washington
  Members-at-Large
  Term expires 1971: Mrs. Julius Alexander, Miami; Henry S. Maas, Vancouver, British Columbia, Canada; Juan Ramos, M.D., Chevy Chase, Md.; Alvin L. Schorr, New York; Edward J. Sette, New York; Malcolm B. Stinson, Los Angeles; George Wiley, Washington
  Term expires 1972: Ellen E. Bullock, Washington; Margaret Hickey, St. Louis; William L. Mitchell, Washington; Ruben A. Mora, New York; Mrs. Aida G. Pagan, San Juan, Puerto Rico; Mrs. Annie Lee Sandusky, Washington; John B. Turner, Cleveland
  Term expires 1973: Eugenia Cowan, New York; Mrs. Alvin Goldman, New York; Phyllis M. Harewood, New York; Mrs. Dorinda Jones, Detroit; William R. Miner, Washington; Mrs. Ammu Menon Muzumdar, Pine Bluff, Ark.; Bernard E. Nash, Washington
  Liaison: NASW–European Unit, Ruby B. Pernell, Cleveland; New England Committee, Pearl M. Steinmetz, Cambridge, Mass.; NCSW Program Committee, William L. Mitchell, Washington; NCSW, James R. Dumpson, New York
  Subcommittee Chairmen: Membership Committee, Ellen B. Winston, Raleigh, N.C.; Nominating Committee, Morton I. Teicher, New York
  Members of Committee of Representatives, ICSW: Ellen B. Winston, Raleigh, N.C.; Stephen P. Simonds, Washington
  Officers of ICSW (residing in U.S.): Charles I. Schottland, President, ICSW, Waltham, Mass.; Kenneth W. Kindelsperger, Assistant Treasurer General, Louisville, Ky.; Kate Katzki, Secretary General, ICSW, New York

NCSW COMMITTEE ON PROGRAM

Chairman and NCSW President: Margaret E. Berry, New York
Past President: Wilbur J. Cohen, Ann Arbor, Mich.
President-elect: James R. Dumpson, New York
Members-at-large: Mrs. Victoria Berg, New York; Miguel Bustamante, San Antonio, Texas; Stanley Hill, New York; Jack David Marcus, New York; Julian Rivera, New York; James Speight, Washington; Al Williams, New York
Representatives of National Social Welfare Organizations: American Public Welfare Association, Florence Aitchison, New York; Council on Social Work Education, Dan Grodofsky, New York; National Assembly for Social Policy and Development, John F. Larberg, New York; National Association of Social Workers, Sam Negrin, New York; National Association of Statewide Health and Welfare, W. James Greene, Columbus, Ohio; National Health Council, Peter G. Meek, New York
Liaison from NCSW Audio-visual Committee: Daniel O'Connor, Washington
Liaison from NCSW Combined Associate Groups: David Jeffreys, Washington
Liaison from NCSW Public Relations and Development Committee: Helen Christopherson, New York
Liaison from Social and Rehabilitation Service, HEW: Shirley Buttrick, Washington
Liaison from Trabajadores Sociales de la Raza: Santos Reyes, Jr., Austin, Texas
Liaison from U. S. Committee, ICSW: William L. Mitchell, Washington

NCSW SECTIONS

SECTION I. ECONOMIC INDEPENDENCE

Chairman: Ewan Clague, Washington
Vice Chairman: Genevieve W. Carter, Los Angeles
Members: Jules Berman, Baltimore; Philip L. Carter, Venice, Calif.; Catherine S. Chilman, Frederick, Md.; Dorothy Daly, Washington; Frances E. Feldman, Pasadena, Calif.; Mrs. Sirel Foster, Los Angeles; Donald V. Howard, Los Angeles; Mrs. Mollie Orshansky, Washington; Mrs. Molly Piontowski, Los Angeles; Juan Ramos, M.D., Chevy Chase, Md.; Philip Rutledge, Washington; Barbara Solomon, University Park, Calif.; Elizabeth Watson, San Diego, Calif.

SECTION II. PROBLEMS OF EFFECTIVE FUNCTIONING

Chairman: Fred DelliQuadri, Milwaukee
Vice Chairman: Joseph McDonald, Cincinnati
Members: Mrs. Besselle Attwell, Houston, Texas; Ed Christman, Houston, Texas; Ada Deer, Stevens Point, Wis.; Mrs. J. Cabell Johnson, Milwaukee; Elizabeth Watkins, Chicago; Frank Newgent, Madison, Wis.; Jack Otis, Austin, Texas; Edward Protz, Galveston, Texas; Orlando Romero,

Denver; Halloway C. Sells, Jr., Cincinnati; Edward J. Sienicki, Chicago; Edward Weaver, Springfield, Ill.; Peggy Riggs Wildman, Dallas

SECTION III. SOCIAL ASPECTS OF HEALTH

Chairman: Mottram Torre, M.D., New Orleans
Vice Chairman: Cecil Sheps, M.D., Chapel Hill, N.C.
Members: Philip Beckjord, M.D., New Orleans; Ashton Brisolara, New Orleans; Andrew Dobelstein, Chapel Hill, N.C.; Kathryn Fritz, Dallas; H. Jack Geiger, M.D., Boston; Geraldine Gourley, Chapel Hill, N.C.; S. Wayne Klein, M.D., East Meadow, N.Y.; Jack David Marcus, New York; Euzelia Smart, Chapel Hill, N.C.; Fred Sutherland, New Orleans

SECTION IV. LEISURE-TIME NEEDS

Chairman: Harry Serotkin, Philadelphia
Vice Chairman: Norma J. Sims, Hartsdale, N.Y.
Members: Elliott M. Avedon, New York; Merrill B. Conover, Philadelphia; Robert W. Crawford, Philadelphia; Julian Euell, Washington; Arthur Kerr, New York; Richard Kraus, New York; Mrs. Jane Lewis, Mt. Vernon, N.Y.; Hugh W. Ransom, Harrisburg, Pa; Robert Russell, Philadelphia; Walter Schatz, White Plains, N.Y.; I. Ezra Staples, Philadelphia; Mrs. Douglas Waller, White Plains, N.Y.

SECTION V. PROVISION AND MANAGEMENT OF SOCIAL SERVICES

Chairman: Mrs. Corinne H. Wolfe, Washington
Vice Chairman: Arthur J. Edmunds, Pittsburgh
Members: Robert Aarons, Pittsburgh; Mrs. Freda Burnside, Washington; Ernest C. Cooper, Cleveland; Leon Haley, Pittsburgh; Mrs. Geraldine Hart, Arlington, Va.; Malcolm S. Host, Houston, Texas; Herbert I. Levit, Carnegie, Pa.; Sherman Merle, Washington; Ruth Pauley, Washington; John Robinson, Arlington, Va.; Santos Reyes, Austin, Texas; Joseph Souflee, Washington; Russell Shelton, Pittsburgh; Marilyn Sullivan, Pittsburgh; Mrs. Murtis Taylor, Cleveland; Rodney Williams, Philadelphia

SECTION VI. SOCIETAL PROBLEMS

Chairman: John H. Ballard, Chicago
Vice Chairman: Leonard Schneiderman, Columbus, Ohio
Members: Warren H. Bacon, Chicago; Louis de Boer, Chicago; Thomas Dilliard, Columbus, Ohio; Harrison Joseph, Columbus, Ohio; Randall Morrison, Columbus, Ohio; Edward Palmer, Chicago; David Peebles, Columbus, Ohio; Warner Saunders, Chicago; Frank S. Seever, Chicago; Rev. Jose A. Torres, Chicago; Nate Vanderwerf, New York; Bernard J. Wohl, Columbus, Ohio

NCSW DIVISION COMMITTEE

Chairman: Duane W. Beck, Atlanta, Ga.
Ex officio: Margaret E. Berry, New York

Members: John Belindo, Albuquerque, N. Mex.; Hyman Bookbinder, Washington; Margery Gross, New York (alternate); Hobart Burch, New York; Matthew Dumont, M.D., Boston; Alejandro Garcia, New York, Gene Guerrero, Atlanta, Ga.; Isaac Hunt, Jr., New York; Lowell Ibery, New York; Ron Linton, Washington; Clarence Mitchell, Washington; Laura B. Morris, Boston; Darwin Palmiere, Ann Arbor, Mich.; Bernard Ross, Bryn Mawr, Pa.; Alvin L. Schorr, New York; Leonard Stern, Washington; Daniel Thursz, Baltimore; Rev. Andrew J. Young, Atlanta, Ga.; Robert Waymer, Atlanta, Ga. (alternate)

NCSW AUDIO-VISUAL COMMITTEE

Chairman: Daniel O'Connor, Washington
Vice Chairman: Lt. Col. Belle Leach, New York
Consultants: Sumner Glimcher, New York; Rohama Lee, New York; Robert Mitchell, New York
Members: James Allen, New York; Jack Bentkover, New York; Mrs. Ann P. Booth, New York; Jeannette L. Burroughs, New York; Robert P. Finehout, New York; Jack Neher, New York; Daniel J. Ransohoff, Cincinnati; Mrs. Marie Stewart, New York

NCSW TASK FORCE FOR SOCIAL ISSUES FORUM

Chairman: Mrs. Ruth I. Knee, Chevy Chase, Md.
Secretary: Thomas C. Moan
Members: Hon. Elmer L. Andersen, St. Paul, Minn.; Robert M. Ball, Washington; Robert S. Burgess, Providence, R. I.; Cecil S. Feldman, Harrisburg, Pa.; Patrick McCuan, Baltimore; Halloway C. Sells, Jr., Cincinnati; John Trevino, Austin, Texas

NCSW TASK FORCE FOR ANNUAL MEETING OF MEMBERS

Chairman: Fred H. Steininger, Atlanta, Ga.
Secretary: Thomas C. Moan
Members: Alexander J. Allen, New York; Harold Baron, Evanston, Ill.; Donald D. Brewer, Athens, Ga.; Mrs. Wayne Coy, Washington; Nelson C. Jackson, New York; Arthur Logan, M.D., New York, Darwin Palmiere, Ann Arbor, Mich.

COMMITTEE ON COMBINED ASSOCIATE GROUPS

Chairman: David Jeffreys, Washington
Vice Chairman: Dorothy Demby, New York
Term expires 1971: American Home Economics Association, Mrs. Nathalie D. Preston, Brooklyn, N.Y.; American Public Welfare Association, Benjamin O. Hendrick, Chicago; National Association for Mental Health, D. Douglas Waterstreet, New York; National Association for Statewide Health and Welfare, Mrs. Tina G. Howell, Boston; Planned Parenthood–

World Population, Samuel Taylor, New York; Social Work Vocational Bureau, Mrs. Esther Bernstein, New York

Term expires 1972: Association of Junior Leagues of America, Clara J. Swan, New York; National Council of Jewish Women, Mrs. Helen Powers, New York; National Council on Alcoholism, Helen Christopherson, New York

PROGRAM CHAIRMEN OF ASSOCIATE GROUPS

AFL-CIO Department of Community Services: Harvey Anderson, Jr.
American Association of Homes for the Aging: Lester Davis
American Association of Retired Persons: Mrs. Lora Buckingham; Bernard E. Nash
American Council for Nationalities Service: Harry W. Morgan
American Foundation for the Blind: Dorothy Demby
American Friends Service Committee: Frank J. Hunt
American Home Economics Association: Mrs. Nathalie Preston
American Humane Association, Children's Division: Vincent De Francis
American Immigration and Citizenship Conference: Mrs. Sonia D. Blumenthal
American Jewish Committee: Mrs. Ann Wolfe
American Legion–National Commission on Children and Youth: Fred T. Kuszmaul
American National Red Cross: Mary Helen Merrill
American Public Welfare Association: Benjamin O. Hendrick
American Social Health Association: Earle Lippincott
Anti-Defamation League of B'nai B'rith: Oscar Cohen
Army Community Service–Department of the Army: Lt Col. Frank F. Montalvo
Association for Voluntary Sterilization: Jane Pendergast
Association of the Junior Leagues of America: Clara J. Swan
Big Brothers of America: George Katz
Child Study Association of America: Otis B. Turner
Child Welfare League of America: Helen D. Stone
Community Development Foundation: Dr. Andre Karam
Council of Jewish Federations and Welfare Funds: Charles Zibbell
Council on Social Work Education: Daniel Grodofsky
Day Care and Child Development Council of America, Inc.: Mrs. Jean H. Berman
Executive Council of the Episcopal Church: Mrs. Ruth Gilbert
Family Service Association of America: William G. Hill
Florence Crittenton Association of America, Inc.: Mrs. Helen Johnstone Weisbrod
Goodwill Industries of America: Donald V. Wilson
International Social Service, American Branch: Sidney Talisman
National Assembly for Social Policy and Development: John F. Larberg
National Association for Mental Health: Douglas Waterstreet
National Association for Statewide Health and Welfare: Mrs. Tina Howell

National Association of Christians in Social Welfare: Dr. Larry D. Hybert-son

National Association of Housing and Redevelopment Officials: Mrs. Dorothy Gazzolo

National Association of Social Workers: Sam Negrin

National Board, YMCAs: C. Lewis Brown

National Committee on Employment of Youth: Eli Cohen

National Conference of Jewish Communal Service: Morton I. Teicher

National Council for Homemaker-Home Health Aide Services: Mrs. Mary Walsh

National Council of Jewish Women: Mrs. Helen Powers; Ben Winitt

National Council of Senior Citizens: Rudolph T. Danstadt

National Council of the Churches of Christ in the U.S.A.: John McDowell

National Council on Alcoholism: Helen Christopherson

National Council on Crime and Delinquency: Robert E. Trimble

National Council on the Aging: Rebecca Eckstein; Marjorie Collins

National Council on Illegitimacy: Ruth V. Friedman

National Easter Seal Society for Crippled Children and Adults: Mrs. Rhoda Gellman

National Federation of Settlements and Neighborhood Centers: Mary E. Blake

National Federation of Student Social Workers: Richard Taylor

National Health Council: Peter G. Meek

National Jewish Welfare Board: Irving Brickman

National Legal Aid and Defender Association: Mayo H. Stiegler

National Public Relations Council of Health and Welfare Services: Seymour Stark

National Retired Teachers Associations: Mrs. Lora Buckingham; Bernard E. Nash

National Urban League: Manuel A. Romero

Planned Parenthood-World Population: Samuel Taylor

The Salvation Army: Brig. Mary Verner

Social Work Vocational Bureau: Mrs. Esther Berstein

Travelers Aid Association of America: Albert J. J. Tarka; Paul W. Guyler

United Cerebral Palsy Associations: Ernest Weinrich

United HIAS Service: Ralph Bergel

United Methodist Church Board of Health and Welfare Ministries: Louise Weeks; Betty J. Letzig

United Presbyterian Church Board of National Missions: James A. McDaniel

United Seamen's Service: Mrs. Lillian Rabins

United Way of America: Herbert Kenny

Veterans Administration, Central Office: Mrs. Natalie Cave

The Volunteers of America: Lt. Col. Belle Leach; Gen. J. F. McMahon

YWCA of the U.S.A.: Norma Sims; Wenonah Bond Logan

Index

Pluralism: cultural, 32; in the Netherlands, 34; structural, 33
"Political Activism for Social Work," 74-83
"Political Economy of the American Health System, The," 90-106
Ponce, Puerto Rico, 23
Populist revolt, 4
Pound, Roscoe, quoted, 38-39
Poverty, 75; culture of, 50; and health problems, 53; in Puerto Rico, 24
President's Committee on Juvenile Delinquency and Youth Crime, 141
Prohibition, 39
Project Head Start, 182-83, 184-85, 186-87, 188, 189-90, 191-92, 193-94
Puerto Rico: drug addiction in, 21; economy of, 23; education in, 20; family needs in, 16-17; Health Department in, 26; health in, 21; housing in, 21; people of, 15-27; Planning Board of, 27; population of, 23, 25; poverty in, 24; public assistance program in, 25-27; rural areas of, 23; urban areas of, 23
Puerto Rico, University of, 20

Rangel, Charles B., paper by, 84-89
Reagan, Ronald, 48, 65, 88
Reform of health system, 95
Rein, Martin, 131n., 141; cited, 171, 184; quoted, 183, 184
Resources Development Fund, 117
Reuther, Walter, 114
Richardson, Elliot L., 113, 127
Rockefeller, Nelson, 48
Roosevelt, Franklin D., 75
Roosevelt, Theodore, quoted, 32
Rosen, Sumner, quoted, 91
Ryan, William, paper by, 41-54

S. 3 (Senate bill), 115-21
San Antonio, Model Cities Program in, 159-67
San Juan, Puerto Rico, 23
Sand Creek Massacre (1864), 34
Sanders, Irwin T., quoted, 183
Saxbe, William, 115-21
Schlesinger, Arthur, Jr., quoted, 6-7

Schottland, Charles, 114
Seebohm Commission (Great Britain), 133
Shannon, James A., cited, 94
Shay's rebellion (1786), 3
Slavery, 29, 57
Slum Clearance Act, 22
Small Business Administration, 94, 165-66
Social services, 130; definition of, 131n.; experimental structures in, 157-58
Social welfare, 47-48, 81; crisis in, 84; and federal budget, 55-62
Social work, 74-83; education in, 80
"Social Welfare Client, The: Blaming the Victim," 41-54
Source Catalogue, 157
Southern Tenant Farmers Union, 4
"Southwest, The: Aspirations of the Mexican Americans," 10-14
Spiegel, Hans B. C., cited, 178

Taft, Robert, Sr., 68
Task Force in Urban Education, 187
Technological innovation, 66
Texas War of Independence (1836), 10
Thursz, Daniel, cited, 176; quoted, 181
Townsend, Claire, quoted, 108
Tribalism, 35
Tumin, Melvin M., 15

United Cerebral Palsy, 185
Urban Renewal and Housing Corporation, 22
Utuado, Puerto Rico, 23

Versailles, Treaty of, 28

Warren, Roland L., paper by, 140-58; cited, 159, 163-64
Weismantel, William, cited, 181
Wilson, Vernon, quoted, 123
Wilson, Woodrow, quoted, 30
Woodcock, Leonard, paper by, 107-22
Workingmen's societies (1820), 4-5

Young, Whitney M., Jr., 114

Zangwill, Israel, quoted, 31

Other Papers from the 98th Annual Forum

Papers presented at the 98th Annual Forum may also be found in *Social Work Practice, 1971,* published by Columbia University Press:

Organizational Patterns to Combat Racism   *H. Frederick Brown*
Instructed Advocacy and Community Group Work   *Paul Abels*
The Process of Group Goal Formulation in Social Work Practice   *Maeda Galinsky* and *Janice H. Schopler*
Child Neglect in Appalachia   *Norman A. Polansky, Christine DeSaix,* and *Shlomo Sharlin*
Social Work with the Family on Release from Prison   *Harris Chaiklin*
A Family Approach to the Treatment of Alcoholism   *Merrilee Atkins*
Drug Abuse Treatment Programs for Underprivileged Black Areas   *Ashton Brisolara*
Social Services for the Aged in a Community Center   *Phyllis R. Miller* and *David Guttman*
Private Enterprise Tackles a Senior Adult Program   *Lynn Hubbert*
Redefining the Role of Hospital Social Work   *Emanuel Hallowitz*
Homemaker–Home Health Aides: Coordinated Service Delivery   *Lillian Feldman*
The Paraprofessional as a "New" Social Work Student   *Lynne Riehman*
Heterosexual Development of Adolescent Blind Males   *Marcialito Cam* and *Merle Broberg*
Redesigning a Social Service Delivery System   *Ruth M. Pauley*
The Voluntary Agency and the Purchase of Social Services   *Benjamin A. Gjenvick*
Improving the Partnership between Private Foundations and Social Welfare Programs   *Samuel J. Silberman*